William McKendree Bryant

The World-Energy And It's Self-Conservation

William McKendree Bryant

The World-Energy And It's Self-Conservation

ISBN/EAN: 9783744714624

Printed in Europe, USA, Canada, Australia, Japan

Cover: Foto ©ninafisch / pixelio.de

More available books at **www.hansebooks.com**

THE WORLD-ENERGY

AND ITS SELF-CONSERVATION.

BY

WILLIAM M. BRYANT.

"In each there is something of all."—*Anaxagoras.*

CHICAGO:
S. C. GRIGGS AND COMPANY,
1890.

PRESS OF
KNIGHT & LEONARD CO.
CHICAGO.

PREFACE.

THE present volume owes its origin to studies that began more than twenty years ago. The studies themselves were prompted by a desire which soon became imperative. And that desire was to find a satisfactory answer to the question: What is "Man's Place in Nature?"

Many things highly interesting and suggestive were said from time to time by the naturalists upon this theme. And yet, as I came at length to notice, the question itself seemed to be ambiguous. For, whatever answer might be given it, all must depend at last upon the answer to this further question, namely: What is that reality which we call "Nature?" Allowing that man is a product of "Nature," there still seemed no other way to learn the real nature and destiny of man than through a successful inquiry as to the essence, the inmost *nature* of "Nature" itself. If this term "Nature" should prove to have a wider, and even so much wider as to be a radically different, significance from that which it is usually assumed to represent, then our estimate of "man's place in Nature" must be correspondingly modified. And this might very likely mean nothing more nor less than that man's "nature" is far more complex than could be inferred from anything we are able to learn through what is commonly understood by the descriptive phrase "Natural Science."

At the same time, the results in this particular field of inquiry show a vitality in the method of inquiry through which the results are obtained, that could not be lightly esteemed. Indeed, the more I learned of the "speculative" method of inquiry on the one hand, and of the method of inquiry in Natural Science on the other, the more did it appear to me that so far as men really *think*, the method of their thinking not only *must* prove, but actually *does* prove, to be one and the same. The method may be consciously pursued, and thus may, or rather must, itself become the object of investigation—in which case it shows itself as explicitly "speculative;" or, on the other hand, it may be unconsciously pursued and applied (for example) in the investigation of physical phenomena; in which case it is still "speculative," though it is so only implicitly—its form here being that of "hypothesis."

It appeared, then, that in the scientific movement of the present time we have the conspicuous external counterpart, or rather complement, of the speculative movement, which first assumed an explicit scientific character with the Greek schools of thought, and which again developed into special vigor and effectiveness in Germany during the closing years of last century and the first quarter of the present.

In short, the famous Hegelian dialectic is in truth nothing less or else than the speculative aspect of the doctrine of the Conservation of Energy, which constitutes the vital element of all that is known as "Modern Science." The former presents the principle of Evolution in its most abstract, but also in its most rigidly consistent form. The latter unfolds the "dialectic" under the form of the necessary relations or laws that "govern," or rather constitute, natural (in the sense of physical) phenomena.

Thus, instead of being contradictory the one of the other, these two great movements are in reality but complementary and increasingly adequate phases of the ceaseless struggle on the part of the human mind to bring itself into harmony with the actual world in its essential, and therefore ultimate, significance.

It is true that on his part Hegel treated slightingly the work of the empirical school, which had already developed admirable results in his time. And the members of this school have ample revenge when they point to the astounding absurdities to be found in Hegel's "*Naturphilosophie;*" a work which, it cannot be reasonably denied, consists in great part of a series of perverse assumptions defying all observed facts. But, on the other hand, empiricists who scoff at that method which they (wrongly) assume to be fairly illustrated in this work, have on their part only too often attempted to interpret "Nature" without the guidance of any clearly defined speculative principle; and precisely for that reason they have been now and then betrayed into speculations that would grace the most arbitrary pages of Hegel's "*Naturphilosophie.*"

What Hegel needed was a better appreciation of the empirical aspects of inquiry. What the empirical scientist needs is a better appreciation of the speculative aspects of inquiry. And clear indications are not wanting that the true relation between the empirical and the speculative is coming to be better understood by many in both these special schools of thought.

If this be true, we may infer that the scientist of the future will not be content, nor even feel secure, without a "speculative" training; while the specialist in speculative studies will not dare, even if he should desire, to remain in ignorance of the special methods and results of the so-called empirical sciences.

Indeed, as was just intimated, these sciences are already far from wanting in sufficiently daring speculations. And it is to be added that the culmination of these speculations, in their most elaborate and most consistent presentation, we owe to Herbert Spencer. It is for this reason that I have never been able to separate the work of Mr. Spencer from that of Hegel, widely as these two are contrasted in many respects. Evolution, and fixity of order in Evolution—that is the key-note of both systems. The one develops this conception in the form of the necessary process of Thought itself. The other traces the evidences verifying this conception throughout the realm of "Nature" considcred as the physical universe. The system of Hegel has been named: *Absolute Idealism.* Mr. Spencer calls his own system: *Transfigured Realism.* The latter begins with the external and simpler forms of Reality and traces them through their relations to their ultimate source—to which indeed he would evidently find satisfaction in applying the term: Absolute Being, though he refrains from using any more definitely descriptive name than: Persistent Force. Hegel begins with the simplest, most abstract concept which it is possible to form, and names that concept "Being." And this name, it is all-important to notice, is the name of a concept only; that is, the name of a concept corresponding to which there is no reality other than the concept itself. But to become aware of the fact that there is no *outer* reality corresponding to the inner real concept of mere pure being, that is to form in the mind another concept with reference to this outer no-reality. And it is a fact sufficiently familiar to all that to this other concept the term *Nothing* is applied. It turns out, then, that the term *nothing*, equally with the term *being*, represents a real concept, while yet in each case there is equally no objective reality to which the concept or its corresponding category can apply. Hence the often repeated and seldom understood expression of Hegel that "Being and nothing are the same."

But in these barren concepts it is impossible for thought to rest. On the contrary, it is driven onward by its own nature to more and more concrete concepts until there is reached the concept expressed in the category of Totality with all that this implies; in short, until there is reached the concept of Cause in the sense of a totality that is eternally complete in its own self-activity. And this, as it seems to me, is just the Persistent Force to which Mr. Spencer's system leads up —only with far more adequate and consistent definition than Mr. Spencer gives it. Mr. Spencer traces out an "established order" in the world of Things. Hegel traces out the necessary or "established" order in the world of Thought.

Thus far these two systems seem on first view to be merely antithetical. And yet, as I have attempted to show in the argument of the present volume, the established order of the world of Things is what it is precisely because it is the outer expression, and nothing else than the outer expression, of the "established"— that is, the necessary or logical—order of Thought. In other words, Thought and Things are but the necessary complementary aspects of the one Totality of Existence.

In short, what I have attempted to do is: To trace out, and thus to render explicit, the speculative thread that is already present implicitly as the vital principle of the modern scientific movement. It will thus be manifest that my purpose has not been "critical" so much as interpretative. I have not been concerned to discover the momentary weaknesses of that movement so much as to find its central, permanent elements of power.

Feeling the need of help in my efforts to solve for myself the problem that involves the whole significance of life, I have not hesitated to seek for help wherever there seemed promise of finding help — being no less grateful for a clue in the realm of empirical science than for one in the realm of speculative science. Thus, at length, it became clear to me that Nature is not something apart from Mind. On the contrary, it became manifest that Nature is nothing else than the outer mode of, and hence has its only truth in, Mind. And this conviction seemed to already present, at least in germ, that solution for which I had been seeking. For now the relation of man to "Nature" was seen to be in truth his relation to the Mind which manifests itself in Nature—a conclusion which gives to the question as to man's Nature and destiny an immeasurably more hopeful aspect than Natural Science in the usual acceptation of the term would seem to warrant.

And not only so, but there appears to be here presented a basis for the complete reconciliation of what have only too commonly been regarded as contradictory views of the world. As already indicated, the empirical and the speculative aspects of thought are by no means necessarily antagonistic. On the contrary, when rightly estimated, they are but the complementary phases of all true inquiry. Nor is this all, for in the given view (justified, as I hope, in the following pages) we have a secure basis for the complete reconciliation of all science, whether predominantly speculative or predominantly empirical, with any Religion that is worthy the name. For according to this view the whole course of Science, whatever aspect may for the hour be predominant, really tends to prove beyond all reasonable doubt that the one all-inclusive Substance is in its very nature a conscious Energy; or, in other words, that it is the one absolute Person.

On such view, it is evident that the "conflict between Science and Religion" is rather imaginary than real; even though an occasional dogmatic scientist should still persist in announcing, as by authority, the overthrow of Religion as nothing more than an old wives' fable; and though here and there a skeptical theologian should more or less scoffingly declare that Science is only a collection of idle fancies, having their origin in the unregenerate pride of man.

In short, just as the empirical and the speculative aspects of science cannot be separated from each other without destroying science; so Religion approaches only so much the nearer to gross superstition the less it is pervaded by the scientific spirit. To bring one's thought into unison with the established order of the World— itself a world of Reason—that is the religion of the intellect. To deliberately bring one's conduct into harmony with that order—that is the religion of the will. To harmonize one's feeling, the entire range of his sentiment, with that order, so that he delights in doing whatever is consistent with the rational World-order— that is the religion of the emotions. And yet these three are but the essential and complementary aspects of Religion in its genuine, practical, concrete significance.

To decry science is to commit oneself to the perpetuation of superstition. To decry religion is to threaten the existence of the ultimate motive leading to any and every effort in the field of science. Equally true is it, whether in the realm of science or in the realm of religion, that nothing can survive save that which is adapted to its environment. And in the outcome the one real environment of human thought, as of human faith, is the abiding Truth of the World.

While, then, it may be true that "man is what he eats (*Mann ist was er isst,*") it is equally true that man *is* what he *thinks* and what he *does* in pursuance of his thinking. So that "man's place in Nature" is essentially his relation as a thinking (and therefore indestructible) agent to the ultimate Reason, which constitutes all that *is* of the reality we call "Nature."

Such are the convictions at which I have myself arrived. Whether the following discussion will justify these convictions to the reader must, of course, be determined by the reader himself.

I have only to add that for the carefully prepared index accompanying this volume, I am indebted to the kindness of my young friend, Mr. Charles L. Deyo.

St. Louis, March, 1890.

CONTENTS.

CHAPTER I.
INTRODUCTION.—ELEMENTS AND CONDITIONS OF KNOWLEDGE, . 1

CHAPTER II.
MATTER AND ITS PROPERTIES, ... 40

CHAPTER III.
PHENOMENON AND NOUMENON.—THE ATOM AS FIGURED IN IMAGINATION, ... 53

CHAPTER IV.
TRUTH OF THE ATOM.—PENETRABILITY OF MATTER, . . 65

CHAPTER V.
TRANSITION TO THE QUANTITATIVE ASPECTS OF MATTER THROUGH INCREASE IN QUALITATIVE CHARACTERISTICS, . . . 71

CHAPTER VI.
DEFINITE QUANTITATIVE RELATIONS IN MATTER, . . 80

CHAPTER VII.
AS TO CONTINUITY AND DISCRETENESS OF QUANTITY IN MATTER, 83

CHAPTER VIII.
Extensive and Intensive Phases of Quantity in Matter, 86

CHAPTER IX.
Measure and the Measureless, ... 97

CHAPTER X.
Of the Possibility of Motion in General, . . . 109

CHAPTER X
Of the Nature of Motion, ... 122

CHAPTER XII.
The Laws of Motion, ... 131

CHAPTER XIII.
Energy as Adequate Cause of Motion, ... 143

CHAPTER XIV.
The Law of Universal Gravitation, . . . 150

CHAPTER XV.
Momentum, ... 157

CHAPTER XVI.
Laws of Falling Bodies, ... 163

CHAPTER XVII.
Curvilinear Motion, ... 170

CHAPTER XVIII.

MOLECULAR MOTION, ... 178

CHAPTER XIX.

CORRELATION OF FORCES AND CONSERVATION OF ENERGY, . 196

CHAPTER XX.

DOCTRINE OF CAUSE, ... 207

CHAPTER XXI.

CREATOR AND CREATION, ... 215

CHAPTER XXII.

THE WORLD-ENERGY AS SPIRIT, ... 218

CHAPTER XXIII.

FUNDAMENTAL MODES OF MANIFESTATION OF THE WORLD-ENERGY AS SPIRIT, ... 242

CHAPTER XXIV.

EVOLUTION OF LIFE-FORMS, ... 255

CHAPTER XXV.

FURTHER CONSIDERATIONS AS TO THE EVOLUTION OF LIFE-FORMS, 265

CHAPTER XXVI.

CULMINATION OF THE LIFE-PROCESS IN A LIVING UNIT WHICH IS CHARACTERIZED BY REFLECTIVE CONSCIOUSNESS, . . 286

THE WORLD-ENERGY AND ITS SELF-CONSERVATION.

CHAPTER I.

INTRODUCTION.—ELEMENTS AND CONDITIONS OF KNOWLEDGE.

a.—FACT AND THEORY.

POPULAR convictions have ever tended toward compact embodiment in the form of maxims. Nor in truth is this anything else than the inevitable outcome of the inherent demand of the mind for definition, clear formulation. There is nothing really surprising, therefore, in the fact that examples of this tendency present themselves in the scientific world no less than in the world of every-day affairs.

There is one maxim, indeed, that has found special favor among men of science. No other has, in fact, been received more widely or with less question. This favorite maxim commonly runs thus: "Facts rather than theories." In other words, in all investigations, whether in the physical world or in the world of mind, one ought always to put his trust in facts rather than in theories. The latter are always to be distrusted. The former alone can safely be relied upon.

From the confidence with which this rule has commonly been urged, it would seem that there could be no question as to the precision and adequacy of its significance. And yet it can require no very prolonged or very profound reflection to discover that if a fact is to be truly a fact *for us*, it must first be subjected to interpretation by us. We can never know a fact until we have given it some sort of interpretation. And our knowledge of the fact will depend, for its completeness, precisely upon the adequacy of our interpretation.

But "interpretation" is substantially the construction of a "theory." For theory is primarily just a looking-at or contemplation, which in turn unfolds into a conviction of the mind requiring nothing but conscious formulation to render it clearly recognizable as a "theory," in the ordinary sense of the term. Hence a fact becomes real and trustworthy as a fact to us, only in so far as we have formed a theory concerning it.

It appears then, that, in *our experience*, "facts," without theories, are just as empty and worthless as are theories without facts. Or rather, it would agree with the truth still more precisely to say that, so far as the experience of any thinking being is concerned, it is impossible that there should be any such thing, either as a fact without a theory or a theory without a fact. The fact may be misapprehended—that is, misinterpreted—but it does not become a fact at all for the individual otherwise than through his giving it his interpretation, however distorted the interpretation may be.

Thus it can become a fact in its *truth* for him only in so far as he gives it a *true* interpretation, only in so far as he forms a rational theory concerning it. And now, recurring to what was said at the beginning, it may be added that a maxim is nothing else than an abridged statement of a theory. Following which it would perhaps not be wholly amiss to inquire whether the "scientific" maxim we have just been considering is wholly exempt from the untrustworthiness so confidently assumed to inhere in all other theories. In truth it is extremely likely to be just that theory which has been least scrutinized, least subjected to criticism, which turns out to be the most untrustworthy.

b.—FUNCTION OF CONSCIOUSNESS.

It is impossible then that a "fact" should come into the consciousness of an individual otherwise than as in part the actual creation of that consciousness. A supposed passive impressibility of the mind is, in truth, but a contradiction in terms. In order that the mind may be impressed *as mind*, it must be no less active than passive. It must receive—that is, actively take up into itself—the element or force tending to produce an effect upon the mind from without.

But this active reception is also a transformation. It adds to the outward element an inner element— namely, that of the mind's own activity—and the two are now fused into a single, indivisible fact of consciousness. The spontaneous activity of the mind itself is a necessary phase of every fact of consciousness, without which phase, therefore, it would be impossible that any such fact of consciousness should ever arise.

The first "facts," then, for which the mind must account are the facts of its own consciousness. Nay, rather the only facts with which the mind can ever deal—the only facts that can exist for it—are the facts of its own consciousness. The only world for me is the world I know.

At the same time, this statement is far from being equivalent to saying that at any given moment the individual, empirical consciousness already possesses all the facts that can ever exist for it. This would indeed be manifestly absurd, for the reason that the individual consciousness has even thus far been unfolded into reality only through the reciprocal activity that has taken place from time to time between the "inner" mind and the "outer" world. On the contrary, it is to be understood as meaning that no new fact can be added to the world of the individual save through the activity of the individual in his character of a conscious unit. And this is as much as to say that each new "fact," as it comes into the consciousness of the individual, passes through a transforming, creative process, the primary element of which process, so far as the individual is immediately concerned, is the spontaneous activity of the individual's own mind, consisting in the seizure and fusion with itself of the given outer element. It is only thus that any "fact" whatever can become known to the individual at all.

Whence, let us repeat, it is impossible that the individual should ever really *know* any fact whatever, otherwise than in so far as it has already come to be a fact of his own consciousness. So that the function of consciousness appears to be primarily this: To seize upon the elements offered it in the outer world of nature and to interpret those elements into the inner world of thought.

c.—RANGE OF CONSCIOUSNESS.

We have next to observe that these facts of the individual consciousness necessarily have relation to a world lying beyond the range of the individual's *immediate* experience. They had a beginning as such facts of consciousness, and with whatever powers we may regard the mind of any individual man as endowed, we cannot include as among those powers the ability to create, out of pure nothing, the facts which go to make up its own world of growing consciousness. If, in a certain sense, the individual consciousness possesses creative powers, those powers can still be regarded as creative only in the sense of being powers of transformation, or rather of transfiguration. It reaches out to a world "beyond itself," and in that world finds material which it seizes upon and appropriates to its own uses. At the same time, this "reaching out" is but a self-expansion of the individual consciousness so as to include in, and assimilate to, its own inner world more and more of what previously belonged to a world that was external and apparently alien to such consciousness.

And yet this gradual appropriation by the individual consciousness of the world which, at the outset, lies beyond such consciousness, could not take place at all, if that world were wholly an alien world. Rather, it demonstrates that the world lying beyond the *immediate range* of the individual consciousness is still in vital relation to the actual present facts of such consciousness.

The limit of the possible experience of the individual then is to be found only where the "outer world" ceases to be in relation to the world of consciousness at all.

It is only because the unknown is fundamentally related to — that is, possesses the same nature as — the known, that it can ever be transformed into the known. Just that and only that which is wholly unlike the known, and hence wholly incapable of ever being brought into relation with the known, is, with the utmost ease and certainty, already *known* as being absolutely "*unknowable.*" It is opposed to intelligence in its very nature, and hence may be at once "recognized" by the intelligence as unknowable, simply because of its sheer vacuity, because of its being absolutely void of any characteristic through which it can or could ever be an object to the intelligence.

The only world, then, which can possibly be known, or even conceived as existing, is a world essentially related to, and hence possessing, in truth, the same fundamental nature as the knowing self. Such would seem, at this point, to be the natural inference.

There is suggested here also this further inference: That the only intelligence I can ever know is of the same fundamental nature as my own intelligence. For I could only know it by taking up its modes of activity into my own consciousness. And that must mean that thus far the modes of my own consciousness are the same as the modes of that intelligence assumed to be essentially different from my own. It is only by an act of my own reason that I could conceive of a reason as different from my own. But in the very act of conceiving it as different from my own I must pronounce such "reason" to be *un*reason. In other words, such conception utterly contradicts itself and thus annuls itself in the very process of its formation.

There is then a universal ideal or type of intelligence to which every particular intelligence, so far as it truly *is* intelligence, must conform. Whence the limit of possible development for each individual intelligence is nothing less or else than the total round of facts and relations capable of being justified to such intelligence as an absolutely rational world.

And further, since the universal ideal of intelligence as such is the true ideal of every individual intelligence realized as a person, it would seem that if the individual can ever trace out the fundamental characteristics of this universal ideal or typical nature common to all intelligences, he will, at the same time, trace out the fundamental nature of all that can ever appeal to reason — of all, therefore, that can be conceived as pertaining in any way to a rational world. In other words, he will trace out the fundamental system of the only knowable — that is, the only possible — world.

It appears, then, that all looking implies a looking within; all investigation, an investigation of self; all judging, a judging of that which pronounces judgment. All seeing is double. Every act of the mind is two-fold. It seizes upon a world beyond itself, and yet, in so doing, identifies that world with itself; or rather, in so doing, it discovers an essential identity as already existing between that world and itself.

The ultimate range of consciousness is thus seen to be commensurate with the total round of the rational world.

d. — SENSATION THE PRIMARY PHASE OF CONSCIOUSNESS.

In any inquiry into the nature and limits of the external world, then, it is essential, first of all, to consider the mode in which such external world comes within the range of the individual consciousness. And it is to be remarked that the simplest phase of the mind's activity is precisely that through which the mind comes into relation with this external world. That the experience of every individual necessarily begins with and in sensation, is a philosophic truism. It is, then, of the first importance to ascertain the conditions under which sensation can and must take place.

It is evident, first of all, that there are two phases of these conditions. The one phase is subjective—the phase in which the mind itself is specially considered. The other phase is objective—the phase in which "objects," in the sense of things of the external world, are specially attended to. Every sensation necessarily implies an act of an individual mind and also an object other than such individual mind, which yet the individual mind seizes upon. Sensation is a concrete relation between subject and object, and its primary condition is the direct "contact" between the two factors concerned.

Of this concrete relation between subject and object there are many degrees. It is that degree of such concrete relation in which the subject seizes upon the object so as to result in a definite and more or less abiding "impression" or "image" in the mind that is appropriately termed *perception*.

But this perception, this seizure and appropriation of the object by the mind, through the sensory organs, implies that the object perceived is specially characterized by externality. It is made up of parts which are outside one another. Whence it is evident that the *object* of sensation is necessarily in *space*.

On the other hand, the *act* of sensation is either after or before other such acts. That is, the *act* of sensation is necessarily in *time*.

It is evident, therefore, that both space and time are necessary conditions of sensation. Without these conditions not a single act of sensation would be possible.

We have accordingly to consider the precise measure in which these conditions determine all our sense-perceptions.

1. *Space as a condition of sensation.*—The object of sensation, as being extended, is necessarily in space. It cannot be perceived save as occupying space. On the other hand, it is perfectly easy to withdraw attention from all actual objects in space and thus *think of* space as itself mere blank extension. Thus we come to recognize that objectively space is at once a necessary condition of the existence of bodies and a relation of body to body. That is its "reality." Otherwise it is mere boundless nothing. Remove bodies, and you remove the one positive characteristic of space.

But space is not merely a necessary condition of all possible objects of sensation. This fact itself is discovered only through, as being necessarily involved in, the further fact that in every possible sensation, space is necessarily presupposed as a fundamental condition of the very act of sensation itself. For sensation is ever a practical, concrete relation between a sensitive subject and a space-bounded and space-occupying object. And this concrete relation completed, shows us the object with its space-characteristics as taken up into the consciousness in the form of an "image," which image is, in truth, just a mode of the mind, of which the outer "object" has been merely the occasion. But the image can no more be dissociated from space than can the object of which it is the image. In any sensation there is an interfusion of a given subject or mind, with a given object or definite quality of matter, and the product of this interfusion is an "image." So that while the image is a subjective fact, it has also an objective origin. It is a creation of the mind and in the mind, but is nevertheless subject to the limitations characterizing the material out of which it is created. Act-of-sensation and object-of-sensation are the necessary complementary factors of every possible sensation. Whence, in every sensation, as well as in every product of sensation, both subjective characteristics and objective characteristics necessarily inhere.

Thus space is seen to be a necessary condition of both object and act of sensation. In so far, therefore, as it is a necessary condition of the *object* of sensation, space is *objective;* while in so far as it is a necessary condition of the purely mental *act* of sensation, space is subjective. It is neither exclusively the one nor exclusively the other, for the reason that it is both the one and the other.

The objective and the subjective, let us repeat, are but complementary aspects of every knowable — that is, of every possible — fact.

It is to be noted, however, that, considered objectively, space is a purely negative factor. It has no positive characteristics or properties. It is pure void, and as such can be known only as relation of externality between object and object, or between part and part of a given object; though this latter case can, of course, be resolved into the former, since the moment one's attention is explicitly directed to the *parts* of an object, those parts become, in turn, mutually exclusive *objects* of attention.

Now, as pure void, space can have no limits. For any possible boundary of space could only be the limit between the given space and another space on the other side of the boundary. Any possible limited space must have geometrical form. But every geometrical form is necessarily bounded by surfaces. Nay, a surface is ever to be regarded as a boundary in a two-fold sense, if we are to accept the guidance of mathematicians by whom in general, and by Professor Clifford in particular, a surface is defined as "the boundary between two adjacent portions of space."*

But a real boundary—that is, a surface constituting a transition between two volumes distinguishable in quality —can have no reality for space as such, since space, merely as space, possesses and can therefore present no positive difference in quality by which one space or portion of space can be distinguished from another.

It is evident, therefore, that any supposed limit *of* space could only be a limit *in* space, the limit having objective reality only through the existence of some object occupying space. So that all talk of a possible "curvature of space" is at once chargeable with confounding extension, as the universal and purely negative possibility of all physical modes of existence, with a particular, positive, material, extended object that might (and must) exist *in* space, but could never coalesce with space.

The distinction here indicated was long ago pointed out and emphasized by Kant in his "Metaphysical Foundations of Natural Science," where he speaks repeat-

* "*Common Sense of the Exact Sciences*" (N. Y. Ed.), p 50.

edly of "empirical space," "relative space," and "movable space."*

Applying such terms to "the sum total of all experience" for the sensuous consciousness, he, at the same time, emphasizes the absurdity of confounding such "empirical, relative space" (by which he evidently means extended objects in general) with "pure, non-empirical and absolute space," which is necessarily presupposed as the universal and indispensable negative condition of — that is, total absence of resistance to — all movement whatever.

In defining space as such, then, we can, it would seem, use no other than negative forms of expression. In space, pure and simple, all definite dimension is annulled. It is true that space presents the possibility of all dimension. Space is formless, and hence wholly indifferent to form. But just for that reason, space is — in a negative sense again — the possibility of all form. That is, it has no characteristics offering any opposition to the development of form. Objects are said to be "in space." At the same time, every definite — that is, arbitrarily selected — portion of space, however large or however small, is still an "outside" to every other portion.

It is further evident that space has no *internality* at all; for that would imply positive or real characteristics by which one portion of space could, on its own account, be distinguished from another portion. On the contrary, it is only through our sensations of objects in space that we can distinguish between space and space, or ever know anything at all about the purely negative, empty infinitude

---

*See Kant's "*Prolegomena*," etc. Translated by Belfort Bax (Bohn's Library), p. 151, and elsewhere.

which we call space. For we can only know space as the negative of body.* It is not even true that space *has* extension, for space just *is* extension, pure and simple. That is its one positive characteristic.* In its objective character, it is nothing else than indistinguishable, immovable, boundless externality. It is the pure blank form of perfect continuity. No power can quarry out a block of space and carry it away.

Subjectively considered, on the other hand, space is, as we have seen, the pure form or mode of all possible perceptions of external objects. So that, on the one hand, space proves to be a universal and necessary condition of the existence of all possible objects of sensation; while, on the other hand, it is seen to be a universal and necessary form or mode of the subjective fact or act of sensation itself.

2. *Time as a condition of sensation.* — But besides perceptions of external objects, there are perceptions of changes in those objects, and not only so; there are also perceptions of internal states of consciousness and of transition from one to another of these states.

These transitions, however, involve, or rather are themselves forms of, *succession.* But it is precisely the relation of succession that constitutes *time.* Thus, just as no object can be perceived except as in space, so no change in a perception, implying change in a perceived object, can take place otherwise than as in time. Time

---

* Strictly speaking, a point is the true negation of space. But it is such merely as the simplest phase of limit; and limit can be *realized* only in and through body. So that the point, which is the abstract negation of space, may be regarded as the initial phase of body which is the concrete negation, that is, the realization, of space. In other words, the point is the transition from pure to empirical space.

is thus the universal form of all succession, as space is the universal form of all physical co-existence.

Transition, in short, is change—a going over from one state to another. But this takes place both in the inner consciousness and also in the outer sensuous object of consciousness. Thus it becomes evident that time, as the universal form of all change, both inner and outer, is also both subjective and objective.

Like space, too, time is, merely as time, an abstraction pure and simple. Just as we could never become conscious of space, save through the perception of objects in co-existence, so we could never become conscious of time, save through the perception of events occurring in succession. And just as space would be meaningless save as a relation of object to object, so time would be devoid of meaning save as a relation of event to event. Both are purely negative factors, and yet, with their utter lack of all positive characteristics, they are precisely the factors in our perceptions of objects and changes in those objects which we find it absolutely impossible to eliminate from our perceptions.

Neither space nor time can be perceived by the senses, and yet it is alone through our perceptions that we become aware of space and time. They are not objects of special perception, and this they could not be, for they are the universal forms of all possible perceptions. It is this fact that lifts the conceptions of space and time completely out of the domain of merely empirical knowledge.

The proposition, "Every force is a form of electricity," is an empirical proposition which has been more or less definitely affirmed at different times within the present century, in spite of the somewhat arbitrary and exclusive way in which it reduces energy, a universal mode of existence, to one of its particular phases. But the proposition, "Every event must take place in time," is seen upon reflection to be necessarily implied in every single instance of the perception of an event. For it would contradict reason itself to say that an event can take place apart from the conditions of time.

It may be noted finally, that, while internal or subjective transitions as such may occur within the limitations of time alone, no external or physical change can take place otherwise than as conditioned by both time and space.

e.—SENSE-PERCEPTION FURTHER IMPLIES CONCEPTION.

We have seen that space and time are the universal and necessary modes of all perception. And yet, on further examination, perception is found to involve as one of its essential factors a mode of mind extending beyond the limits of perception, as such. It has already been intimated that every phase of mental activity necessarily presupposes a two-fold character. We have now to note more explicitly that even the simplest perception is still a highly complex fact. For the sensuous consciousness of an object arises not merely from a fixing of attention upon a given object; it is also a singling out or selection of that object from among an indefinite number of objects all presenting themselves to notice. And still further, it is a direct reference of the perceived object to the self as perceiving.

It is true that in these acts of selecting objects and referring them to himself as a conscious unit, the individual is not necessarily aware of the fact that he is making such selection and reference. Rather, in common experience, the process goes on without the individual's noticing the details of the process. At the same time, however, reflection shows that in every such act the selection itself is necessary in order that the perception may be distinct, and the reference of the object to the self is necessary in order that the perception may exist at all. And thus again the receptivity of the mind in perception is seen to be quite as definitely active as passive; or rather, it is evident that passivity is but receptivity, or *reaction.*

But now this reference, whether of object to object, or of an object to the self (both of which must take place in every act of perception), implies a seizure of a *relation;* and this seizure of relations does not belong to perception as such, though necessarily involved in every act of perception. The office of perception as such is to seize particular objects. The relation of object to object can come into the consciousness in no other way than through a *seizing together* of the objects related. And this seizing together of objects is again a primary, original act of the mind — an act which has appropriately come to be called, in English, *conception.*

Individual sensuous objects are *per*ceived. Relations can only be *con*ceived.

But now let us note that this relation seized through conception is a relation at once of identity and of difference. A number of objects different from one another are yet found to possess some characteristic through which they are all similar to one another. The several objects could not be seized as several — as separate — otherwise than through the seizure of their difference. But this seizure of the difference separating object from object is itself a reference of those objects to one another. Their severalty, or state of *severance*, can not be comprehended in thought save through a corresponding recognition of their unification or identity.

In other words, the recognition of them in their particularity necessarily implies the recognition of them in their universality. These, indeed, are but complementary phases of every possible stage of knowing. The recognition of difference between objects is the negative reference of those objects to each other—that is, the recognition of their dependence upon one another in that, to a greater or less degree, the one has what the other lacks and lacks what the other has. On the other hand, the recognition of their similarity is the positive reference of them to each other—that is, the recognition of their tendency to coalesce into one continuous, independent whole.

The negative reference of object to object is the basis of the recognition of multiplicity. The positive reference of object to object is the basis of the recognition of unity. Whence it is evident that the "one" and the "many" are but complementary aspects of one and the same *total*.

But, let us repeat, both the negative and the positive reference of object to object is the seizure of a *relation;* and while the seizure remains implicit in every act of *per*ception it becomes explicit as an act of *con*ception. Thus perception necessarily implies conception. The single object cannot be seized in isolation. The seizure of it as a single object is already implicitly a seizure of it in its relations. On the other hand, the seizure of a relation between objects necessarily implies that the objects themselves are already, in that very fact, perceived. Whence it is evident that these two phases of the mind's activity—

perception and conception — mutually and necessarily imply one another. However far the one may predominate in any given instance, the other is always involved in the same act. Or, as somewhat picturesquely expressed in a phrase attributed to Kant* (whom we are here substantially following), "Conceptions without perceptions are empty. Perceptions without conceptions are blind." †

Nevertheless, perception is of a distinctly lower rank than conception in the scale of the mind's modes of activity. As we have seen, the former is the distinctive mode by which particular objects are taken up into consciousness; while the latter is the mode by which the more wide-reaching result is obtained of bringing into clear definition in the individual consciousness the complementary relations of identity and difference necessarily involved in the objects which appeal directly to the senses. So that mere sense perception, so long as it predominates as such in the activity of any given mind and thus includes conception only in its implicit phase, is necessarily a very inadequate, superficial stage of mental activity. And the development of conception into its explicit phase as the dominating mode of mental activity is essential to anything approaching adequate knowledge, even of the simplest fact.

Any "fact," indeed, can be truly known in no other way than through its relations; and it is, let us repeat,

* I have to acknowledge my indebtedness in the study of Kant to the expositions of Dr. W. T. Harris, and also to Professor E. Caird's admirably clear "*Critical Account of the Philosophy of Kant.*"

† Kant's own expression is: Gedanken ohne Inhalt sind leer, Anschauungen ohne Begriffe sind blind. (*Kritik der reinen Vernunft.*— Ed. Hartenstein, S. 82.) But the context shows that the form given above — the form used by Professor Caird, and which also exactly translates the words used in Schwegler's exposition (*Geschichte der Philosophie*, 12te Auflage, S. 191), — is a perfectly accurate rendering of Kant's meaning.

only through the power of conception that the fact can be seized in its relations and thus thoroughly comprehended. This remarkable power of the mind, then, which we call conception, is found in its most elementary character to be a subordinate phase of perception. And yet, through its own expansion into its complete, explicit significance and vigor, it transcends perception, includes and subordinates it, and proves to be the mode of activity by which the outer world of objects and relations is brought together or comprehended as a harmonized, unified whole, completely within the grasp of the mind.*

f.—PRIMARY UNITY OF SELF-CONSCIOUSNESS.

It will now be desirable to bring into more explicit statement the significant fact already more than once referred to: That in every act of knowing, whether that act be predominantly perceptive or predominantly conceptive, there is necessarily involved not merely a reference, implicit or explicit, of object to object; but also a reference of every object to a *self* as perceiving and as conceiving. Thus every possible act of knowing necessarily implies a *self-reference* as the fundamental characteristic of the individual consciousness.

Knowing is, first of all, *self*-knowing — a knowing-together, as the word consciousness itself implies. And this collectedness and vital unification of knowing in selfhood has been further emphasized among English-speaking people in the term *self*-consciousness. It is,

* It will be noticed that the term conception is here used in a sense so wide as to include thought—an extension of meaning not without precedent, and not without psychological justification. For just as conception is implicit in every act of perception, so thought, properly speaking, is implicit in every act of conception. Hence the frequent use of the expression "to conceive," meaning "to think."

indeed, precisely in self-consciousness that every possible phase of knowing must, in the first place, take its rise, and in the outcome find its culmination. Nay, the self is in truth the fundamental, vital unity actually constituting the whole manifold series of perceptions and conceptions that take shape in the individual consciousness.

It is, therefore, nothing more than a truism to say that, apart from this unity, the series could never be known, either as a whole or in its parts; for without the unity the series could have no existence. The unity of self is the universal which, at first abstract, brings itself into concrete realization, through its own activity displayed in the development of the manifold particular phases of perception and conception.

Underlying all knowledge, then — nay, rather constituting the very core of all knowledge — is the primary, or rather primordial, unity of self-consciousness.

At the same time it is easy to see that this unity is far from being a simple, abstract, empty unity. On the contrary, it is dual and triple, nay, infinitely manifold. First, as that which knows, it is *subject;* secondly, as that which is known, it is *object;* and thirdly, as that which in its very nature is self-known, it is *subject-object,* which also necessarily implies infinite complexity.

This indeed is substantially the standpoint of all modern philosophy. Descartes, the founder of modern philosophy, finds the ultimate ground of certitude in self-reference. "I think, therefore I am." I, who think, first of all know myself as thinking; and so long as this conscious self-reference continues, I am absolutely assured in that very fact of my own existence. I can indeed conceive of an object as having existence, and yet as being destitute of consciousness. But I find it absolutely impossible to conceive of a consciousness that yet has no existence.

It may indeed prove, in the sequel, that every phase of existence implies intelligence or consciousness; but it is manifest without further demonstration that every phase of consciousness explicitly and of necessity involves existence. Thus it appears that consciousness is the wider, richer term, and involves existence. And it may be that *perfect* consciousness is precisely the highest term of existence, that it is just another name for self-existence. So that existence not otherwise defined, is vastly the poorer, more abstract, and hence subordinate term.

Self-consciousness, then, appears to be the root from which every branch of knowledge springs. If I turn "experimentalist," and apply myself to the acquisition of knowledge of external things, here too, as I have seen, every step imperatively demands, absolutely cannot be taken without, the reference of all to self. Every fact, however simple or however complex, must inexorably be tested by reference to laws which I find in my own consciousness — laws which I find it impossible to think of as undergoing change. For change itself is meaningless, save in so far as it is referred to the permanent, to the changeless, as the standard of judgment.

Nor will it avail here any better than elsewhere to take refuge in the mists of "relativity." For the "relatively permanent" must in the outcome ever prove to be something undergoing change. Such standard is therefore in its very nature self-contradictory, since a changing standard can be in truth no standard at all.

This truth is verified — that is, empirically "proven" — in the ordinary affairs of life. In so far as standards of value fluctuate, they cease to have reality as standards. It is rightly assumed that the value of the changing can be estimated only in comparison with that which is absolutely unchanging, with that which is permanent, in the ultimate and legitimate sense of the term. Even standards of weights and measures are *assumed to be unchanging*. Not a single transaction in commerce, nor an experiment in science ever occurs that does not involve this assumption. Otherwise, indeed, no sane people, and therefore no people at all, would exist to pursue either commercial or scientific or any other interests.

To this it need only be added here that any change *in* consciousness that is not subordinated to the unity and therefore permanent identity *of* consciousness could be nothing else than a complete break in, and hence the utter annihilation of consciousness. And this is as much as to say that consciousness, in its universal character, in its ideal nature or type, can never undergo any change. Underlying the unity of the self, and constituting its fundamental characteristic, is the law of self-consistency, which may be stated in the following form: *Perfect consistency in consciousness is the ultimate and absolute ground of all certitude.*

By this standard every "fact" must be accepted or rejected, every "theory" approved or condemned. Here is the ultimatum of "experimental," as of all science. It is upon the results of the supreme, inner experiment which thought performs upon thought that all knowledge must ultimately rest.

Thus while all really systematic, scientific research begins with the outer or physical, it culminates and must ever culminate in the inner or spiritual. And while these two phases or fields of investigation may appear to be mutually exclusive, they in reality merge into one another; so that the physical may be rightly described as the initial phase of the spiritual, the spiritual as the maturity, the fulfilment of what is only vaguely intimated in the physical.

On one side our knowledge depends upon sensuous experience; on another side it transcends that phase of experience; while finally it coincides with experience in the widest, richest meaning which the term experience can have. Knowledge is, in truth, the very core of experience, and experience is but the unfolding or outer realization of knowledge. Experience is practical knowledge; knowledge, theoretical or reasoned experience.

Evidently, then, sensuous experience is neither all nor the best experience. Rather, the best experience is that which realizes with the most perfect consistency the greatest extent and degree of truth. That, doubtless, is the most "practical" way of life which serves best to symmetrically unfold the spirit into the concrete realization of all its powers.

Once more, then, the sensuous is seen to be the poorest, least adequate phase of experience, for the reason that it is but the simplest, most rudimentary phase thereof; while "experience," in its truth and completeness, is just the total process of the development of man in the entire compass of his nature.

All genuine knowledge is, in truth, experimental. There can be no other. If experimental science has its initial point in the discovery of physical relations, it has its culmination in the discovery of the higher relations unfolded in the world of thought.

g.—THE LAWS OF THOUGHT.

The "necessary laws of thought" are nothing else than the technical presentation in three abstract propositions, expressing successively, with greater explicitness, the conviction above set forth, namely: That perfect consistency in consciousness is the ultimate and only absolute ground of certitude.

The law of identity declares that "whatever is, is." Regarded formally, this is pure, empty tautology. But the statement also contains implicitly the deepest significance. It declares in effect that existence is absolute and uniform. Already in the fifth century before the Christian era, this truth was felt, and Parmenides sought to give it utterance in his dictum that "Being alone is and non-being is not." Aristotle also reaffirmed it in his representation of the "Unmoved mover of the world," while in the modern world it reappears in the affirmation that the total quantity of matter or of energy can never be either increased or diminished.

Thus the first law of thought is, in germ, the doctrine of the conservation of energy. It implies that existence can never be changed into non-existence, nor the latter into the former. So far as existence itself is concerned, there is neither past nor future, but only a ceaseless, changeless present.

This law is, then, the law of consistency under the form of absolute continuity. The truly existent, however great its complexity, however much of mutual opposition there may possibly be between its various multiform phases, can still never contradict itself. The law, as stated, says nothing whatever as to whether multiplicity is or is not necessarily involved in existence. It simply affirms existence as changelessly one with itself.

Nevertheless, this is but vaguely intimated in the law of identity, which thus proves to be sufficiently ambiguous. And yet, as already shown, the formula may be fairly interpreted as meaning that whatever is cannot cease to be, and still more, that whatever is cannot, at the same time, *not be*.

Thus the first law of thought, when unfolded into the negative form, is found to involve also the second law, or the *law of contradiction*, which, in truth, only emphasizes and aids in rendering explicit the law of identity. The law of contradiction declares that "anything cannot both be and not be." And this is simply an advanced form of the law of consistency.

Nor does this advanced form of the law of consistency exclude the dialectic of change inhering in all things finite. This is sufficiently evident even in the form just quoted, and which is the form in which the law of contradiction is more commonly stated. But still less does this law exclude change when stated in the form given it by Aristotle, namely: Τὸ γὰρ αὐτὸ ἅμα ὑπάρχειν καὶ μὴ ὑπάρχειν, ἀδύνατον τῷ αὐτῷ κατὰ τό αὐτό. "It is impossible that precisely the same phase of reality should both begin and not begin at the same time and in the same sense." *

Thus stated, Aristotle declares the law of contradiction to be the "most firmly established of all first principles." And as he makes this statement immediately following the declaration that the philosopher must come provided with a first principle that is "independent of

---

* "*Metaphysics*," Lib. III. (IV.), cap. III.

hypothesis," it is evident that he regarded this as the primal law of the reason, and as such necessarily self-evident in its truth.

With such assurance from such a thinker, then, one may well be encouraged to inquire with care and diligence whether there may not be something more in this law, even in the form ordinarily given it, than the shallow, contradictory abstraction which, as simply the negative power of the law of identity, it has been represented by Hegel as being.* When it is declared that A can not be both A and not A, it is implied in the very form of the statement that A may be either A or not A, *according as it is subjected to this or that set of conditions.* It is simply declared that the two affirmations, "A begins" and "A does not begin," could not possibly both be true at the same time and in the same sense.

But if A possesses any definiteness, that is, any reality, then so far as the characteristics of A are determined by any given set of conditions undergoing change, A must necessarily change as the conditions change, and in so doing must thus far necessarily become not A. For example, with sufficient increase of temperature, a given portion of carbon now constituting a diamond may be vaporized and combined with oxygen; the resulting carbon-dioxide may be decomposed through absorption into a vegetable organism, the carbon that was diamond now becoming woody fiber, to undergo still further transformation, perhaps into coal, etc., etc.

Thus the same group of carbon particles may be both diamond and not diamond. But if by this declaration it is meant that both these mutually exclusive states can be

* "*Werke*" (2te Auflage), VI., 230.

assumed at the same *time*, by the *same group of particles*, it can be true only in a *special sense*. If true in the *same sense* it can be only in *different times*. At the moment when the particles constitute diamond in *reality*, they can at that moment be said to constitute not-diamond (woody fiber, coal, etc.) only in the sense of *potentiality*. Or, in general terms, any given quantity of matter can be in one and only one state at one and the same time; so that, whatever the number of states possible for such given quantity of matter, those states can be realized by and for it only serially, or through successive periods of time.

Thus the law of contradiction might also be called the law of consistency as exhibited in the actual world — the law of precision in the modes of existence.

It would seem then that the true significance of the law of contradiction is rather this: *First*, that whatever the forms successively assumed by any portion of substance, that portion of substance, through whatever transformations it may pass, still exists absolutely, and is wholly excluded from non-existence in the sense of mere nothingness; *secondly*, throughout its transformations a given portion of substance can as a unit assume at any given moment but one consistent grouping of its parts, from which it follows that no two contrary descriptions could be true of it at the same time. It is perfectly consistent with our conception of the existent that it should assume all possible forms of existence; but it is wholly inconsistent with that conception to suppose that the existent in any of its possible aspects should ever become utterly null or non-existent.

It is to be noted, too, that while the law of identity would seem on first view to exclude change, and while it does exclude change from existence as a whole, yet the law of contradiction, which is but a more explicit form of stating the same truth as that contained in the first, distinctly assumes change to be perpetual for every finite form of existence. Any given thing is perpetually in process, and can "begin," at any given moment, in this or that particular phase of the process only.

The first law declares the permanence and continuity of existence as a whole. The second law declares that the particular aspects of existence are in a ceaseless process.

Again let us regard A as a symbol of the totality of all that exists. Then it becomes evident that while all change is involved *in* A, there can never by any possibility be any change *of* A.

We find ourselves thus contemplating that absolute Identity which includes all possible difference within itself. Here the seemingly negative law of contradiction is found to negate the non-existent absolutely, and thus to be the positively developed form of the law of identity in that it is the absolute affirmation of all reality.

The "law of excluded middle" finally, announces that the existent and the non-existent exhaust the possibilities of thought. "A thing must either be or not be;" there is no third or "middle" possibility. Whatever is, not only must *be*, but must be in a state of perfect definiteness.

The first law of thought affirms *positively* that what exists is self-consistent; the second affirms the same thing *negatively* in declaring that the existent cannot contradict itself, either by being at the same time non-existent, or by presenting the same portions of itself at the same time under mutually exclusive forms; while the third law reaffirms *absolutely* the self-consistency of the existent as being *necessary*.

Rightly understood, then, these laws are valid and vital as the laws of thought. They affirm under a progressive series of forms the primordial law of perfect consistency in consciousness as the *absolute test of certitude*.* They are "necessary laws," not in the sense in which Professor Jevons seems to think that expression must be understood, namely, in the sense that they are "laws which cannot but be obeyed;"† but rather in the sense that one's thinking must inevitably be self-contradictory in just so far as it fails to be in conformity with those laws. They are the laws in accordance with which one *must* think *if* he is to think *truly*. The order of the only world we can ever really *know* is the order of reason, of self-consistency. And this is a "necessary" order, in the sense that it can never change without destroying itself. Whence no thinking can really be true thinking — that is, self-consistent thinking — unless it follow this law of the inner necessity of reason itself.

Doubtless it is in this sense that one ought to understand the remark of Hegel that, "True thinking is the thinking of necessity." ‡

h.—THE LAWS OF THOUGHT ARE THE LAWS OF THINGS.

It is certainly not without significance that while these laws are *named* the laws of *thought*, they are nevertheless *formulated* as the laws of *things*. At first view this seems a radical inconsistency. And yet it is not necessarily so. They are rightly named "laws of thought," because, as has just been pointed out, they are the three

---

* This appears to me to summarize the aspects of truth involved in the three laws of thought; though Prof. Jevons expresses doubt as to the possibility of such summary statement. "*Principles of Science,*" (3d ed.) p. 6.
† Ibid. p. 7. ‡ "*Logic of the Encyclopedia,*" § 119.

essential forms—positive, negative and infinite (or absolute)—under which the primary law of the necessary unity and self-consistency of thought may be presented. But they are equally the laws of things, since the only "things" with which thought can really deal, and hence the only things concerning which affirmations possessing any real significance can be made, are the facts of the world such as they present themselves in consciousness; that is, in thought. But thus presented in consciousness, these facts, so far as they are really facts for the individual, are just the perceptions and conceptions which the individual has formed in his own mind.

No doubt any given perception has taken place in any given mind only in consequence of certain stimuli which such mind has received from outer "things." But to say this, is only to describe another conception which the individual has formed concerning the conditions under which perceptions and conceptions in general can arise in his mind. That is, while such statement emphasizes the fact, that in one sense, we can never get beyond our own perceptions and conceptions, and that thus all our knowledge seems purely subjective; yet the very consciousness of these subjective states necessarily involves a reference of them to some external exciting cause and thus proves that knowledge is no less objective than subjective in its nature.

It is especially worthy of note in this connection, too, that even in the ordinary use of language it is the subjective phase of mental activity that is called thought, while the objective aspects of that activity are denominated "things." And again, this implicit rationality of the ordinary consciousness is developed into more explicit form by the psychologist, who points out the fact that the only "objects" which we can ever know are in reality *our own perceptions* of what *seems to us* to be objects lying beyond and independent of us and of our perceptions.

The complementary relation between thought and things thus indicated, is made still more evident if we follow out the clue and consider

i.—THE VARIOUS ASPECTS OF IDEALISM.

The first aspect of idealism is that in which the idealist presents himself in his subjective, most elementary stage of development. In this stage he puts his own interpretation upon the fact to which the psychologist has drawn attention. "Yes," he declares, "the only 'things' I can ever know are, indeed, just my own states of consciousness. That is the only real world for me, and hence for me the only true world. What I really think, that is true for me and the only truth. Allowing the existence of an 'objective' world, I can never know anything of its real nature and can not even find any valid proof of its existence. So, also, allowing the existence of other minds, their convictions, however valid for them, can have no significance for me, to whom there can be no truth apart from my own mental states."

Such is the standpoint of what may be called *subjective idealism*, pure and simple; or, as it has commonly been known since the time of the later Greek thinkers, it is the standpoint of sophistry. It has appeared again and again with more or less elaborateness and subtlety of form and presenting a greater or less degree of substantial truth.

But such one-sided view could not but be confronted by its opposite—that is, by *objective idealism*.* Naturally, too, the latter is marked by distrust of the "human intellect" and its powers. "Speculation" is regarded as idle and mischievous. If one is ever to put himself in possession of the truth, he must abandon the absurd effort to find it in the empty depths of his own consciousness, and must turn his attention to the real objective world. It is in the world of nature alone that one can hope to find continuity, consistency, truth. Here the "ideal" is that of an outside, solid, *material* world. It is of a world already given, but given one knows not how.

Doubtless the investigator in this field would prefer to be known as a *realist*; and indeed the "speculations" that inevitably force themselves into formulation here as elsewhere do lead up to a very lofty phase of idealism which has been named (by Herbert Spencer) "*transfigured realism*." And yet this transfigured realism is itself a speculative or ideal representation of the objective world, as that world is conceived to be in its essence.

Finally, there comes a third idealist and appeals in turn to each of the other two. To the subjective idealist he says: "You have abandoned reason and in its place have substituted caprice. You are right in declaring that thought is all one can know; but radically wrong

---

*The reader familiar with the history of philosophy will notice the difference between the use here made of these terms and that given them in Germany in the early part of the present century. At the same time I cannot but think that the crude form of subjective idealism specially referred to in the text is in reality nothing more nor less than the initial aspect of what in its subtler form develops into such theories as that of Berkeley; or even, in another direction, into theories like that of Fichte. It is scarcely necessary to add that the "objective idealism" here referred to is that (apparently for the most part unconscious) aspect of idealism involved in the current movement in natural science.

in your assumption that the mere private, and very likely wholly undisciplined, thinking of the individual is the only attainable form of thought, or that it is necessarily true *thought* at all. If the thinking of each individual is the truth for him, then there can be no truth at all, since the untrained mind makes no effort to avoid contradictory thought, nor does it even recognize the fact that contradictions are constantly arising in its own thinking. And yet thought can only be true, as thought, in so far as it is consistent with itself. The contradiction of thought by thought must be the utter negation of thought; that is, must prove that what was taken for thought is in reality not thought at all.

"If, therefore, you are sincere in your search for truth, you must recognize that your standpoint is one-sided and superficial, and therefore requires to be supplemented and deepened through fusion with another element. That element is the objective phase of thought. Thought, as such, is universal and necessary in its nature. It is absolutely consistent and unchanging. That is the fundamental characteristic of thought; and because no subjective caprice which you or I may entertain can ever, in the least, affect this fundamental nature of thought, as such, the latter may very properly be called *objective* or *true* thought, in contrast with our own subjective, often self-contradictory, and in such case necessarily untrue thought.

"I readily admit, and with you emphatically declare, that it is only by our own individual thinking that we, as individuals, can reach any conclusion at all. But I also declare, with no less confidence, that we must ever and inevitably be led to the conclusion I have just been stating, if we carefully put our individual thinking to the crucial test of self-criticism. For self-criticism must ever culminate in the clear recognition of the fundamental law of *perfect consistency in consciousness* as the absolute, unchanging, and hence *objective* test of certitude as to the truth in any given case of inquiry. It is only when the thinking of the individual unfolds into this objective character that it becomes genuine, true thinking."

So, again, this third idealist will appeal to the idealist of the second type, and say to him: "Admirable as are your work and the results of your work, there is, nevertheless, a phase of your method that remains as yet almost wholly implicit; and this fact proves at times to be the occasion of serious error. You say rightly that truth is to be attained only through a searching examination of the objective, real world. But you seem to have not sufficiently regarded the fact that the only way by which a real knowledge of the 'objective' or outer world can be attained is through the exertion of your own subjective or inner powers. You are thus led to look upon the objective world as something independent of your own mind, or even as independent of mind in any and every sense. So that when you discover necessary laws in 'nature' you not only regard the necessity of those laws as a 'natural' necessity, but also make the unwarrantable assumption that 'natural' is synonymous with 'physical.' And yet, as a matter of fact, you can scarcely fail to admit, upon reflection, that 'natural' means the same as 'rational,' if it means anything. For whatever contradicts reason, the reason cannot but regard as unnatural; and it is only through reason that we can pronounce upon this, or, indeed, upon any question whatever.

"Do but remember that the 'nature' in the study of which you find such delight, and whose orderliness and symmetry you have so superbly demonstrated, is by no means all *there* in space — is by no means objective merely in the sense of being outer and foreign to mind; but rather that it is 'objective' in the sense of being the embodiment of consistency, of necessary truth, and hence as involving mind or reason as its very essence. Indeed, with every advance in your investigation of nature, you develop more and more conclusive proofs that nature is an embodiment of 'laws' that justify themselves to the trained reason as possessing universal and necessary validity.

"Thus there is constantly increasing ground for confidence in the justice of the maxim which virtually underlies all your work. And we may well go to nature and trust to the guidance of its "facts" if we would find the truth. At the same time, it is of the utmost importance that we should know, as precisely as possible, both the character and the extent of the significance which the maxim contains.

"And, on careful examination, this appears evident enough. Thus the maxim implies that truth is in Nature, and that the truth thus embodied is not beyond the reach of thought. For it is, indeed, only through thought that we can go to nature, or 'go' anywhere in search of truth.

"If, indeed, nature were something wholly distinct from thought, then the proposal to go to nature in order to find the truth would imply that thought must absolutely go beyond itself to find the truth. In which case thought must itself appear to be something untrue. At the same time, taken in the absolute sense of the term, the demand that thought should 'go beyond itself' is wholly self-contradictory, and therefore destitute of meaning. It is only when taken in a special, limited sense that the expression is found to be consistent and to possess real significance. Thus, the 'thought' of the individual human mind, considered in the sense of the actual state of consciousness of a given person at any given moment, may indeed, be developed or 'expanded' into greater complexity and consistency. But it can do this only because it already contains implicitly in itself, *as its own fundamental nature*, objective universality and truth.

"In so far, then, as the individual consciousness develops or 'expands' itself, it is only harmonizing or identifying its real self with its ideal or true self. That is, in 'going beyond itself' it is merely going beyond its present immature, untrue self, and in so doing is *coming to* its substantial, universal, true self.

"But now, you who insist upon the truth that the total quantity of energy forever remains unchanged, must admit that the individual human mind has no power to produce out of pure nothing any phase of reality whatever, least of all the richest of all phases of reality—realized reason itself. The human mind doubtless has the power to discover and transform, but not the power to create, in the sense of producing something which absolutely had no existence before. So that every step by which the individual mind 'goes beyond itself' as an imperfect embodiment or realization of reason, implies of necessity, that both the phases of reason already reached, and also *all the phases possible to be reached*, by such mind must already possess perfected and permanent realization in the universe as a whole. Otherwise the growth of the individual as a power-to-think, must ultimately involve a change in (and of) the total quantity of energy.

"But thus, again, it becomes evident that wherever the individual as a power-to-think can 'go,' there thought is of necessity already present in realized form. The 'where' of thought proves to be just the total round of the possible modes of thought itself; which modes, to be possible at all, must be already realized in the universe as a whole. Whence it appears that the thought of the individual can 'go' to nature on this one condition alone: that thought, in its universal character, is already there present and realized in nature.

"You would separate nature from thought as if nature were something objective and thought a merely subjective process. And this is right as far as it goes. But it remains only a half-truth until supplemented by the recognition of the fact that in the strict sense of the term the only possible objects of thought are precisely thought itself, and the modes of thought in their manifestations.

"And, in truth, your maxim really conforms to this view. For our examination of it has already shown substantially that the thought of the individual can go to nature only on the condition that thought in at least some of its essential modes is already there in nature. But thought can only be 'in' nature by being fused with nature.

"I submit, therefore, that this is the real truth of the case: *Nature is the external and thought the internal;* internal, that is, in the sense that thought is the inner, vital principle, which manifests, unfolds, utters or outers *itself* in nature. So that, nature is 'object' not in the sense of being *external to* thought, but rather in the sense that it is the *externalization of* thought. It is, in short, as a mode of thought, and only as a mode of thought, that nature is accessible to intelligence in any degree whatever.

"Thus, it appears that the separation between nature as object, and mind as subject, is valid only in so far as concerns the experience of this or that individual mind. To the untrained mind nature, and still more, all the more complex modes of thought, are quite foreign or external. On the other hand, as the untrained mind 'goes to nature' and expands its own powers into fuller realization, it approaches more and more nearly to the apprehension of that great truth that, in the final outcome, subject and object are but the necessary complementary phases, not merely of each individual human mind's experience, but also that they are the necessary complementary phases of the one only world or universe.

"On this view it is perfectly 'natural' (*i. e.* rational) that on the one hand the individual mind in its investigations of nature should discover everywhere in nature the most beautiful manifestations of the law of consistency, harmony, continuity, *rational system;* and that on the other hand the testing and verifying this discovery should lead at length to the recognition of the fact that this law is, in truth, one and the same with the law of consistency, harmony, continuity, *rational method* underlying the very nature of thought itself.

"Thus the laws of thought and the laws of the only things that can ever be known by thought prove to be identical. And the truth is to be attained, not by an exclusively 'subjective' method, as if one could exhaust the possibilities of thought by a mere examination of his own inner consciousness; nor by an exclusively 'objective' method, as if one could possess himself of the whole or even the highest phase of truth by a mere examination of that outer world of appearances occupying space, and which is commonly called 'nature.' On the contrary, the *truth*, in its vital reality, is to be attained only through a complete blending of these two methods; that is, through a constant recognition of the true relation between the outer and the inner, between the objective and the subjective, as the mutually complementary modes of existence in its ultimate reality and perennial vigor as the ever-living truth."

Such would be the appeal of our third idealist, who, as insisting upon this: that the absolute fusion of the subjective and the objective is the truth alike of things and of the method of inquiry concerning things, proves to be the representative of *absolute idealism*.

And because this mode of viewing the world appears to bring us to, or at least to point us toward, the ultimate equilibrium of thought, it is the mode of view which we would hope to maintain in all our further investigations.

What follows in the present volume is an attempt to develop dialectically the fundamental characteristics of nature. This logical process of thought in the investigation of nature leads up to a conclusion in which there is found to be represented the logical presupposition of nature. Our final discovery is the primal Fact.

CHAPTER II.

"MATTER" AND ITS PROPERTIES.

IN the introductory chapter, it has been shown that every object of sense-perception must necessarily occupy space. It must, in other words, be extended. We come, then, to ask, in the next place: What is the necessary significance of this characteristic inhering in the matter of sense-perception?

a.—RESISTANCE OR REPULSION.

To answer this question, we have but to reflect that our impression of an object as extended is due primarily to the resistance which the object offers to our activity. Without such resistance we could never even know that the object exists.

But the resistance which an object presents to our activity necessarily implies that the parts of which the object, as a whole, is composed, must themselves be mutually resistant. I attempt to compress a given object. I feel the object as resisting. That is, the object presents itself to my consciousness *as resistance.*

Thus the object, as object of perception, is not only, by that fact, necessarily extended, and hence made up of mutually exclusive parts; but this very mutual exclusion is found to be realized under the form of mutual resistance. The entire body resists my efforts to compress it, because the parts of which the body is composed resist any effort, either to bring them into mutual *in*clusion, or to alter their positions relatively to one another.

In other words, while the mutual resistance of the component parts of a body would seem, on first view, to be a merely positive characteristic, consisting of the simple action of a force from the center outward, it really proves, on further examination, to be quite as much negative as positive. It is not merely that the body holds together in a given positive form, but also that each component part *excludes* every other part. And in this respect the parts or particles are negative, as toward one another, and thus give to matter the negative, or at least negatively named, characteristic, of impenetrability. That is, so far as we regard matter merely under the aspect of resistance, it is evident that we can have no doubt of the impossibility of any two bodies ever occupying the same space at the same time.

Apparently, then, the truth of anything I can know as a body is found in the characteristic of resistance, or, otherwise named, *repulsion*. And yet I have but just noticed that the resistance which any given body offers to any effort I may make to change its form consists in part of the resistance which the parts composing the body present to any change in their positions relatively to one another. But this can only mean that the parts are positively connected with one another, that they hold fast upon one another so as to hinder my efforts to bring them into a relatively different position. That is, they attract, as well as repel, one another.

Besides, were the negative characteristic of repulsion the sole truth of bodies, we must be driven to a conclusion wholly at variance with the very idea of body. For unrestrained repulsion, as between all portions of matter — between the smallest, no less than between the largest — absolute continuity of repulsion must have the effect to infinitely diffuse each body through space. Whence, not only must every particular body lose all outline or boundary, and thus contradict the conception of body as something both extended and also limited; but every particular body must thus penetrate every other body completely, and hence occupy the same space at the same time. In other words, there would be but one uniformly diffused mass, which, by the very fact of its infinite penetrability, must forever remain wholly unknown to us.

It appears, then, that a "matter" which should consist solely of resistance must, by that very fact, be infinitely diffused, and hence infinitely penetrable, or absolutely non-resistant. And this is the same as to say that the conception of matter as consisting solely of resistance is a self-contradictory conception — a conception wholly at variance with the law of consistency, the central law of all thought and of all reality that can ever be known by thought.

Our conclusion is, then, that though mere resistance may be the truth of matter as *extended*, it is far from being the *whole* truth of matter.

We have, then, to make this further inquiry: What is the real truth involved in the conception of resistance?

We have certain impressions, to the objective phase of which we give the name "body," or "matter." And for us body or matter consists of a resistance which we name repulsion. We cannot account for these impressions in any other way. And yet, thus accounting for them, we find ourselves involved in contradiction. From this contradiction we are to seek a way of escape.

In doing so, let us assume any series of particles, as:

    (1)   (2)   (3)   (4)   (5)

If repulsion is an essential characteristic of matter, then each of these particles must repel every other in the series. Hence (3) repels (2) and (1) on one side, and (4) and (5) on the other side. But each of these repels (3) in turn. That is, repulsion is a relation of reciprocal action. One particle cannot repel the other without being in turn repelled by it. Indeed, there can be no exertion of force in any direction except in so far as there is opposition or resistance from that direction. There can be no push without something to push against — no action without a corresponding reaction. And the degree of force actually exerted in either direction will depend upon the degree of force actually exerted in the opposite direction. So that, no matter what possibility of force there may be in (3), it can actually repel (2) only in so far as it is repelled by (2). And the same is true of whatever pair we may consider.

But (3) repels (2) not merely by its own isolated power of repulsion (setting aside for the moment the question of the possibility of such isolated power), but also with the added impetus which it receives from the repulsion exerted upon it by (4) and (5). It is evident, then, that not only do (1) and (2) mutually repel each other, but also that (2) is actually driven toward (1) by the cumulative repulsions between itself and (3), (4) and (5).

It is true that while (4) and (5) repel (2) through (3), they also repel (1) through both (3) and (2); so that it would seem as if (1) must be driven from (2) still more powerfully than (2) is driven toward (1). At the same time, however, it must be remembered that (1) is the limiting particle of the series on one side. As such its repulsion for (2) and for the remaining particles in the series must be less than that of (2) for those remaining particles. For the repulsion of (2) for (3), (4) and (5) is intensified by the repulsion between (1) and (2), which thrusts (2) back upon (3), but only to be the more powerfully urged toward (1) again.

Thus the tendency of the repulsion between (2) and the particles of the series beyond (2) is to cause an actual *approach* of (2) toward (1). And it is to be also noted, at the same time, that the repulsion between (1) and (2) counteracts in a measure the tendency toward separation between (2) and (3); and so throughout the series.

But, again, it has already been incidentally observed that each intermediate particle in the series exerts its repulsion in two precisely opposite directions. In the case of (3), indeed, these repulsions in opposite directions must balance each other. Hence, (3) is the point of equilibrium in the series. And it is to be noticed especially that the repulsion of this middle particle for those on either side presents this peculiar aspect: that in thus exerting its power of repulsion in opposite directions, it necessarily *concentrates upon itself.* And this brings to explicit utterance the truth that no particle, under any conditions whatever, can push outward in any direction from itself save by pressing in upon itself in the same act.

Repulsion, then, even in so inadequate an example as the one assumed, proves to be something more than a mere tendency toward indefinite diffusion. Instead of being merely a more explicit phase of externality, of matter as the extended, it proves to be a tendency toward concentration as well, and hence to involve internality no less than externality. And this will become only the more apparent the more concretely it is viewed.

Imagine the particles in such series as that above represented to be retained in the same relative positions, and the whole revolved about the central one in such way that the several other particles shall describe concentric circles in the same plane. It is evident that every possible diameter of the circles thus described has been represented in succession by the line joining the series of particles, and that the same relations would be true in every position assumed by the series.

If, now, the distances of (1) and (2) from (3) in the original series be assumed to be different from the distances separating (4) and (5) from (3), then we should have four circles, each with a material circumference about a common material center. In such case it is evident that the complexity of relations must be vastly multiplied, since the repulsions will be exerted not merely between the members of each series in any given diameter, but also between each member of each series, and every member of each and all the other series as well.

But, again, let us imagine each diameter to be rendered material throughout its whole length through the further multiplication of particles. We should then have a continuous disc, involving still further complication of repulsions and counter-repulsions—the lines of relation running out from each particle to every other particle in the whole disc, and thus forming a most minutely complicated web of relations.

And yet, once more, suppose the disc itself to be revolved about one of its diameters, so as to describe a sphere. The described sphere would be a material one, such that every section through a great circle of the sphere would present a set of relations identical with that of the revolved disc. We should then have not merely an indefinite repetition of the web of relations existing in the disc, but also a wholly new and immeasurably more complicated network of relations, consisting of lines of repulsion between each particle and every other particle throughout the entire sphere. Each particle would be repelled by every other particle; that is, every particle within the sphere would be repelled in *all directions*. Hence it would be driven *toward* as well as *from* every other particle. And, still further, each particle, as exerting repulsion in all directions, is driven in upon itself from all sides; so that the more intense and complicated the repulsion exerted by it, with only so much the greater energy must it concentrate upon itself.

Finally, let the sphere—since there is no necessary limit to its volume—be regarded as co-extensive with space; that is, let it be regarded as infinite. The repulsion of part for part would then necessarily react in such way that the tendency to concentration would, in the total quantity of matter, exactly balance the tendency toward expansion. In other words, the "repulsion" must prove in its very development as repulsion to constantly unfold into its own opposite, and to be in its very nature attraction no less than repulsion. For "attraction" is the name we give to the inherent tendency of matter toward aggregation or concentration upon itself.

And here it is to be remarked, that not only is there no *necessary* limit to the ultimate "sphere," or total volume of matter in the universe; in reality it would seem that no such limit is *possible*. For, on the assumption that such limit existed, the particles of matter at the surface would then be bounded on one side by pure space. That is, in all directions from the center there would be repulsion outward, which would, indeed, on first view, seem to develop itself into attraction about the center of the sphere. But, on the other hand, at the surface there would be complete absence of reaction; that is, there would be absolutely no resistance to the thrust outward from the center. Hence the sphere must go on expanding indefinitely through space, and result at length in the complete dissipation of whatever energy may be allowed to have been accumulated, by whatever incomprehensible means, upon the supposed center in past time.

Thus I find that in reality it is impossible for me to conceive that any definite portion of "matter" should be so aggregated as to present a definite surface and an appreciable resistance (through which alone I could ever become conscious of its existence) otherwise than upon the condition that the total volume of matter is co-extensive with space; that is, upon the condition that the total quantity of matter is infinite.

It appears, then, that every portion of matter exists, not merely on its own account, but also and necessarily— that is, in its very nature — for every other portion of matter. It has just been seen that resistance—the primary characteristic of the objects of sense-perception — proves this to be true. And the conviction that such is the case — a conviction arrived at, apparently, by no very explicit dialectic — has long since become general under the form of the "impenetrability" of matter, which term is defined as meaning that "no two portions of 'matter' can occupy the same space at the same time."

It is especially important to notice, too, that though presented in the negative form, the definition is expressed as having universal and absolute validity. If no two portions of matter can occupy the same space at the same time, then we but alter the mode of statement in saying that every portion of matter is necessarily related as repellant to every other portion of matter — that every portion of matter exists not merely by itself, or in isolation, but also for all other portions of matter; that is, in essential relation to them. Nor is the mutual repulsion of all portions of matter for one another a merely negative relation. It is also, as we have seen, a positive relation or connection, which we can only name *attraction*.

If again, we still further consider the nature of repulsion, it is evident that this universal characteristic or property of matter is essentially a strain of separation. And yet a strain in one direction, let us repeat, necessarily implies a strain in the opposite direction. Already, in the very conception of repulsion between two bodies, there is necessarily implied that the bodies are related to each other positively as well as negatively. For the fact that the action of a force is required to separate them, or to widen the already existing separation between them, necessarily presupposes that there is already in action a force drawing them toward each other. Repulsion would therefore be absolutely meaningless were there not constantly presupposed in it its own correlative phase of force, that is, attraction. And in tracing the dialectic of repulsion we have seen how, in its own activity as repulsion, it necessarily develops into its own opposite, that is, into attraction. Thus it would seem that either of these two modes of force is wholly unthinkable apart from the other. They appear to be but different aspects of one and the same force or energy. And this becomes only the more evident as we trace out the dialectic of attraction from the assumption that it is an independent mode of force.

b.—ATTRACTION.

Throughout the scientific world attraction is constantly referred to as if it were regarded as pre-eminently the one universal mode of force. And in some of its phases it does *seem* to act quite independently. It will be well, then, to examine it in its seeming independence.

Objects of sense-perception present definite boundaries, and we have seen that they offer resistance to any force tending to compress them. But they also offer resistance to efforts made to change their shape, or to divide them. Evidently then the particles hold fast upon one another—*attract* each other.

Thus at once it comes to light that the resistance which a body offers to pressure is due, not merely to the repulsion of its particles for one another, but also quite as much to the relation of attraction between them holding them in fixed relative positions. So that the impenetrability of bodies proves to be a repulsion, which in large measure has its truth in attraction. If I press a piece of moist clay between my fingers it yields, not because of the lack of repulsion between the particles in the immediate line of resistance, but rather because of the feeble attraction between particles in other directions.

But let us trace out the nature of attraction in the same way as that in which we examined into the nature of repulsion. Assume the same series of particles, and regard them now under the aspect of attraction. Remember also that attraction, to be attraction at all, must be mutual. No *relation* can be wholly one-sided.

Each particle in the series, then, attracts and is in turn attracted by every other. Applying this in detail, (3) evidently stands in the relation of mutual attraction with (1) and (2) on one side, and with (4) and (5) on the other. But in this double relation it is drawn at the same time in contrary directions. And since the drawing is partly its own, it draws itself in contrary directions.

But this drawing in contrary directions thus proves to be an opposition of the particle against itself, tending to separate it from itself. So that the middle point of the central particle as the "center of gravity" of the whole series is precisely the point where gravity cancels itself and becomes null ; or rather it is the point where gravity, or attraction, undergoes transformation into its own opposite, that is, into repulsion. And this must be true in greater or less degree of every intermediate particle in any series, since such intermediate particle must, in the very fact of its being intermediate, be drawn, and hence must draw itself, in opposite directions at the same time.

Thus attraction proves to involve not merely the approach of particles toward each other, but also their separation from each other — nay, it involves with each and every particle a tendency toward separation from itself. For every particle situated between two other particles is, we have seen, necessarily drawn, and even necessarily draws itself, in opposite directions ; and thus the particle inevitably tends toward its own infinite division. On the other hand, as we have already seen, the repulsion which a particle exerts in opposite directions must have the effect to concentrate such particle upon itself.

In further consideration of attraction we need hardly do more than mention briefly that, as before, our single series of particles may be conceived as revolved about the middle one, so as to form a series of concentric circles in the same plane, while these circles may be conceived as having their perimeters made up of actual particles, thus forming circular bands, through which every diameter will present the same conditions as the series we have just considered. Thus at the same time we should have the additional attractions between each particle in each series, and every particle in every other series, with the same results of counteraction and transformation of attraction into repulsion throughout. And this complication must go on increasing with the increased complexity of grouping of particles, as the circular bands are conceived to coalesce into a solid disc, and the disc, by revolution on its own diameter, to unfold into a sphere.

At the same time there should be borne in mind the vastly complex network of attractions and counter-attractions, involving the connection of every particle with every other particle throughout the sphere, and the consequent tendency, not merely toward infinite concentration of the total mass upon its own center, but also toward the obverse phase of its expansion, and even of the disruption, not only of the sphere itself, but also of every particle of matter in the entire sphere.

Lastly, conceive the sphere to be the total quantity of matter in the universe, in which case it is evident that we should again have the total of attractions so reacting upon itself as to unfold into an exactly balancing total of repulsions. For in the physical universe as a whole (that is, the only extended universe we can ever know) the sum of reactions in attraction, just as the sum of reactions in repulsion, must be equal to the sum of the actions.

And the more fully to satisfy ourselves that this is the case, we have only to repeat that the action of a force in any given direction necessarily implies that there is resistance to overcome. In other words, there can only be action in so far as there is reaction. In the sum-total of the physical world it could not, in the nature of things, be otherwise than that "action and reaction are equal, and in opposite directions."

Thus, once more, attraction and repulsion prove to be but the complementary modes of an all-pervading force or energy, which constitutes the fundamental characteristic, the inmost essence, of "*matter*" — of whatever is real and at the same time extended. They are thus the truly *essential* " properties of matter."

CHAPTER III.

PHENOMENON AND NOUMENON.—THE ATOM AS FIGURED IN IMAGINATION.

IT is now to be further noted that, as implied in our investigation of particles in their relation to one another in any series, there are present in inseparable union throughout the minutest possible portion of matter both attraction and repulsion, as the necessary complementary phases of that force which constitutes the substance of matter. Neither of these phases can exist anywhere, in however limited a sphere, except through the co-existence of the other phase throughout the same sphere.

There is latent here, indeed, the long-vexed question of the relation between phenomenon and noumenon, between appearance or manifestation, and reality. Plato would have it that there is a world of ideas or archetypal forms constituting the real, the eternal and unchanging world; while the world of man's experience is the world of appearance, of change, and hence a vanishing world. So, again in modern times, Kant urged that we can only know phenomena, while the noumenon, or thing-in-itself (*Ding-an-sich*) is forever beyond our ken. And again, in quite recent times, it is confidently affirmed that while appearance may be regarded as fairly within the grasp of the finite mind, the *reality* must forever remain to such mind something wholly unapproachable, absolutely *unknowable*.

It would seem worth while to note, however, that the phenomenon, otherwise called appearance or manifestation, must at least be allowed "reality" *as appearance,* and that thus it cannot be absolutely separated from reality. Similarly also, the reality can only be known as reality through its manifestation. And, since it is the only "reality," the manifestation so far from being something apart from reality, is simply the reality manifesting *itself.*

Indeed, Mr. Spencer himself declares that by no mental effort is it possible to suppress the idea of absolute being, that the unknowable, as absolute being, manifests itself, and that this self-manifestation is in accordance with an "established order."* And from this standpoint it would seem that one ought to recognize the truth that all reality exhibits or manifests just its own essential being precisely in unfolding *itself* in phenomena. In other words, manifestation is not "something" apart from reality. It is *nothing* unless the manifestation *of* reality. Whence it would seem that the ultimate Reality or Absolute Being can be rightly called the Unknowable only in a relative sense; that is, in the sense that we can only progressively learn all there is to know about it, that we can never absolutely know it in the sense of having attained an absolutely complete, exhaustive knowledge of it in all its infinitely manifold details.

The term *noumenon* has indeed already faded away into what might very properly be styled a mere phenomenon. It simply marked a confused phase of thought, which must therefore prove a vanishing phase.

* "*First Principles*" (N. Y. Ed.), pp. 117, 122, and elsewhere.

It is to be further noted that physical science has long used forms of expression clearly implying the inseparability of reality and manifestation. Certain of the "properties of matter" have been classed as *essential*—an expression which can mean nothing else than that these properties are the very *essence* of matter; that matter exists in and through these properties, and could have no existence without or apart from them. This, indeed, we have seen to be the case in our tracing of the simplest relations necessarily involved in the objects of sense-perception, which are, in general, the sum of things extended or characterized by externality.

And yet physical science has not been able to prevent the re-appearance of the shadowy noumenon within its own domain. For, from the unquestionably just opinion that there can be no action save as there is something to act upon, the conclusion has been leaped to that *force* can act only upon *matter* as a something apart from force.

Of course physicists have not failed to note the contradiction involved in this conception. Thus Thomson and Tait, in their "*Elements of Natural Philosophy*" (§ 173), after remarking that they "cannot, of course, give a definition of *matter* which will satisfy the metaphysician," proceed to say that "the naturalist may be content to know matter as *that which can be perceived by the senses*, or as *that which can be acted upon by, or can exert, force.*" To which they immediately add that "The latter, and indeed the former also, of these definitions involves the idea of *Force*, which, in point of fact, is a direct object of sense; probably of all our senses, and certainly of the 'muscular sense.'"

This remarkable paragraph, in which the identity between matter and force is fairly asserted, concludes with the statement that "To our chapter on the 'Properties of Matter' we must refer for further discussion of the question, *What is matter?*"

The part of the joint work of these two physicists containing the promised chapter on the properties of matter does not seem to have appeared. But a volume under that title has been published by Professor Tait, while Professor Thomson has also separately developed his own theory upon the subject; from which it may be guessed that the two could not entirely agree as to what should be said upon this particular theme.

Indeed, after certain introductory remarks, Professor Tait declares (p. 11) that these "have been brought in with the view of warning the reader that we are dealing with a subject so imperfectly known, that at almost any part of it one may pass by a single step, as it were, from what is acquired certainty to what is still subject for mere conjecture." To which he adds that:

"An exact or adequate conception of matter itself, could we obtain it, would almost certainly be something extremely unlike any conception of it which our senses and our reason will ever enable us to form."

A little further on (p. 14) this declaration of nescience on the part of the scientific man concerning matter is even more emphatically set forth. He has been indicating the various theories concerning the constitution of matter, and, referring especially to W. Thomson's theory of vortex atoms, declares that this "has the curious peculiarity of making matter, as we can perceive it, depend upon the existence of a particular kind of motion of a medium which, under many of the definitions above, would be entitled to claim the name of matter, even when it is not set in rotation."

After thus indicating that the theory which his former associate had developed, with a view to explaining the constitution of matter, has the "curious peculiarity" of assuming the thing it was proposed to prove, Professor Tait adds: "But as we do not know, and are probably incapable of discovering, what matter *is*, what we want at present is merely a definition which, while not at least *obviously* incorrect, shall for the time serve as a working hypothesis."

He therefore chooses to "define, for the moment, as follows:

"*Matter is whatever can occupy space;*" and this for the following reason:

"Experience has proved that it is from this side that the average student can most easily approach the subject." * * *

The point of view from which we have set out in the present essay, then, is not one that the strictly scientific mind would call an "*obviously* incorrect" one. And it is reassuring to have such confirmation from one who has gained the right to speak as one having authority, and not as the scribes, or "paper scientists."

Amid such uncertainties, too, it would seem to be not wholly unwarrantable for even the "mere metaphysician" to throw in his conjecture also, though, from the expressions Professor Tait uses, it can hardly be expected that such conjectures will be estimated above the merest infinitesimals by the—mere (?)—mathematician.

Even the infinitesimal has its value, however, and so we proceed upon the line of our argument, not without some glimmer of hope.

The course of the argument thus far has tended toward the conclusion that the essence or truth of matter is force or energy. And we have seen that such eminent physicists as Thomson and Tait define matter to be "that which can be acted upon by, or can exert, force." We have also seen that Professor Tait accepts as a tentative definition of matter, "whatever can occupy space."

In either case matter cannot be a something apart from force, but, rather, must be identical with force, so far as we can ever know anything about it. For, as already noticed, it is only through a counter force opposing the force we ourselves exert that we can know anything about "whatever occupies space," or about space either, seeing that we become aware of extension only through the extended.

But that which is extended, or "can occupy space," is in that very fact divisible, at least theoretically, without limit; and it is divisible, experimentally, far beyond our powers of observation. Whence all bodies *within* our experience must be aggregations of infinitesimal bodies *beyond* our experience — at least beyond our *sensuous* experience. Nor is there any necessary contradiction between the "metaphysical" conception of the infinite *divisibility* of matter, and its practically limited *division*, as will perhaps become more evident with the further progress of the argument.

The Democritean conception of the atom, or ultimate division of matter, has, of course, long been given up. Instead of the minute, absolutely hard, and therefore inelastic and eternal, body named "atom" in the ancient doctrine, physical science has first cautiously defined the atom as the smallest division of matter arising in chemical reactions, and has lately come to look with favor upon the conception of the perfectly elastic and plastic vortex atom as somehow existing in, as parts of, a perfectly elastic fluid pervading all space.

That the atomic theory has been an instrument of wondrous efficiency in the furtherance of physical science there can be no question. And this can only be because there is an essential truth involved in that theory. At the same time, as leading scientists themselves clearly recognize and explicitly affirm, this does not necessitate the conclusion that the *atom*, as a necessarily permanent, unalterable unit, is anything more than a mere product of the "scientific imagination"—something, indeed, not so very far removed from things "metaphysical."

So long as modern science held fast to the conception of rigid atoms, it was under the necessity of also assuming the "void," in so far as "pores" were indispensable to the elasticity of a body. But this again led to another assumption. As "action at a distance" is unthinkable, according to Newton, and also according to anyone else who has done any genuine thinking, and as atoms, nevertheless, act upon one another, though separated from each other by the void "pores," it was assumed by Clausius and others that each atom was surrounded by a sphere of force which was elastic, but which also prevented the enclosed atom from ever coming into contact with any other atom.

With the impact theory, on the other hand, the force-sphere seemed no longer indispensable. Each atom, having an irrepressible and more or less irresistible way of beating about among its neighbors as if it were a "little demon," preserves its own eminent domain inviolable. The impetus given in such impacts would produce the phenomena of repulsion, while the rebound, allowing the atoms to be elastic, would give rise to like phenomena in opposite directions, and the approach of atom to atom in either way would likewise give rise to the phenomena of attraction. At the same time, the "void" appears here in its primitive simplicity.

Indeed, this theory approaches nearest to that of Democritus, the difference, in one respect at least, being that the cause of motion in the atoms is left as something unknown, if not inexplicable, while, in the other, the atom is assumed to have an inherent eternal motion— a kind of self-activity. From such crude "science" as that of Democritus, indeed, one could hardly expect the mythical element to be wholly excluded. Accordingly, with him the atom seems to have been a sort of unconscious symbolical eternizing of the beautiful, self-complete divinities of the Greek popular faith. Thus, with the father of the atomic theory, matter, or substance, was absolutely discrete, and "bodies" such as those appealing to our senses could only result from the accidental and temporary aggregation of the ever-self-sufficient and, in some sense, divine, atoms.

It is also to be noted that, however superior the modern methods of science, the impact theory still leaves us no alternative. From this theory we must also accept the absolute discreteness of matter, and thus find ourselves forced into irreconcilable contradiction with the conception of the continuity of matter. And this is as much as to say that it is irreconcilable with the theory of the all-pervading, perfectly elastic fluid, which fluid would seem to be in its very nature perfectly continuous in spite of its seeming discreteness as developed in the vortex atom.

To this it may be added that, on the supposition that matter consists solely of atoms, and that it is therefore absolutely discrete, then the essential properties of matter must really be the essential properties of the atom. Thus, in the first place, the atom must be pervaded throughout by attraction at least, since, being of a definite volume, it must be drawn together by an infinite force in order that it may be able to maintain its integrity as against all forces tending toward its disintegration. And yet, as we have already seen, the attraction thus demanded for the assured existence of the atom must appear, in however limited a compass, as the complement of repulsion. Nay, the incompressibility of the atom is itself once more a manifestation of repulsion, which is at the same time equally the infinitely vigorous truth of its attraction. In other words, here, as everywhere, the existence of attraction at any point necessarily implies repulsion at the same point, and equally the contrary.

It may be added, too, that, on the supposition of rigid atoms, in order that the atom may retain its rigidity in form and volume, it would be necessary that the relations between the attractions and repulsions within it should never be disturbed. And this again would require that the external relations of the atom should forever remain unchanged. In other words, the atom could only be and remain absolutely rigid upon condition that the whole universe should likewise remain absolutely rigid, and hence wholly destitute of motion in any and every sense.

On the other hand, should the external conditions change, then the relations between the attractions and repulsions within the atom must change, following upon which—or, rather, necessarily accompanying which—the volume and the form would undergo change. That is, the "atom" must then prove to be itself an aggregate of an indefinite number of parts, each of which must in the same way prove to be changeable in volume, and hence also to be made up of parts, and so on until the atom slips completely from our grasp, and the irritating, if not terrifying, "metaphysical" conception of the infinite divisibility of matter once more stares us in the face.

In fact, there is here presented to us an intimation that there is some other relation between the discreteness and the continuity of matter than that of their mutual exclusion. And, it may as well be added, this is the one valid excuse for introducing the foregoing discussion of the rigid atom.

What that other and truer relation really is will, it is hoped, appear in the further course of the argument.

In resuming, it may be remarked that the tendency of the argument thus far is to show that while, of course, force cannot act save as there is something for it to act upon, the "something" required is not a "matter" as apart from force, but rather it is force itself. Force can in truth act upon nothing else than force. It can, let us repeat, prove itself to be force no otherwise than in the opposition of contrasted phases. Force is exerted only in opposing force, and force not exerted is no force at all.

In the common acceptation of the term "matter," there is implied just the passive phase of the physical world, while "force" is the active phase. Or, to use

G. H. Lewes's form of expression, "Matter is the passive aspect of existence."* But we have already seen that force is, in its very nature, at once active and passive. So that the conception of a matter apart from force only darkens the stream of thought with a sediment having no corresponding reality in nature.

The theory of Clausius, already referred to, has a germ of suggestiveness which may be put to use along with the theory of Boscovich. In the theory of the former, the material atom is surrounded by a sphere of force. In the theory of the latter, the atom or ultimate element of matter is a mathematical point, from which radiate out to a greater or less distance, both attraction and repulsion.

In either case the force-sphere, as limited, must still present the difficulty of "action at a distance." It is also evident that in the theory of Clausius the atom itself plays absolutely no part whatever. All that is done is done by the force-sphere surrounding the atoms. Whatever action is directed toward an atom is already received and reacted upon by the sphere of force in which the neither active nor passive atom is imprisoned—in blissful unconsciousness, it may be presumed—to all eternity.

It seems evident, then, that any supposed matter as apart from force, is the veriest fiction; that, in short, the "atom," as generally figured, is simply an unscientific creation of the insufficiently restrained phantasy; that is, of the *un*scientific imagination. In other words, it is simply the re-appearance, under a changed and scarcely improved form, of the mysterious, unapproachable, metaphysical *noumenon* of the Middle Age modes of thought, from which it might reasonably be supposed that the

* "*Problems of Life and Mind*" (Boston Ed.), II., 302.

progressive science of the nineteenth century should long ago have freed itself.

And mainly, indeed, this has actually been accomplished. The word "atom" is used more and more in a symbolic sense, and now really involves no contradiction with the conception that matter, as that which is extended, or which can occupy space, simply consist of its properties manifested in various degrees, under various conditions. And let us recall that, thus far in the present essay, two opposite and complementary forces, or modes of force, have appeared as constituting the very basis or essence of matter as that which is extended.

From whatever side we view the subject, then, force appears to be the sole reality of matter; while the "atom," as a something existing apart from force, proves to be nothing else than a phantasmal product of that "bad metaphysics," which is, perhaps, indulged in most of all by those who know least of, and therefore have least patience with, metaphysics, properly speaking.

CHAPTER IV.

TRUTH OF THE ATOM.—PENETRABILITY OF MATTER.

NEVERTHELESS, as already stated, the conception of the atom has served an excellent purpose in the progress of physical science. And we have next to inquire what the truth of this conception is.

We have seen that the really essential elements of matter in its most rudimentary state must be the two complementary modes of force, attraction and repulsion, and thus have grounds for the assurance that matter consists of, and is nothing apart from, force. It has also become evident that neither of these modes of force can exist in reality, save as in completely blended unity with the other. Indeed, when either is assumed as real, the other necessarily proves to be already contained in it. Or, more strictly speaking, each is not itself merely, but is itself and the other.

It cannot be too strongly emphasized, then, that in every minutest possible portion of whatever is real, and at the same time characterized by externality, attraction and repulsion must be present in completely blended unity. Or, it may just as well be said, each must be present, both as itself, and the other. And this is but to say that everywhere where "matter" exists there must be *at every point* a center whence force radiates in every direction, and with an intensity diminishing uniformly with increase of distance from that center.

Thus far, indeed, it would seem that matter would necessarily be distributed uniformly through space, and that therefore "body" would have no meaning. To this objection an answer will develop in the further course of the argument.

What we have now to note is that the force radiating from the centers everywhere appearing in whatever occupies space, would not, according to the conception of the constitution of matter thus far developed, ever reach any absolute limit. And this would seem to be the same conception as that which would result from the fusion of the two theories before mentioned. The "atom" of Clausius vanishes into the non-extended point of Boscovich, and from such focus a sphere of force extends indefinitely, though with gradually diminishing intensity. That is, the points of force in the one case and the atoms in the other are seen to be each in reality just a focus of force. That, it would seem, is the truth of the "atom."

But, this once recognized, a number of important inferences are seen to logically follow. In the first place, if the atom is in truth nothing else or less than a focus of force, it is evident that it has no absolutely fixed boundary. Its nucleus must indeed possess a maximum of tension, but as it radiates outward in all directions, its extent or volume must be *indefinitely great*.

Hence, *secondly*, we would express the truth more precisely if, instead of using the formula, "every particle of matter attracts every other particle of matter," we were to say: Every focus of force, through its unlimited expansion, takes hold upon every other focus of force. And thus, *thirdly*, instead of the atoms, or foci of force, being merely side by side in space, and therefore characterized in their absolute isolation by externality solely, it is evident that each in its unlimited expansion *includes all at the same time that it is included in all.* In other words, each "atom," in its relation to every other "atom," includes the whole physical universe. It therefore has in some sense internality as well as externality; that is, the greater its extent, the greater also would seem to be its intent or content.

Nor in saying this is there any latent purpose to trifle with the reader's time. We are attempting to examine the "atom" in its nature and essence. That is, we are endeavoring to trace out its fundamental characteristics and relations. And in so far as this is really accomplished, there lies open before us the fact that this so-called ultimate, simple division of matter is in truth a highly complex phase of the physical universe. It exists not merely by itself, or in isolation—that is, within absolutely fixed boundaries—but rather it exists for all else that is extended—just as all else that is extended exists reciprocally for it.

That is, the total sum of the extended can only be conceived as an indivisible *unit*, which is at the same time an immeasurably complex *manifold;* though in our present investigation only the relatively simplest phases of this manifoldness have as yet received explicit statement.

The next thing, indeed, that lies on the surface after what has already been developed is the solution of the contradiction between impenetrability and compressibility as properties of the extended. Even in the diffusion of gases "matter" shows itself to be practically in greater or less degree penetrable. And while this is usually explained on the theory of the "porosity" of matter, yet in every chemical combination there is evidently a genuine interpenetration on the part of the elements, so that at no minutest point is there to be found any particle of either element untransformed. "Atoms" *combine*, become interfused, mutually penetrate, whenever a chemical reaction takes place.

Thus, even empirically, the porosity theory, in explanation of so-called impenetrability, is found to be unnecessary, at least in such cases, seeing that in such cases "matter" is really penetrable. And on the theory which we have seen reasons to adopt—namely, that the atom is just the nucleus of an indefinitely extended force-sphere—porosity appears to be in its ultimate character simply a fiction, having its only claim to reality in the complementary fiction of the absolutely rigid "atom."

Nor can we too strongly emphasize the proposition that this force-sphere constituting the truth of the "atom" (and, hence, constituting the truth of "matter") is a *reality*. And because every "atom" is indefinitely—or, rather, infinitely—extended, then there can be no part of space where there is no force, no physical reality. Doubtless this plenum presents various and varying degrees of tension, but everywhere it would appear that there must be *some* degree of tension, some degree of reality.

Thus, what are called "pores," or inter-atomic spaces, are to be regarded as relative degrees of density in the matter that fills all space. So that when the atoms or molecules of two gases mutually occupy the "pores" of one another, it would seem that the gases really penetrate one another, according to the law that motion takes place in the direction of greatest traction *or of least resistance*. *Least* resistance, not *no* resistance.

But, still further, and leaving aside such concrete example, which at the present stage of our argument must be considered an anticipation, it is evident that the relations of force running out from every minutest center, and connecting it essentially, really, with every other center, must penetrate each other to an unlimited extent. It is, once more, the mutual inclusion of each in all and all in each.

It appears, then, that impenetrability, as already hinted, is but the negative aspect of resistance or repulsion, which, as we have seen, also necessarily involves attraction—the opposite but also the necessary complement of repulsion. Whence we may conclude that a body is "impenetrable" in this sense, and this sense only: That in so far as it is real it is simply a nucleus of force; or, if one prefers, it is a compacted cluster of such nuclei. It cannot, therefore, be infinitely compressed—that is, reduced in volume to a point, or to no-volume—because, if that is to be accomplished, whatever force is brought to bear upon it must be applied *on all sides.* That is, the applied force simply unites its own volume with, by completely surrounding, the body to be compressed, and then presses in upon that body on all sides. In other words, since what is to be compressed is enfolded in and now constitutes the central portion of that by which it is to be compressed, the whole now constitutes in reality one continuous system, which to all intents and purposes can compress nothing but itself. It is a proposed self-crusher.

But the greater the strain applied *toward* the center the greater the strain developed *from* the center. As the hollow golden sphere forces its way into the enclosed water, the water at the same time forces its way out through the enclosing sphere. It is an initial metamorphosis, in which the outer shows its readiness to become inner, and the inner an equal readiness to become outer. But as to crushing anything out of existence—that can never be done; not even were the whole universe to join in the attempt. For it would still be the universe straining at self-annihilation, and all the while in such effort, nay, as the very consequence of such effort, only succeeding in bringing into fullest manifestation or realization whatever could possibly lie within it as hidden or potential.

"Matter" is impenetrable, then, in this sense, and in this sense only: That action and reaction are, in the long run, absolutely equal and in opposite directions, and that therefore force or energy is forever *indestructible*.

At the same time, as previously noticed, so far as there may be local changes of relation between attraction and repulsion, bodies will inevitably alter in volume. The bringing external pressure to bear is itself a change of conditions; and a change of such character as, within certain limits, to diminish the volume of—that is, to compress—the given body. Limited portions of matter (bodies) are measurably compressible, but not indefinitely so. Compressibility is, in fact, just a relation between attraction and repulsion, the two elementary factors of matter.

CHAPTER V.

TRANSITION TO THE QUANTITATIVE ASPECTS OF MATTER THROUGH INCREASE IN QUALITATIVE CHARACTERISTICS.

HERE, we may now observe, there is already presented to us the ground of the varying states of "matter," or the extended. Attraction tends toward concentration, repulsion toward diffusion, of matter. According, then, as the former or the latter predominates at any given moment in any given portion of matter, the tension will be increased and the volume diminished, or the contrary. With the predominance of attraction, the given portion of matter will be in the solid state. With the approach toward a balance of the two complementary modes of force, the solid will become viscid. With further increase of the relative degree of repulsion, the liquid state will be reached; and the continuance of increase in this tendency must result at length in the matter assuming the gaseous state.

Similarly, on the contrary, relative increase of attraction over repulsion must result in a given gaseous mass becoming condensed into a liquid, and again in the liquid passing into the solid state. Of this, indeed, something more remains to be said at a later stage of our inquiry.

What has just been said concerning the relation between attraction and repulsion brings us to note this further point: That there is doubtless more in the distinction between ponderable and imponderable matter than modern scientists are for the most part disposed to admit. "Ponderable" matter is matter that has weight. But weight is, properly speaking, an accident of matter, not a necessary property. It is wholly erroneous to regard it as identical with attraction. It is, as Professor Tait points out, a relation between bodies; or, as we should here prefer to say, weight is simply the excess of attraction or centripetal force over repulsion or centrifugal force. Even in the ordinary text-books on physics, indeed, it is pointed out that the "weight" of a given body is less at the equator than at any point distant from the equator, and that the greater "weight" always corresponds with greater distance from the equator. Of course this difference in the weight of a body, corresponding with difference in latitude, is due chiefly to centrifugal force—that is, to the mass of the body itself combined with, or "multiplied into," the "tangential velocity." And one need only recall the frequently repeated calculation that, were the equatorial velocity increased to seventeen times its present rate, the weight of bodies at the equator would be just *nil*. That is, even solid bodies would become thus far "imponderable."

But in another way matter may become imponderable. Weight, as we have seen, is the measure of the excess of attraction over repulsion, or centrifugal force. We have also seen that in respect of the states of matter, the excess of attraction over repulsion is the condition essential to the solid state (the production or retention of matter in the solid state through pressure, being but a special phase of attraction). Thus what we know as "ponderable matter" is directly associated with a large mass of solid matter—the earth. On the other hand, it would seem that imponderable matter is in this sense just that phase of matter in which repulsion is so highly developed that within a given volume (of any finite extent), the tendency toward separation is vastly greater than the tendency toward concentration, and that therefore in such volume even gravity is masked, while weight would have no existence at all.

Thus, as all matter consists primarily of the interaction of attraction and repulsion, and as there is no absolute limit to the degree in which this interaction may vary locally, so there is no absolute limit to the possible diffuseness of matter in any given portion of space.

It would seem, then, that throughout the spaces far removed from large, dense masses of matter, there is diffused what may properly be called imponderable matter. And there seems no good reason why we should not adopt for this imponderable matter the name, *ether*. It is the "unseen universe"; nay, in some sense the unseeable universe, since it is that part of physical reality which, as such, must forever elude all efforts to bring it to the test of the chemist's balance. It seems in some sense to especially court inquiries of the metaphysical kind, and more or less to refuse answer to questions put in any other form.

Doubtless the reader has already observed that the proof of the possibility of any change whatever in matter, considered as constituted of absolutely balanced modes of force, is not as yet by any means forthcoming in the present essay. It is well, at least, to have this explicitly called to mind, in order that the demand for such proof may not be forgotten or in any degree slurred over. Nor shall we omit to look carefully for such proof as we proceed.

For the present, however, we must leave the question in abeyance. Change unquestionably does take place in the extended world which constitutes the object or sum of objects of our perceptions, however these changes may be ultimately accounted for. What has thus far been proven is that the truth of the extended world is force, which in turn is a complex of mutually inclusive, everywhere interpenetrating, attractions and repulsions. What is proven is, *that* the world is so constituted. What remains to be shown in this connection is, *how* such balance of forces can result in an active universe.

What follows will, it is believed, be seen to join on naturally to the already completed portion of proof, and furnish an important stage in the movement leading up to the more adequate developments of the argument.

It has already been shown that increase in the number of atoms or radiant centers, within a given compass, must increase the complexity of lines of relation between those centers. From this it is to be inferred that with the advancing concentration of matter in any given locality from any cause, there could not fail to be increased intricacy of interpenetration of the indefinitely extended dynamical spheres.

But increased complexity of dynamical relations can only be manifested as increased complexity of material characteristics. On the contrary, the more widely separated the radiant centers are, the less intricate and less tense must be the dynamical relations, and hence also the less must be the complexity of material characteristics.

While, then, attraction is a strain toward simple unity, in that it tends to concentrate all into a single totality, it proves also to be a strain toward the heterogeneous, in that it tends to develop a multiplicity of qualitative differences within that total. And so, also, on the other hand, while repulsion is a strain toward infinite multiplicity, in that it is a continuous outputting or development of yet other ones from the total one, it proves also to be none the less a strain toward the homogeneous, since it is, after all, a development of "ones," each qualitatively indistinguishable from the others; the result being a cancellation or annulment of qualitative differences. Condensation means increased tension, and increased tension means increased complexity of matter; just as, on the contrary, rarefaction means decreased tension, and decreased tension means decreased complexity of matter.

Such is the logical conclusion to which the argument thus far leads. And this conclusion is distinctly in agreement with the results of the most searching investigations in physical science, and especially with the brilliant results achieved by means of the spectroscope, in connection with the nebular hypothesis.*

It is well known that, previous to the invention of this remarkable instrument, there was no means of answering the question whether certain cloud-like patches in the heavens consisted of diffuse incandescent matter, or of star-clusters so distant that, to the eye of an observer from the earth, their light blended together. With the invention of the spectroscope, however, scientists found themselves in possession of an instrument that revealed

---

* See the special works on "*Spectrum Analysis*," by Schellen and by Lockyer, the latter in the "*International Science Series.*"

instantly whether or not the light received into it was from a body in the gaseous state. Not only so, but in addition to this it also revealed the remarkable fact that each of the so-called elements has its own peculiar and exclusive spectrum.

With this instrument the vexed question as to the reality of true nebulæ was at once set at rest. The spectrum of nebula after nebula was found to present unmistakable characteristics, showing that these were actual masses of matter in extremely attenuated gaseous form.

But what is especially to our present purpose is the fact that of these nebulæ some were found to consist of but few elements, mainly hydrogen and nitrogen; while in the spectra of others there are lines indicating a greater number of elements, and so on, until the continuous spectrum indicating the presence of all the known elements is developed from the sun and other incandescent bodies in the solid or in the liquid state.

From these grounds alone, the logical or natural—that is, rational—inference is that increase in multiplicity of elements, which is the same as increase in complexity of matter, goes hand in hand with, and is a consequence of, the increased complexity of those force-relations constituting matter which must inevitably result from the condensation of nebulous masses in space. Thus it seems that the more diffuse the nebula, the more simple the spectrum; that is, the more simple the constitution of the "matter" composing the nebula; while the more advanced toward solidification, the more complex must be the spectrum; in other words, the more complex the constitution of the "matter" composing the nebula.

What shall we say, then, of the claim that all matter is permanently divided into seventy or more elements, all differing essentially from one another? It is true that chemists themselves are beginning to doubt the finality of their analyses; and while the tendency still is in the main to look to a further increase in the number of elements, there is already arising here and there a guarded query as to whether, after all, the elements may not prove to be only specialized conditions of a "matter" that, theoretically at least, is primarily homogeneous.*

I say "theoretically," because it is evident that there can be no actual case of concrete matter which can be strictly homogeneous. This we have already seen in the attempt to form a conception of matter as consisting solely of repulsion. It was found that such conception cannot be formed, because no sooner has the representation of such assumption been made than it becomes evident that any real repulsion must develop attraction as a necessary aspect of such real repulsion; just as any real attraction must include, as a necessary phase of itself, repulsion also.

In this connection the following significant paragraph from Lockyer ("*Spectrum Analysis*," N. Y. Ed., p. 196) may be cited. "It is," he says, "abundantly clear that if the so-called elements, or, more properly speaking, their finest atoms—those that give us line spectra—are

* It was not until after the foregoing was written that I read Mr. Spencer's "*Principles of Psychology*," and found therein (N. Y. Ed., Vol. I., p. 155) the following statement: "Moreover, there is reason to suspect that the so-called simple substances are themselves compound, and that there is but one ultimate form of matter, out of which the successively more complex forms of matter are built up." Other suggestions of a similar nature had been previously made—as that hydrogen is the ultimate form of matter; though this has the obvious fault of regarding one of the various differentiated phases of matter as itself the primal undifferentiated aspect of matter.

really compounds, the compounds must have been formed at a very high temperature. It is easy to imagine that there may be no superior limit to temperature, and therefore no superior limit beyond which such combinations are impossible. Because the atoms which have the power of combining together at these transcendental stages of heat do not exist as such, or rather, they exist combined with other similar atoms, at lower temperatures. Hence association will be a combination of more complex molecules as temperature is reduced, and of dissociation, therefore, with increased temperature there may be no end."

To this conclusion, indeed, the facts brought to light by means of the spectroscope clearly point, and thus, as already remarked, offer a strong confirmation of the argument we have presented above in abstract form, showing that increased complexity of "matter" must necessarily result from increase of condensation, involving, as that necessarily does, increased complexity of concrete relations in the mass; while, on the other hand, this complexity must grow less and less with the diffusion of matter into wider space.

We can but conclude, then, that matter is not only constituted by and of force, and that it is thus ultimately (at least in a relative sense) homogeneous, but also that the seeming complexity of matter—that is, the multiplicity of "elements"—is in reality but the increasingly complex grouping of and multiplied tension between the indefinitely-extended dynamical spheres which constitute the initial phase of the development or manifestation of force—the added complexity of grouping and increased intensity of relation being due to the steadily accumulating strain incident to the condensation of nebulous masses into stars and suns and their attendant spheres.

It is a notable fact, too, that even by artificial means a gas may be subjected to so great a pressure as to cause it to give off a continuous spectrum. It is as if, out of a single element, the increased complexity of grouping of centers of force together with the intensified strain between those centers corresponding to increase in the number of elements by the analogous process exhibited on the grand scale in nature could thus temporarily be reproduced at will in the laboratory.

CHAPTER VI.

DEFINITE QUANTITATIVE RELATIONS IN MATTER.

WE have seen that as the qualitative relations of matter develop into increased definiteness they necessarily involve quantitative aspects also, though this has appeared thus far only in the form of indefinite multiplicity. We have now to trace this quantitative aspect into its more precise forms.

The elements of which we have just traced the origin constitute in large measure the subject-matter of what is known as modern chemistry. It was largely in the interests of chemistry that the atomic theory was revived in modern times; and it is directly in the field of chemistry that the more elaborate part of the theory in its specially modern character, and particularly in its quantitative aspects, has been developed. The "atomic weights" of the several elements have been ascertained with at least the appearance of great precision.

Nor is there any sufficient reason to call in question the substantial accuracy of these results, so far as they are understood merely as the expression of the quantitative relations necessarily involved in matter. And, as we have already mentioned, the more advanced chemists themselves regard the "atom" as hypothetical, and even look to an entire change of view respecting the so-called "elements."

What has thus far been said, then, far from conflicting with the assured results of science, proves rather to be quite in harmony with those results. The only conflict developed is with what scientists themselves have already begun to call in question, and which they are definitely prepared to set aside as forming no necessary part of any of the various phases of truth which science has brought to light and verified beyond all reasonable question.

It will be quite in the direct line of our inquiry to trace some of the more characteristic of the confirmations which science presents to our theory, and to develop such consequences as the theory thus confirmed may be found to involve.

We may recall that the development of the interrelations of attraction and repulsion necessarily involve on the one hand the unifying of matter in that at every point there is a center of attraction fundamentally related to the whole of the material universe. This, as has been shown, is involved in the received statement that every particle of matter attracts every other particle of matter, —an expression which, developed so as to explicitly conform to the conception that matter has its substance in force, would take the form: Every nucleus of force radiates outward to the farthest points of space and takes hold on every other nucleus of force.

Thus, it may be remarked by the way, the physical universe, regarded as commensurate with space, is a veritable sphere whose center is everywhere and whose circumference is nowhere. It is also manifest that there is no possible object in space that can be in absolute isolation, since even the simplest force-center still radiates outward into the whole of immensity.

The smallest thing in the universe, then, is still, in its truth, commensurate with the universe itself. The small is not merely included within the great; the great is also included within the small. Each presupposes the other and could not exist without the other. Force regarded as attraction, let us repeat, then, unifies the extended world absolutely, gathers the physical universe into an absolutely indivisible One.

On the other hand, however, we have also seen that the complementary mode of force, namely, repulsion, puts restraint upon this unifying tendency and gives rise to an infinitude of independent centers within the all-embracing one. And yet this one itself is but the totality of relations between attraction and repulsion. Thus the One, as this totality of relations, itself gives rise to an infinitude of ones within itself, each of which in turn is essentially related to the whole, and thus also to all the other ones.

Thus the phase of unity finds its necessary complement in an infinite multiplicity which, however, still proves to be but a mode of the unity itself. The appearance of multiplicity is but the unfolding of the unity. The qualitative distinctions as they emerge into view prove to already necessarily involve quantitative distinctions also. Each center of force is already something definitely opposed to, as well as connected with, every other center of force. And each in comparison with every other is seen to be necessarily a greater, or a less, or an equal, as regards that other.

CHAPTER VII.

AS TO CONTINUITY AND DISCRETENESS OF QUANTITY IN MATTER.

AT this point we come upon the question as to the relation between continuous and discrete quantity in matter. And in our search for the answer to this question we have but to revert to what has already preceded. We have seen that matter, as constituted of force, is simply a manifestation of the relations between the complementary modes or phases of force—attraction and repulsion. But the interaction of these phases of force cannot but result in the focusing at every point in space of a greater or less intensity of strain between those phases.

And yet each of these foci of force necessarily extends outward so as to act upon, and in turn to be reacted upon by, every other focus of force. Thus constituted, then, matter is necessarily *continuous*. At the same time, however, the very focusing of force through the interaction of its two complementary modes is a setting up of distinctions which necessarily mark off or limit one portion of matter as thus far separate, at least quantitatively, from every other portion. Whence it is to be concluded that matter is not merely continuous, but is also at the same time, and not less truly, *discrete*. That is, the same totality presents itself under the two different but also complementary aspects of discreteness and continuity.

Thus in a concrete sense the continuity of matter necessarily implies the absolute fluidity of matter; just as, on the other hand, the discreteness of matter no less necessarily implies its perfect rigidity. But it is precisely in this concrete sense, as we have already seen, that matter (that is, force) in its very character of the continuous develops within itself infinite discreteness. The infinite fluidity of the extended is nothing more nor less than the varying relation between the complementary aspects of force, known as attraction and repulsion, whereby any and every given quantity of "matter" is constantly undergoing expansion or contraction, and whereby, at any given moment, therefore, the complete disruption of the given quantity of matter may begin; following which, or even accompanying which, such given quantity may become completely fused with other quantities and thus undergo entire re-constitution. And it may be that the conception here presented is not so very far removed from that of the perfectly elastic fluid which, in the vortex-atom theory, is assumed to fill all space.

Here, then, the puzzle of the infinite divisibility of matter finds its solution. Considered as continuous merely, matter is, like space, infinitely divisible; for as simply continuous matter must be as absolutely indifferent to division as is space itself. But, on the other hand, matter considered as merely discrete—and such the atomic theory makes it—cannot possibly be thought as undergoing infinite *division*, since it has already undergone *final* division, and hence consists of ultimate, unalterable particles.

It would seem, then, that the reconciliation of these two apparently irreconcilable views is found in the foregoing conception of matter as force which necessarily so unfolds itself as to present everywhere two primary and complementary aspects rendering matter fluid throughout its whole extent, and at the same time specializing it into more or less complex and distinct, but still more or less unstable, concrete masses. As is well known, the densest mass still retains the character of fluidity. And this must be true of the minutest "atom" no less than of directly perceptible masses.

CHAPTER VIII.

EXTENSIVE AND INTENSIVE PHASES OF QUANTITY IN MATTER.

IT is to be noted that, in so far as matter is considered as merely continuous, its qualitative characteristics do not appear. On the other hand, its discrete character arises from distinctively qualitative phases of the relation between attraction and repulsion. It is precisely through qualitatively developed differences that discrete quantity is perceivable in matter.

But the more and less of strain, as between the concentrative and the expansive tendencies, within any given sphere involves still another quantitative contrast. With diminished strain there is a canceling of qualitative differences and an increase in mere space-occupancy. As the tension diminishes the extension increases. That is, the intensive quantity proves to be inversely as the extensive quantity.

Here, indeed, then, comes to light the deeper meaning involved in the contrast between extensive and intensive quantity, as set forth in the ordinary formal logic. There the term having the greatest extent of meaning is ordinarily understood to be merely the most abstract term, since, in order to increase the number of objects included within it, the term must be restricted to fewer and fewer distinguishing characteristics. That is, with increase of extent there must necessarily be decrease of intent or content.

So that, formally, the intensive phase of quantity must be completely set aside in precisely the same measure that the extensive phase is brought into prominence.

But "set aside" may also mean, "held in abeyance," rendered latent or potential. It is evident, for example, that the matter of a nebula is, in the first place, quantitatively extensive; and yet the *quantity* will not be diminished by its development of the intensive phase through condensation into a planetary system, with the resultant unfolding of chemical elements, followed by the appearance of the whole vast order of compounds in vegetal and animal organisms.

Doubtless through this development (which is also an envelopment) there will be a differentiation of tendency toward the merely extensive phase of quantity in the substance through the radiation of the most diffusible phases of the substance into space as the concentrative process goes on. But also in this concentrative process the tendency toward diffusion, toward mere extensive quantity, still remains as a necessary factor in every stage of the condensation. For while the latter is the process in which the intensive phase of quantity is realized, there is also necessarily involved in this the development of the tendency toward expansion, toward diffusion, toward the extensive aspect of quantity. Or, in the more concrete terms of physical science, pressure toward a common center must inevitably develop its complement, heat, which is pressure away from the common center.*

* Professor Helmholz's calculation showing that the continued high temperature of the sun is fully accounted for by its continued concentration upon its own center will doubtless occur to the reader as verifying what is said in the text.

In the same way, also, the extensive term in logic implies, though it does not explicitly include, all the characteristics of all the special objects included under it. The term "rock" formally excludes all the special characteristics which distinguish granite from sandstone, and either from marble. But since the term "rock" includes all these, there is implicit in it all that belongs to whatever objects it may be applied to.

The quantity of steam used in propelling a ship in safety from New York to Liverpool would, if developed instantaneously in its boilers, inevitably shatter the ship to atoms. The quantity might be precisely the same in either case; but in the former it would be predominantly extensive, while in the latter it would be predominantly intensive. In either case the qualitative result depends upon the relation between the extensive and the intensive aspect of the quantity of force in exercise.

With continued preponderance of attraction, as we have already seen, there is also corresponding increase in the development of qualitative characteristics, from the diffuse, almost qualitiless nebula, to the solid earth, with its intense strain of forces and endless wealth of qualitative developments. At the beginning of this process of concentration the quantity of matter is indeed mainly extensive, and hence only in the simplest degree specialized in point of quality. At the very outset, indeed, this extremely diffuse matter is already found to qualitatively distinguish itself into the two opposite but complementary phases of attraction and repulsion.

Now, extension is itself a universal form of all physical magnitude, while magnitude, as a phase of extended *reality*, is a given quantity of matter, which must necessarily be both extensive and intensive, these phases appearing always as reciprocals. So that attraction and repulsion are, in the first place, the initial and fundamental qualitative differences, constituting the reality of matter, or the extended. And the varying relations between these complementary phases of the extended must involve the whole series of relations between extensive and intensive quantity.

At the same time, the transition in matter from the state in which its quantity is predominantly extensive to that in which the quantity is predominantly intensive proves to be a process of qualitative evolution. That is, the increase in the degree of strain between attraction and repulsion within any given quantity of matter results necessarily in the increased complexity of qualitative manifestations within the matter.

Attraction and repulsion, then, appear in the first place as if merely qualitative; but as the complementary phases of the *extended* they prove also to be quantitative, while their varying quantitative relations under the reciprocal forms of extensive and intensive quantity again give rise to an infinitude of qualitative determinations. So that quality and quantity prove to be but different aspects of the same sum of facts in the physical universe. And science has for its special mission to unfold into explicit form the orderly representation of this entire sphere of relations.

A few illustrations, selected mainly from chemistry, may serve to make clearer the truth of what we have just been saying.

It has already been more than once remarked in the present inquiry that the condensation of a nebulous mass into solid spheres must, through an increasing strain between attraction and repulsion, develop as a phase of that strain a correspondingly increasing tension in and between the local centers of force constituting the substance of the sphere, and that increase of such local tension is the real secret of the development of the so-called chemical elements. It is now to be added to this that the farther this process of condensation has advanced in any given portion of the developing system the greater will be not only the actual number of these elements, but also of the actual number and complexity of the combinations of these elements. All chemical compounds appear as manifestations of the special phase of attraction known as "affinity." At the same time chemical decomposition also appears as a negative aspect of chemical combination; for the separation or dissolution of a compound may be due to the approach of an element between which and one of the elements of the compound there is a still stronger attraction or "affinity" than exists between the elements already in combination. That is, the breaking up of an existing compound may be involved in the very process of the formation of a new compound. One degree of attraction is annulled *in its qualitative result* by the interposition of a greater degree of attraction, bringing about a different result.

On the other hand, the phase of repulsion, as such, must tend toward the complete disintegration of all compounds. As the separative phase of force it still further tends to dissolve all solids and to dissipate all liquids into vapor, and again to still further attenuate the vapor until it ceases to belong to the type of ponderable matter at all, and thus comes to exist in the state of imponderable space-filling substance, where, as we have previously intimated, it is the true *ether*. Such would seem to be the legitimate inference. And in any case it is evident that where the separative tendency as yet greatly overbalances the tendency toward concentration, the number and complexity of chemical compounds must be correspondingly limited. So that in the sun, for example, with its enormously high temperature—that is, with the still existing relatively intense repulsion or strain toward separation—the number of chemical compounds must be exceedingly few and those compounds must be of the simplest character. More explicitly, it is impossible that oxygen and hydrogen should there realize their combinative tendency in the actual formation of water, even in the vaporous state, while not a single one of the whole series of known carbon compounds can possibly exist otherwise than in the purely potential state.

It is to be noted further that the whole of modern chemistry is built up from the precise quantitative relations existing between the "elements." So that on this side chemistry is simply one form of applied mathematics. As M. Berthelot declares in closing his remarkable work, "*Essai de Mécanique Chimique*," chemistry "approaches more and more nearly to that ideal conception, followed out for so many years by the efforts of scholars and of philosophers, in which all speculations and all discoveries tend to establish (*concourent vers*) the unity of the universal law of natural movements and forces." That is, chemistry is coming more and more to be regarded as simply a branch of mechanics in the general sense of the term in proportion as chemical phenomena are found to be capable of mathematical treatment. At the same time this in no way obscures the fact that each new compound developed through change in quantitative relations exhibits new qualitative characteristics. Take, for example, the simplest cases—those of allotropic substances. Oxygen combines *with itself*, the result being what is called ozone. The quantitative change is simply one from extensive to intensive quantity. Externally the only change is a reduction of one-third in volume. So, too, carbon presents the three strikingly different states of graphite, coal, and diamond, by mere variety in the combination of carbon particles with carbon particles.

The same remarkable development of qualitative difference through mere change in quantitative relation is seen again in all those cases where one element combines with another in more than one ratio. A conspicuous example is found in the various oxides of nitrogen, where a constant quantity (28 parts by weight) of nitrogen combines successively with five different quantities (16, 32, 48, 64 and 80 parts by weight) of oxygen, producing as many qualitatively different results. It is noticeable that each succeeding quantity of oxygen in the series is a simple multiple of the first. And chemists have often called attention to the fact that no combinations take place between these elements in other proportions than those given. It was precisely such facts as these that led Dalton to enter upon those investigations which resulted in his revival of the atomic theory under a genuinely scientific form.

The core of Dalton's discovery is that this combination in definite proportions is the universal characteristic of all chemical activity—that chemical compounds are, without exception, dependent upon precisely fixed quantitative relations. Nor is it without significance that in Dalton's theory the numbers representing the proportions in which the elements combine have direct reference to the *weights of the combining atoms*. For weight, as we have seen, is simply the excess of attraction over centrifugal force in the neighborhood of a gravitating body like the earth. So that the relative weights of the atoms of different elements really means the relative excess of attraction over centrifugal force as between the earth on one side, and the atoms or force-centers in the elements taken severally.

Now, the weight of an atom of hydrogen being taken as 1, the weight of an atom of nitrogen is 14, and that of an atom of oxygen is 16. But the simplest compound of nitrogen and oxygen known to take place consists of two parts of the former and one of the latter. Hence the combining numbers for these two "elements" expressed in their atomic weights are: 28 for nitrogen and 16 for oxygen. And since the "atoms" can only combine as wholes, the next more complex compound, supposing the quantity of nitrogen to remain fixed, would be that in which the quantity of oxygen would be doubled, and so on.

Allowing, then, that the atom is real, not as an infinitely hard, absolutely fixed particle of something existing independently of force, but rather as itself simply a focus of force which constitutes a relation that must remain fixed so long as the surrounding conditions remain approximately the same; allowing this, we can see that the law of multiple proportions only becomes the more significant, without losing in any degree its simplicity.

This law, indeed, but expresses the fixed relation between the general mass of the earth in its present relatively matured stage of condensation and the various classes of force-centers constituting, through their varied intensive quantities, the qualitatively different phases of force-substance known as the elements, *and in any given case arbitrarily assumed not to be of the earth's mass.* In reality, the mass of the earth holds these force-centers in definite relation to itself, and in definite relations to one another. Thus many compounds take place "naturally" (the mass and temperature being what they are) which would be impossible as "natural" compounds on the surface of a sphere of very much less mass, or of very much greater temperature. In short, all chemical compounds must arise as the realization of inherent relations of attraction and repulsion between definitely determined force-centers, which, doubtless, there is no harm in calling atoms. And should there be more than one compound possible between any two elements, as in the example of oxygen and nitrogen cited above, it is evident that the several compounds formed must show in the successive groups of atoms that the combining numbers of one or the other element stand to each other in such relation that all after the first are exact multiples of the first.

The law of multiple proportions, however, presents the external conditions of chemical combinations; or, more precisely, the qualitative relations here presented are figured rather as the relations of extensive quantity. On the other hand, the phase of intensive quantity is shown in *affinity*, properly speaking—in the energy of attraction between the particles themselves. At the same time there is, as must ever be the case, a variation of the intensive quantity presented in the compound, through a variation in the extensive quantity of combination. And this variation of the intensive quantity is precisely what determines the qualitative differences of the several compounds. Thus, the several oxides of nitrogen already referred to present each its own group of distinguishing qualitative characteristics.

The whole of chemistry is, indeed, but an extended illustration of this, so that we need here do no more than call special attention to the immense number of exceedingly complex compounds which carbon forms with one or more of the three other elements, oxygen, hydrogen and nitrogen—the great number of the compounds being rendered possible, as the chemists assure us, by a "fundamental and distinctive property of carbon itself." That property is the power, possessed by no other element in so high a degree, of *combining with itself*, and forming a variable basis for multitudes of complicated compounds involving one or more of the other elements just named.

The point we have here specially to emphasize is, that the mere variation of the quantitative relations in the combinations of these four elements gives rise to the entire series of qualitative differences which lend such immense variety to the products, both of the vegetal and of the animal world.

To what has been said respecting the relation between extensive and intensive quantity as illustrated in chemistry, there may be added the following, from what is known of electricity. Statical electricity is said to be characterized by *intensity*, while dynamical electricity is distinguished by its *quantity*. And yet these two modes of electricity do not differ in *kind*, but rather in the mode of their development, which fact becomes explicit in the alternative names: frictional and chemical electricity. Not only so, but a Leyden jar may as well be charged from a Voltaic battery, as from an electrical machine.

The real truth of the relation between statical and dynamical electricity comes out in the estimate of Faraday,* that a current of dynamical electricity which would decompose a single grain of water by acting upon it during three and three-fourths minutes would, if its whole force were expended instantaneously, be equal in intensity to a powerful flash of lightning. Here the *quantity* of force is evidently the same. Acting through a longer time, it is *extensive* quantity; while the instantaneous expenditure of its whole energy presents the same quantity of force under the character of *intensive* quantity.

Statical electricity, then, is a phase of force, whose quantity is characteristically intensive, while dynamical electricity is a phase of force whose quantity is characteristically extensive. And, as is well known, all that is necessary in order to concentrate the extensive quantity of the latter, so that its manifestation shall be specifically intensive, is to introduce into its circuit an induction coil.

It is evident, then, that the "intensity" of statical electricity is simply intensive quantity, while the "quantity" of dynamical electricity is quantity manifested under the specific character of extensive quantity. And when it is said that quantity and intensity are inversely the one as the other in electricity, it is evident that this is but a loose way of saying that in any given quantity of electricity—as of any other phase of force—the extensive and the intensive aspects are reciprocals.

* See his "*Experimental Researches in Electricity,*" (2d Ed.) I., 250.

CHAPTER IX.

MEASURE AND THE MEASURELESS.

WE have thus seen that the extended world is first known to us through the qualitative differences of attraction and repulsion; that these in turn, through their necessary interactions, develop, or rather are seen to involve, an unlimited complex of quantitative relations; and again, that these quantitative relations reciprocally serve to render completely explicit a whole world of qualitative characteristics. It is also evident that these mutually inclusive qualitative and quantitative relations constitute the reality of the extended world.

Let us now inquire further of this extended world and obtain, as far as we may, a more adequate knowledge of its fundamental character and modes of existence.

In the first place, it is evident that whatever knowledge we possess of the quantitative relations of this extended world must involve comparison of one phase with another. But these comparisons also imply a fixed standard. And comparison with a fixed standard constitutes *measure*.

At the same time, we must soon become aware that all standards of measurement in the extended world must be arbitrary, and hence the measure must be purely relative. Hence, it may be remarked by the way, there can be no absolute distinction between extensive and intensive quantity. On the contrary, a given quantity may be regarded as either extensive or intensive, according to the standard of comparison. The rending force of gunpowder would be regarded as intensive compared with that of freezing water, while on the other hand, it would rather bear the character of extensive quantity, when compared with dynamite. In other words, any given quantity of energy is not merely extensive *or* intensive; it is both extensive and intensive. The distinction between these phases can never be suppressed, while, at the same time, their unity is inseparable.

And yet all measure proves to be relative, even *absolutely relative*. So that, as it seems to turn out, we *know absolutely* that *all our knowledge,* especially our *exact* knowledge, is *relative*. It is a hopeful-discouraging outcome. Assuredly, if we are anywhere to obtain knowledge that may be called absolute, it must be in the realm of *measure,* which is pre-eminently the realm of the exact sciences. There is, at least, one science universally acknowledged to be exact—the science of pure quantity, or mathematics. And yet, even here, there have been skeptical murmurings, not to say loud protests. The very axioms of mathematics have been called in question.* And not only so, but here and there, especially in the applications of mathematics, there is full confession of the necessity of approximation, as will be seen more fully when we come to consider the subject of motion. So that a momentary shadow of suspicion arises lest the very science in which men have so long confided with absolute serenity may prove to be, after all, only the exact science of approximation. And so much the more as those sciences which have come to be called "exact," through the

---

* See, for example, Helmholtz's criticism on The Axioms of Mathematics, in his *Popular Scientific Lectures* (Second Series).

application of mathematics to them, must keep *within the limits of measure*, seeing that they have constantly to do with the quantitative phases of the extended world, and must, therefore, bear the mark of "relativity" inherent in all things within the realm of measure.

In sober truth, that the application of mathematics to the actual extended world may be brought within the range of finite powers of thinking, it is necessary to confine the calculations to a simple set of relations more or less arbitrarily chosen, and to regard this set of relations as if completely isolated from the rest of the universe. For example, Thomson and Tait, in their "*Treatise on Natural Philosophy*," call special attention to the fact that even in so simple a case as that of the investigation of the lever it is necessary to assume that a lever is a bar, perfectly rigid, inflexible, and without weight—an assumption which, of course, can never be realized.

In short, the assumption made in every single instance in the application of mathematics to the concrete sciences is more or less in direct contradiction to the actual facts. Or, if not exactly this, at least all except certain more or less arbitrarily chosen aspects of those facts are of necessity ignored in each and every problem proposed.

It is true that the very purpose of the mathematical phase of the sciences is to discover the exact measure of things. And yet the *really* exact is not the *approximately* exact. The former is, no doubt, that which is desired, though the latter is the utmost that is ever actually attained. The "exact sciences" propose an ideal which they can never hope to realize; and this is inevitable from the very nature of the case. The so-called exact sciences are necessarily restricted to the realm of *measure*—that is, to the realm of the *finite*. For in every such case measure consists in the comparison of any given object with an arbitrarily chosen, and therefore finite, standard. Everything *measured* is by that fact *limited*. Hence it is that the realm of mathematics is the realm of finite thought.

At the same time, we have seen that the sum-total of the extended world is necessarily a *unit*—a whole of which the infinitely varied phases constitute the specific objects of all sense-perception. That is, these objects are but the precisely defined forms resulting from the activity of the total World-Energy.

But *measure* is the comparison of these various forms, one with another, or with some purely conventional standard. That is, these forms present the only realm of the actually measurable; so that the world, as a whole, thus proves to be *measureless*.

And yet these forms, we have just seen, are not only the specific objects of sense-perception, but they are also the direct product of the activity of the World-Energy. They are modes of its manifestation. In other words, the measurable proves to be just a phase of the measureless. Or, again, the measurable is found to constitute the modes in which the measureless manifests itself. Nay, Mr. Spencer himself, as we remember, allows that even the "Unknowable" has an established order of self-manifestation.

Thus the measurable is found to be the finite, while the measureless is the infinite; so that the finite is not something contrasted with the infinite, but is in truth a mode or phase of the infinite. Otherwise the infinite would have to maintain itself in contrast with, or in opposition to, the finite. It would then be in external relation to the finite—that is, it would be *limited by the finite*, in which case it would itself prove to be something finite, and not the true infinite.

Thus the infinite and the finite prove to be but the more adequate aspects of what were previously called continuous and discrete quantity.

But here something further suggests itself. It is this: As the true infinite must include the finite within itself as phases of itself, then the infinite must be the comprehensive total of all reality. And as such it must be absolutely equal with itself. It can be compared with nothing else than itself, for it is itself the only reality. It is, then, absolutely immeasurable by any finite standard, and yet at the same time it is the eternally *self-measured*.

Thus the finite is seen to constitute nothing else than the endlessly varied modes of the self-measurement of the true infinite. The world as a whole is, therefore, a mighty process in which all that is finite or measurable is dissolved and absolutely fused in the infinite or measureless.

In this connection a significant hint is found to be latent in the most elementary phase of mathematics. The beginner learns that "once one is one." At a later stage he learns something of the "powers" of numbers. He learns that 2 multiplied by itself produces 4, while 1 multiplied by itself is still 1. Unity, he is assured, is peculiar to itself in the fact that it remains unchanged, however persistently it may be multiplied by itself.

Surely that is a wonderful property—wonderful, indeed, if true! Let one attempt its verification in practice and see what the result will be. If 1 is a line, then 1 x 1 is a surface—still 1, it is true, but 1 having a quite new value. So again 1 x 1 x 1, is a solid. It is still 1, but 1 with added wealth of meaning.

And what do the higher "powers" of numbers signify but varying degrees of "solidity"? And what are those varying degrees of solidity but varying degrees of tension within a given mass, resulting in *qualities*—that is, in enriched modes of existence? That plaything of modern mathematics—the "fourth dimension in space"—is in truth a symbol representing the transition from extensive to intensive quantity. And the higher "powers" of numbers in general are nothing else than abstract expressions hinting obscurely at the concrete fact that the more intensive a given quantity of energy becomes, the richer does it become in quality.

In other words, what is commonly called quality as distinguished from quantity is in reality, let us repeat, nothing else than intensive quantity, which is the reciprocal of quantity in its aspect of extent.

But again, the abstract formula, $1 \times 1 = 1$, not only *seems* unquestionable. It *is* unquestionable from *two points of view*. The first is that point of view (the usual one) from which the formula is taken in its purely abstract sense. In pure or formal mathematics the expression: $1 \times 1 = 1^2 = 1$ is faultless. On the other hand, the second point of view is that in which unity is taken in its richest, most concrete significance. From this point of view it is equally unquestionable that the absolutely perfect unit, the total, self-sufficing Energy, maintains its eternal self-equality by the faultless continuity of its fusion, its combination, its multiplication of itself with itself. And here indeed the formula is no longer $1 \times 1 = 1^2 = 1$; but $1 \times 1 = 1 \propto = 1$.

Again, zero is commonly defined as a symbol which, when standing alone, expresses no value. That seems simple enough. And yet on further examination the symbol 0 represents, even in its very lowest term, a product of very abstract thinking. It *really* represents the negation in thought of all *reality*. That is, its subjective meaning may be said to be greatest when its objective meaning is least. Or if, as is sometimes done, we take the term "objective" to mean *valid, true*, then we would have to change the mode of our expression, and say that the objective significance of the term zero in its ultimate abstraction consists precisely in its subjective character. For in its ultimate abstraction the term zero represents a perfectly valid concept to which there is no corresponding reality other than the concept itself. It represents just that negative concept which consists in the recognition that beyond reality there is absolutely no limitation, for limitation is itself a mode of reality, or, if the technical reader prefers, a mode of *actuality*.

But still further, in concrete science zero represents a multitude of values on occasion. In the higher geometry a right line is represented by an equation, of which one member is 0. Again, in physics zero of temperature (Centigrade) represents that balancing of the molecular attractions and repulsions in water, the slightest disturbance of which one way or the other will (under given conditions of pressure) cause the water to assume the solid state or assure its remaining liquid. But this is by no means all. The theoretical "absolute zero" ($273°$ below 0 Centigrade) gives a scale in which 0 Centigrade is found to represent an "absolute" positive temperature of $273°$.

It seems worth remarking, too, that the "absolute zero" logically represents the complete absence of molecular repulsions, and therefore also the complete absence of molecular attractions. But this can only mean the complete absence of matter—that is, complete vacuum (such vacuum itself being in great danger of collapse, one might suppose).

But not to extend illustrations further, we may say in general that in concrete science zero represents a positive value; and that value is always of precisely one character. It is invariably a point of indifference, or *equilibrium*. And this is the clew to the ultimate, most concrete significance of zero. For, as representing the equilibrium of concrete modes of energy in general, it becomes evident at once that the ultimate, most concrete significance of the symbol, is that of the equilibrium, the perfect self-poise of the total Energy; just as 1, in its richest meaning, represents the absolute wholeness of the total Energy.

Finally, the formula $\frac{1}{0} = \infty$ is meaningless if 0 stands for pure nothing. Or, if it represents any positive quantity, the formula is absurd if 1 stands for any finite quantity. It can have genuine concrete significance only when 1 represents the absolute totality of existence, and 0 the absolute equilibrium of that totality, in the sense of the absolutely perfect method of the totality, as self-consistent energy. In the first of the supposed cases it is a formula of division, representing no-division. In the last case it represents, not the division of one quantity by another, but rather, the absolute self-division of the total Energy; and such self-division is nothing else than the self-specialization, the self-differentiation, that is, the self-realization of the total World-Energy.

Thus, there comes into something like distinct view the one central conception which has been gradually focusing into definite utterance throughout the whole of our inquiry, thus far.

Before proceeding with the further stages of the argument, it seems worth while to notice that the result here reached is altogether in agreement with the doctrine regarding the relation between substance and its attributes, as defined by Spinoza. That is, to use his phrase, "attributes are what we may know of substance." So, also, the same results may be reached through a consideration of the interdependence of the categories of Aristotle.

It has been claimed that Aristotle gathered his categories together in more or less arbitrary fashion, from the current speech of his time. But it is also to be borne in mind that his writings have reached us in exceedingly fragmentary form, and that our judgment regarding the arbitrariness of his mode of procedure ought to be guarded accordingly. In any case, the categories as they stand in the list handed down to us as the one he proposed, are open for interpretation. And it seems but reasonable and just to allow that the most adequate and consistent interpretation which can be given them is the one which Aristotle himself put upon them, in more or less explicit fashion. Or if not so much as this, at least it ought to be allowed that such interpretation is not inconsistent with the general estimate he gave them.

Let us see, then, what interpretation will be borne by these categories as presented in the Organon. They are as follows: Substance ($οὐσία$), Quantity ($ποσόν$), Quality ($ποιόν$), Relation ($πρός τι$), Where ($ποῦ$), When ($ποτέ$),

Position (*κεῖσθαι*), Possession (*ἔχειν*), Action (*ποιεῖν*), and Passion (*πάσχειν*).

It is true that in the logical treatise of Aristotle these categories receive a treatment that seems rather formal than essential. And yet, even here, and still more strongly in the metaphysics, Aristotle intimates his conviction, not only that substance must be (logically) prior to its attributes in any given object, but that substance is one and indivisible, as well as primal and primordial.

Doubtless this would be a somewhat violent interpretation if taken from the logical treatise alone. But its justification is found to be fairly complete through the frequent references to, and even extended discussions of, substance in the metaphysics, where it is represented as equivalent to the very being, essence or nature of a thing, and where the conception that substance must be primarily *one* is explicitly referred to with approval, and something approaching proof of its necessity. And when taken in connection with the outcome of the discussion of the nature of cause, with which he identifies substance, it is fairly evident that the *οὐσία* was to him what substance is in modern thought—namely, that which supports and unifies all attributes, or rather, that which enfolds all "attributes" within itself, as nothing else than modes of itself. Thus, evidently, it is that without which the attributes themselves could not be.

From this point of view it is manifest that quality and quantity can be real only as attributes of substance. They are simply the what-kind and the how-much of substance. Similarly, *relation* can exist, in the first place, only as between substance and the attributes inhering in substance, and secondly, as between the attributes themselves. Indeed, in our present discussion, we have seen that substance, so far as the extended world presents its developed reality, is just the unity (relation) of *quality* under the form of mutually opposed and yet mutually inclusive forces, on the one hand, and *quantity*, on the other hand, as measure or limitation, and hence as a phase of differentiation, or the rendering explicit what lies latent in substance.

"Where" and "when" are manifestly relations respectively of time and place. "Position" indicates attitude or relative place, including relation of part to part in the thing having position. "Possession" is but a relation between a superior (more complex) and an inferior (less complex) phase of substance. So that thus far, we have in reality but three categories as attributes of substance—namely quantity, quality, and relation.

At the same time it is noticeable that these three attributive categories could have no existence apart from substance, nor could substance exist without involving what those categories imply. They are essential phases of substance.

So, too, the remaining categories show themselves at once to be only mutually implying modes of substance. For the reality of substance can be shown only in its activity; and as substance contributes the sum-total of reality, it must be no less truly passive than active, since, as the total, it must receive the whole of its own activity. Passion or passivity is simply sufferance or receptivity. But receptivity is not merely passivity; it is just as truly activity. It is, in short, but another name for *reaction*. It may be remarked by the way, then, that in his categories Aristotle presents us with the simplest possible scheme of thought. For those categories are nothing else than the names, first, of that which is necessarily presupposed in all thought, and, secondly, of those fundamental modes in which alone it can be comprehended in thought. We may criticise the list as we will. It still is a series of names representing concepts without which thought and things would be alike impossible.

Let us now remind ourselves once more that the fundamental qualities of the matter or substance of the extended world are, primarily, attraction and repulsion, and that these are opposed and yet also mutually inclusive phases of force. Whence it appears that action and passion are but further (that is, more explicit) aspects of the necessary interrelation between attraction and repulsion. They are the phases of action and reaction in the total process of the *self-measured*.

We have already seen how quality finds its truth in the intensive phase of quantity. It now appears, too, that quality and quantity are but modes of substance, or of the self-measured Total. So that the ultimate truth of relation is found to be the self-relation of the Total.

The substance of the extended world, then, is Energy, which presents itself as an all-inclusive *process*, whose fundamental phases are *action* and *reaction*. This is the essence, the very nature, the true internality of the external world. It is the noumenon or reality bringing itself into open manifestation through—or, rather, *as*—the all-pervasive, all-energizing process of the world. This, indeed, brings us to the consideration of motion, which involves not merely the space-relations already brought under review, but also the fundamental relations of succession—that is, time-relations.

CHAPTER X.

OF THE POSSIBILITY OF MOTION IN GENERAL.

THE doctrine of Heraclitus that all is a becoming was unquestionably the most important phase of the pre-Socratic philosophy. It unified the elements which had previously been brought into definition, and which in the Eleatic school were not only opposed to each other, but were also held in mutual exclusion. The central doctrine of Parmenides, the chief representative of that school, was that "being alone is, and non-being is not."

This doctrine involves the conception that everything *is* all that it can *ever be*. It therefore has no potential phase, and so can by no possibility pass out of its present state. Hence no change, quantitative or qualitative, can ever take place. All seeming change is mere illusion. The senses only deceive us. It is by reason, and by reason alone, that we can ever attain a knowledge of the truth. The senses tell us that the things of the world change; reason assures us that no change whatever is possible.

Thus, in defense of this doctrine, Zeno's dialectic comes to have an exclusively negative employment. Its central, if not its sole, purpose is to prove that the conception of motion (and hence of change) is a self-contradictory conception, and hence impossible. A thing, he says, must move either where it is or where it is not. On the one hand, however, it is impossible that it should move where it is; for the moment it begins to move, it must in that very fact leave the place where it is. On the other hand, it can not move where it is not, since it is impossible that it should be in more than one place at the same time. Hence it is impossible that anything should move; or, in other words, motion of any kind whatever is impossible.

It was doubtless a very effective sarcasm on the part of Diogenes when, on hearing this argument through, he silently and contemptuously filliped a pebble into the brook with his not too tidy great toe, though it could scarcely serve as a philosophic answer to the argument.

The fallacy, in fact, lies in the ambiguity of the expression, "where it is." In truth, the *place* where anything is is absolutely indifferent as regards *space in general;* while, on the other hand, the place where a thing is is no less absolutely inseparable from the *thing itself*. No matter, then, whether the thing be moving or motionless, the "place-where-it-is" pertains absolutely to the thing itself, and is indifferently any portion of space whatever.

Thus, the "place-where-it-is" is by no means to be understood as an absolutely fixed division in or of absolute space. On the contrary, space is simply an infinite series of indifferent "places," each of which in turn comes to be the "place-where-it-is" as the thing passes into it, and comes again to be the place where it *was* as the thing passes out of it—that is, again, if such "place" could possibly be defined apart from body.

It is not true, then, that, in order to move, the thing must leave the "place-where-it-is;" for the "place-where-it-is" is not a fixed portion of absolute space, but is, instead, precisely the abstract externality or volume pertaining to the thing itself, and inseparable therefrom. It can occupy only just so much of space as corresponds to its volume, neither more nor less; and thus, in a certain sense, it carries with it the "place-where-it-is", the latter being, in short, nothing else than a given quantity of what Kant calls "movable space." It may also be said that the whole of pure space is the "here" of every particular body, since it is impossible to say where, in space as such, the body is. It can, in fact, be *located* only with reference to other bodies. Apart from body, then, "place" has no meaning, so that a body cannot leave the "place-where-it-is", simply because it cannot separate itself from its own volume. On the other hand, as to the particular portion of abstract space which the body is in, it is impossible for us ever to know whether a body is moving or not, so long as the body is viewed apart from other bodies. As will be shown more fully below, neither motion nor rest could ever be ascribed to an isolated body in abstract space. Motion and rest are terms that cannot be applied with any meaning to a body, save as expressing a relation of that body to some other body.

Thus motion proves to be the very first and simplest phase of "becoming" or change in any portion of the extended world. That is, in such "change" the object is found theoretically to undergo change or modification only in a purely external sense; for there occurs no real change *in the object*, but only a change in the purely external relations which the given object sustains to other objects.

It may be, indeed, that even such external change necessarily involves internal change also, though that is not immediately apparent. Nevertheless, as was already seen at an earlier stage of the argument, any change in the relative position of any given force-center must involve a change in the strains to which it is subjected, and hence must develop greater or less modification within the force-center itself; and not only so, but it would seem that the continuity of substance must render such interrelation inevitable in every sphere of existence. Of this we will see more as we proceed.

Another form of Zeno's argument is as follows: Granting that motion is possible, an arrow, for example, can never actually pass through any assigned space. For since space is infinitely divisible, there will be an infinite number of divisions or spaces between the point of beginning and the assigned terminus of its flight. At the same time, it must occupy a definite portion of time in passing through each of these spaces. But, as there is an infinite number of spaces to be passed over, the arrow will necessarily occupy in its flight an infinite number of moments or divisions of time. That is, an infinite time will be required for the arrow to reach its terminus. Therefore no assigned space can be traversed by any object in any finite time.

It is as if all velocities were subdivided into what the acute eye of modern science has been able to recognize as "infinitely small" velocities, which in truth is but a calm adoption, with or without recognition, of the dreadfully metaphysical conception of the infinite divisibility of both time and space; for "velocity" is just the product of space and time.

Here, indeed, the fallacy is not so very deeply hidden as has been sometimes supposed. Space is assumed to be infinitely divisible. Then a finite space is assumed to be *actually divided* to infinity. Then one of these "infinitely small" divisions is assumed to have absolutely *no dimensions at all*. That is, an "infinitely small" portion or extent of space is assumed to be identical with the *point* which, so far from being a space, even an "infinitely small" space, is just the absolute negation of space.

On the contrary, no matter how far the division of space may be considered to have been carried, even though it be to "infinity," yet will the smallest actual division still be *space*, and will thus have actual dimensions. So that, each extending over a definite part of the distance, there will be but a finite number of spaces to pass through.

But, again, as Aristotle did not fail to observe, time is infinitely divisible, as well as space. And, hence, a portion of time, however small, may be stretched out to infinity by the same process, and thus a fictitious infinite time produced to render the passage of the arrow through the assumed fictitious infinity of space reasonably successful and prompt.

Nay, let the same mode of proof be applied to the arrow itself (since matter is also infinitely divisible), and it will be found that the arrow consists of an infinite number of parts, each of which has a certain extent. Whence the arrow, as a whole, has infinite dimensions, and thus offers a solid bridge whereon one may safely pass from the earth to the remotest star in space! For thus, evidently, the arrow itself is already the star and the earth, and all things else extended. Hence, too, it is already at the point of destination without even leaving the point of departure.

But one fallacy is not explained, still less explained away, by putting another by its side. A really valid answer to the one here under consideration is found in the contradiction involved in the expression, "infinite number."

Doubtless there may be, and is, a reality corresponding with the expression, infinite *quantity;* and mathematics is commonly defined as the "science of quantity." Nevertheless, as we have seen, mathematics deals, and from its nature can only deal successfully, with the finite aspects of quantity. To quantify in the mathematical sense means to find a definite measure. And whenever a "mathematically exact" result is reached, that result is represented by some definite number. But number, *as a given definite number*, is and can only be finite. Any given number may be added to, or may be multiplied either by itself or by any other number. Hence the expression, an "infinite number," has really no meaning in the strict sense of the term. The infinite is beyond all number, and no given number can ever represent the infinite. So that the phrase, "infinite number," is an "expression," indeed, but an expression of nothing more than the vague conception of a quantity very great, but as yet undefined; *unmeasured,* but by no means absolutely *measureless.*

In short, the Zenonian fallacy can possess even the color of truth only so long as one fails to recognize the essential relationship between the continuous and the discrete aspects of quantity—the true relation of the measurable to the measureless.

A valid reason is found, as I think, for the attention here given to the fallacies of the Zenonian dialectic, in the re-appearance of those fallacies under varying forms in modern science. In this connection it will suffice to mention the mathematical theory of "variables and limits"; in which it is supposed to be shown, for example, how a polygon may actually become a circle;* and, as a typical case in physical science, that of work done by 0 weight with a lever of infinite length. Mathematics struggles courageously toward the infinite, and produces magnificent results—within its appropriate domain of the finite.

In contrast with the Eleatic doctrine that "Being alone is and non-being is not," Heraclitus declared that "Being no more is than non-being." In the former the conception of "being" is equivalent to that of absolute reality, while by "non-being" is evidently meant the absolutely unreal; that is, mere nothing. In the latter or Heraclitean doctrine, on the contrary, the term "being" evidently represents the present state in which any given phase of reality is, while the term "non-being" stands for any state that a given phase of reality may assume other than that which it now is in. That is, Heraclitus seems to have been the first to see clearly that nothing in the finite world is ever at any one moment all that it is possible it should be—the first to see at all clearly the true distinction between the *real* and the *potential*. Thus, according to his doctrine, any individual object has *being* at any given moment in just so far as its potentialities

---

*In some mathematical works it is, indeed, explicitly stated that the "limit" can never be actually reached; though the conception of a number "becoming infinite" seems to present no difficulties.

are realized in that moment. On the other hand, whatever of its potentialities are unrealized at any given moment, such potentialities constitute its non-being.

But these unrealized phases of potentiality belonging to an object and constituting its non-being are no less constituent factors in the total significance of the object than are the phases which are for the moment realized, and which thus constitute its being. The being of an object may cease as being and come to *be* as *non-being;* but it can do so only on condition that some phase or phases of its non-being shall cease as non-being, and thus come into the state of *being*. Thus his somewhat enigmatical saying that being no more is than non-being is seen to be entirely justified. It is an explicit announcement of the condition necessary to any and every change or becoming. Whence his doctrine is called the doctrine of Becoming, emphasizing as it does (in opposition to the changelessness of Being as affirmed by the Eleatics) the evident fact that all things are in a ceaseless process—that all things perpetually flow or become.

It seems probable, too, that we have here the clue to the peculiar form which Aristotle gave to that law, which he regarded as the fundamental law of all true thinking. As has already been stated (in the introductory chapter) the "law of contradiction" as formulated by him declares that "a thing cannot both *begin* and *not begin* at the same time and in the same sense." It is as if Aristotle wished to emphasize in his formulation of this central conception of all real science the truth of the doctrine of Becoming, and the necessity of its recognition in all rational inquiry.

And that this is by no means a strained interpretation is shown in a remarkable passage of the "*Metaphysics,*" (Lib. XI. [XII.] cap. II). The entire book is devoted to a discussion of substance. In the second chapter change is especially considered as pertaining to that phase of substance perceptible to the senses. In the preceding chapter he has remarked that in this phase of substance there is an eternal element or factor. Here he indicates that this permanent factor in the midst of the changing is to be called matter ($ὕλη$). Directly after is found the passage to which reference is made above, and which is as follows: "If there were four modes of change—one as to type ($τὸ\ τί$), one as to quality ($τὸ\ ποιὸν$), one as to quantity ($ἡ\ ποσὸν$), one as to place ($ἡ\ ποῦ$); and if simple integration ($γένεσις$) and disintegration ($Φθορὰ$) [were to take place] according to the first of these modes, increase and diminution according to that of quantity, change, [in quality] according to passivity, and motion according to place; then in every case change would be a contradiction." Thus far, as if with reference to the Zenonian arguments in disproof of the possibility of change. But he adds immediately a statement that seems to refer distinctly to the Heraclitean doctrine of Becoming as the essentially true one in respect of change. The statement is this: "Whence, of necessity, all possible change in matter is two-fold [or of reciprocal nature]. But, since being is two-fold, everything changes from potential being ($δυνάμει\ ὄντος$) into real being ($ἐνεργείᾳ\ ὄν$); as, for example, from light potential to light real. Similarly with increase and diminution. Whence it is by no means accidental that all things are developed *recipro-*

cally from non-being and from being" (ἐκ μὴ ὄντος, ἀλλα καὶ ἐξ ὄντος).

Thus Aristotle interprets into clearness what remained a somewhat obscure theory with Heraclitus, namely, that non-being *is* as the reciprocal of being, and that, as potentiality, non-being may be of any degree whatever—the greater the degree of reality in any given case the less the degree of potentiality; the less the degree of reality the greater the degree of potentiality. When the rose-bud is real, the rose is the next natural phase of potentiality. When the rose is the real, the next phase of potentiality is decay, etc. And the *actual* rose is the total round of possibilities of the rose, both the realized and the unrealized. That is, the actual total world is the entire range of both reality and potentiality, of being and of non-being; and every object of the world appealing to the senses, is in constant process or rather it is itself a constant process with both beginning and ceasing, with both being and non-being, as the necessary reciprocal factors of its protean existence.

Thus motion is inevitable. It is not so difficult to conceive its existence as to conceive its non-existence.

To this it need hardly be added that Hegel takes, as the starting-point of his famous (though, it is to be feared, little known) dialectical development of the categories of thought (and of reality) this same doctrine of Heraclitus concerning the relation which being and non-being sustain to each other in becoming, though of course with a subtle refinement upon these concepts as they were left by Heraclitus.

It appears, then, that motion, activity, *becoming*, has long been considered as constituting the vital truth of the world. And modern science is but tracing out in more precise details what the greatest "metaphysical" thinkers of preceding ages have shown, each in his own way, to be the one truly rational theory of the world. What is, perhaps, wanting more than anything else in the work of modern science, is the clear guidance of the universal principles which these great thinkers have outlined with such admirable consistency, and which modern investigators themselves are seeking after, through their so-called inductive methods. In reality, the fundamental principles of all science are discovered rather by reflection than by pursuit of details. And what are called discoveries are commonly nothing else than the outward, conspicuous verification of the accuracy with which the inward inconspicuous process of thought has traced out this or that fundamental principle in nature. Thought anticipates experiment. Experiment is the process of measuring one's thought by applying it to the unvarying standard of nature.

Doubtless thought, to be successful, to be real as thought, must in a certain sense be experimental, must keep in view the "facts" of nature, though, again, these "facts" could only be known as such by means of thought. Similarly, on the other hand, no experiment or observation is worthy the name unless thought is present as the very soul of the process so named. As we saw at the outset of our inquiry, it is absurd to suppose that theory and fact are separable elements in human inquiry. No theory is trustworthy that did not more or less have its origin in "experiment," and that does not constantly find its confirmation in experiment. But, equally true is it that no "experiment" is of any real significance unless it has begun in thought, and is continuously guided by thought. And, after all, the supreme "experiment" is that which thought performs upon itself, clarifying itself by self-criticism, and thus making sure of its own consistency, of its own harmony with the supreme law of thought—which law, let it be ever remembered, is also the central law of all reality. This is the value of the universal logic which, as Kant expresses it, is a "cathartic of the ordinary understanding."

To resume, then, Heraclitus is seen to have solved the contradiction inherent in the doctrine of the Eleatic conception of the world, by the discovery, substantially, that quantity is not to be regarded as *either* continuous *or* discrete; but that, rather, quantity is necessarily *both* continuous *and* discrete—that the discrete or measurable is itself a necessary phase of the continuous, or measureless. And this discovery is also found to be distinctly recognized as the discovery of the central truth of at least all extended reality, by both Aristotle and Hegel. So that, with them, motion, activity, *becoming*, constitutes the central, vital truth of the world.

And what is this but the doctrine of evolution in large outline? Here, too, "all flows." There is no rest in the sense of mere quiescence. Perpetual activity, perpetual motion, characterizes the sum of all reality.

At the same time, it seems well worth noticing, that the first rigidly reasoned and, at least approximately, consistent development of the doctrine of evolution in modern thought, assumed a metaphysical character. And this we owe to Spinoza, who presents the doctrine under the form of a demonstration of the necessary relation existing between substance and its modes—

between the continuous and the discrete aspects of existence.

Having thus shown not only that motion is possible, but also that it is inevitable, in all extended objects, we have next to trace the fundamental characteristics of motion.

CHAPTER XI.

OF THE NATURE OF MOTION.

WE have seen that the question of the possibility of motion engaged the attention of thinkers at a very early period. We also found that the difficulties in the way of conceiving the possibility of motion are due to a misconception of the relation between the extensive and the intensive aspects of quantity, together with entanglement in the fallacy that the "infinitely small" is absolutely without dimensions.

Thus it requires no very extended research to enable us to set aside the arguments of Zeno as having no real force or validity. But we shall find another contradiction in the conception of motion, considered from the modern standpoint, which, at least within the limits of inquiry allowed by anti-metaphysical investigators, is far more difficult to solve than those presented by Zeno. This difficulty will develop of itself as we proceed.

Let us note now that space presents no obstacle to motion. On the contrary, it is a primary condition of motion. It is, besides, a veritable abstraction. It *is*, and yet is— just nothing. It possesses not a single positive characteristic, and has therefore no negative limitations or distinctions by which one part of space can be distinguished from any other part of space.

So far as space itself is concerned, then, neither Zeno nor anyone else could by any possibility ever tell from the closest scrutiny of a given body, in its relation to space merely, whether such body were moving or motionless. Granted that space could be emptied of all objects with the exception of one single body, that body could not be said either to be at rest or to be in motion. For, space being "infinite," in the double sense that it is without limitation both externally and internally, there could be no possible fixed point in space as such with reference to which the body could be said to be either stationary or moving.

On the supposition, however, that two definite bodies are in existence, it is evidently possible to recognize whether the distance between the two remains the same, or increases, or diminishes. And with the aid of the spectroscope this would be possible, even though the observations were taken from one of the given bodies, though, of course, on condition that the other body should be incandescent.

But, again, in such case it would be impossible to judge whether the *system* composed by the two bodies were moving or not, for the same reason that it would be impossible to judge whether the single body in the former case were moving or at rest. Nor would it be possible to tell whether the one, or the other, or both the bodies composing the system were moving, in case the distance between them were ascertained to be increasing or diminishing. And, again, the two bodies might be revolving about each other with any velocity, and the fact must remain forever unknown to an observer from either body, supposing an axial rotation in each exactly corresponding with the motion of their revolution about each other. Or, supposing an axial rotation in the body from which observations are taken, and not corresponding with any given movement which the bodies might have about one another, the observer could never detect the axial rotation in his own sphere. On the contrary, he must inevitably attribute to the observed body a movement about his own sphere, even though the bodies were at rest with reference to each other. While, in case an actual revolution existed, it could in no way be detected, and the apparent motion might be exactly opposite to the actual one. The former case is sufficiently illustrated by the apparent revolution of the sun around the earth; the latter by the apparent motion of the moon contrary to its actual motion about our planet—discrepancies which could never have been discovered save through observation of the motion of many bodies.

Finally, what has been said of the relativity of motion must be true in any system composed of any number of bodies. Any motion of the system as a whole could never be detected, save in comparison with some body, or group of bodies, outside the system. That is, no positive judgment could ever be formed of any state of motion or rest respecting the bodies composing the system, save with reference to one another.

Thus, we may perhaps be permitted to say, we know absolutely that all our knowledge of the motions of bodies must be relative—though the special discussions of those motions constitute several of the most important of the "exact sciences" which, as such, ought, it would seem, to lead us to absolute knowledge of some sort. Perhaps, after all, it will yet be discovered that these are the absolute sciences of the relative.

A striking example of the absolute relativity of our knowledge of motion is given in Clerk Maxwell's admirable little treatise on "*Matter and Motion*" (p. 36). He says: "If, when referred to a certain point, the body appears to be moving northward with diminishing velocity, we have only to refer it to another point moving northward with a uniform velocity greater than that of the body, and it will appear to be moving southward with increasing velocity."

We may, in short, heartily agree with the same author when he declares it to be "unscientific to distinguish between rest and motion, as between two different states of a body in itself, since it is impossible to speak of a body being at rest or in motion, except with reference, expressed or implied, to some other body."

It is assuredly "unscientific," not to say unphilosophic, to attempt to set up a distinction in thought where it is "impossible," even absolutely impossible, to discover any distinction in fact.

It would seem, then, that there is a possible contradiction involved in the conception that *all* our knowledge of motion is relative in its nature. It would seem that, so far as we have knowledge at all, such knowledge must belong to us as a phase of our own consciousness. So much, at least, we may fairly be allowed to know absolutely. And further, we know, by an application of the law of contradiction — which, we have seen, is also to be regarded as one phase of the larger law of consistency — that the only space we can truly think; that is, the only space we can ever *know*, in any rational sense of the term — is, in its very nature, absolutely unlimited. We know absolutely, also, that, as there are no distinguishing points whatever in space, considered merely as space, it is wholly "unscientific to distinguish between rest and motion as between two different states of a body in itself." And still further; we know absolutely that if the actual distance between two bodies increases or diminishes, one or other, or both the bodies, must move. By the law of consistency, thought must accept this as true and must utterly repudiate any asserting by which it is contradicted.

Motion, therefore, is primarily a *change in the space-relations of two or more bodies*. And this, too, we may fairly claim to know absolutely.

But now another phase of the subject presents itself. We have just seen that all our knowledge of motion is a knowledge of change in space-relations between actual bodies. But change of any kind can only take place in time. Whence it appears that our knowledge of motion is a complex knowledge, involving the relations both of time and of space. At the same time, however, it is to be noted that though our knowledge of motion is, in its nature, a *knowledge of relations*, it by no means necessarily follows from this that all we can know of motion is to be counted as merely *relative knowledge*.

It seems well worth while to notice, by the way, too, that the ambiguity just noticed is precisely that which underlies the whole theory of the relativity of knowledge — the advocates of which seem to find not the slightest difficulty in knowing with absolute certainty that absolutely nothing can ever be certainly known. Nor are they likely to become aware of such difficulty until they have learned to distinguish between knowledge of relations and relative knowledge.

It is relations, indeed, that constitute the marrow, the essence, all that has substance and vitality in our knowledge; for relations constitute the core of all reality. It is for this reason, and not because of the hopeless limitations of our powers of knowing, that we can learn so little concerning space. For space is utterly destitute of relation within itself. It has, as already noticed, no qualitative differences by which one portion of space can be distinguished from another. This is the reason why it is "unscientific" to speak of motion or of rest as pertaining to an isolated body in space. Thus, as being without inner or qualitative relations, space is barren of reality. Hence, not a single positive proposition can be made concerning it. Space has no secret save an infinitely wide open one. It has and can have no relation to bodies beyond the purely negative one of absolute non-resistance to their movements. Hence there is neither fixed nor fixable position or direction in space apart from bodies in space. Position and direction could, in fact, have no possible meaning apart from bodies.

In short, space *is* only as a relation between bodies; though still only the purely negative relation of mere separation.

Our interest in "absolute space," then, can only be our interest in the emptiest, the most "absolute" of all abstractions; our interest in boundless *nothing*.

On the other hand, as we have already intimated, our interest in *motion* is an interest in the changes of relation of bodies to each other in space. The only directions that can come within the possible range of our knowing are those determined by the relations of bodies to each other.

Such relations are fixed or absolute in the sense that they are inseparable from the bodies. If the bodies exist the relations also exist necessarily or "absolutely." Thus in every case of the relation of body to body in space coming under our observation we have an example of absolute knowledge, though it is also a knowledge of relations.

But again, when the relations between the parts of a physically constituted system are considered, such relations will be found to undergo change. It is here, indeed, that we find the appropriate realm of measure and of relativity in estimate of values. A change of distance, or of velocity, or of direction, is equal, or greater, or less, in comparison with some other change of distance, or of velocity, or of direction. And these changes are represented in empirical space; that is, in a space rendered significant by the presence of objects.

But also, with such changes of relation, there is introduced the element of possible confusion. A given body, A, considered with reference to a given other body, B, will appear to be moving in one direction; while, in comparison with a third body, C, it will appear to be moving in a contrary direction. Thus motion appears to contain its own dialectic, through which it exhibits its own *absolute relativity*. For example, suppose any three bodies, a, b and c, to be moving in the same direction along the same straight line, c being first and a last. If c has the greatest velocity and b the least, then b will appear to be moving away from c

toward a; and a will appear to be moving away from c, but also toward b. That is, b will have the appearance of moving in the opposite direction from that of its real velocity, while a will be moving in one direction with reference to c, and at the same time in the opposite direction with reference to b.

Again, both a and c may be revolving about b with any velocity, and, so long as their directions from one another remain unchanged, this revolution could never be detected save with reference to some body outside the system (as we saw before in case of a system of two bodies).

Once more, suppose an "infinite" sphere, of uniform density, to occupy an otherwise empty space; the sphere might be revolving on its axis in any given direction and with any velocity, while yet the fact of its revolution, and still more the velocity of its revolution, must be absolutely undiscernible. And yet, at the same time, its revolution must constantly involve motion in an infinitude of opposite directions. That is, every point not in the axis of motion must move in a direction precisely opposite to that in which the corresponding point on the other side of the axis moves.

Nay, the revolution of such sphere must also involve all possible velocities, from the "infinitely small," at the axis, to the "infinitely great," at the infinitely removed "circumference."

Finally, it is easy to see that this "infinite sphere" without differentiation of any kind, is but a materialized image of space itself, whose content is nothing but the abstract and purely negative possibility of all motion.

Evidently, then, all motion is relative, though our knowledge of such motion is in many respects absolute. Among other things, we know, with absolute certainty, that the expression, "absolute motion," is a contradiction in terms; or, in other words, we know *absolutely* that no motion of a body can be really conceived save as *relative* to some other body.

What further is to be known of motion in its general character has long since been formulated with at least apparent "exactness," or, in other words, with absolute precision. Our next task, then, will be to examine these formulas.

CHAPTER XII.

THE LAWS OF MOTION.

IT has been seen that a single, isolated body in space could not be said to be either at rest or in motion. Motion can only be of one body with reference to another body. It is, to repeat, a *change of relation* between bodies in space, and can no more be said to belong to the one than to the other. It is simply an approach or a recession — an increase or a diminution of the distance between them — and is thus essentially mutual.

But since motion can only take place on the part of bodies with reference to each other, it must be occasioned by some fundamental connection between the bodies themselves; and this connection, or concrete relation, we have already seen developed in the discussion of the fundamental nature of matter, or the extended, of which "bodies" are but the local aggregations.

Force or energy being the substance of the extended world, its modes of manifestation, or phases of differentiation, give rise to infinitely multiple relations of force, some of which, in turn, appear under the form of "bodies" in space. And these bodies, thus constituted, must, in the nature of the case, be fundamentally related, each to every other.

Each body is, in fact, itself a force-center, involving necessarily both phases of force — attraction and repulsion. And this not merely within itself, but also with reference to all other bodies. For, as has already been shown, even an atom is a force-center, which is also a force-sphere, extending infinitely and laying hold on each and all other such spheres.

The relation of distance between any two bodies will therefore depend upon the deeper relation expressed in the algebraic sum of the centripetal and the centrifugal forces constituting the complex relation of the bodies to one another, and which must determine whether they shall approach each other or become more widely separated from one another.

Thus every actual change of relation in space between any two bodies is seen to be necessarily nothing else than a manifestation of force. And since the motion can only be a change of relation in distance, or direction, or both, as between two or more bodies, such change resulting from, or rather being itself a manifestation of, the predominance, either of attraction or of repulsion, between them, it is evident that motion cannot be conceived as taking place save in a multiple world of objects.

It is further evident that no single body possesses within itself alone the power to put itself in motion, as a whole, in any direction whatever. And this implies also that, once put in motion, it can never, of itself, change either the direction or the rate of its motion.

It would seem, then, that impulse toward motion or hindrance from motion must come from without. And yet, not *wholly* from without, since the force-relation is ever essentially a mutual one.

Here, indeed, we have an intimation of the primary condition of all actual motion. We shall see, too, that a careful consideration of the accepted "laws of motion" will lead us toward the full development of that condition and of its central significance.

FIRST LAW OF MOTION.

This law was formulated by Newton as follows: "Every body continues in its state of rest or of uniform motion in a straight line, except in so far as it may be compelled by impressed forces to change that state." *

We have, indeed, already developed the complete justification of this law which is absolutely universal since it is implied in the very nature of the extended world. It cannot, therefore, be classed under the category of "relative knowledge," though it affirms that without external relations any and every single body is absolutely helpless and inane.

But the law, in affirming the absolute incapacity of an isolated body either to move itself, or in any way to change the direction or quantity of motion which may have been imparted to it, expresses a most significant limitation of extended objects. The law does not affirm a positive characteristic of the external world, but a wholly negative one. It does not declare what material objects possess. On the contrary it declares unquestionably what they do *not* possess, and that is the power of self-movement. Every body, every object in the material universe, moves, or changes the direction or velocity of its motion only from external causes. Such body can act only in so far as it is acted upon.

This law is then very appropriately styled the law of *Inertia*, which is in truth nothing else than the law of

---
* This, with the statement of the second and third laws, given below, is the rendering of Newton's Latin given by Thompson and Tait.

indifference. The extended is the indifferent, the *unconscious*, and is therefore capable of action only by way of reaction. And even thus its action, according to this law, is still only of the most external character. It is primarily nothing more than a change of space-relation—mere motion of translation.

But again, since the movement can take place only from external impulse, it is evident that the direction and quantity of the motion will depend upon that impulse. In other words the motion must, both in direction and in quantity, be directly and absolutely proportioned to the impressed force.

Here, then, is a further fundamental condition of all actual motion. And this condition is formulated in what is known as the

SECOND LAW OF MOTION.

Newton's statement of this law is that: "Change of motion is proportional to the impressed force, and takes place in the direction of the straight line in which the force acts."

This statement, it will be noticed, assumes that all bodies are in motion, and that motion can therefore never be produced, but can only undergo change. This change, however, can only take place by transferrence—by one body giving up its motion to another. For thus only can we conceive a force to be "impressed" upon a given body. But this amounts to saying that on the whole motion can neither be increased nor diminished, that the total quantity of motion in the physical universe must forever remain unchanged.

Still further, in direct opposition to the Zenonian opinion that motion is impossible, it assumes on the contrary that *rest* is impossible. And this again follows evidently from the conception of the extended world as constituted by and of force. For force, to be force at all, must act, and the action of force must necessarily involve motion.

But let us inquire what are the further implications of this second law of motion. And first we have to notice more explicitly that the second law is but the positive expression of what is negatively announced in the first. The first law declares substantially that no body has the power to move itself. If it moves it must be moved from without; that is, by an "impressed force." But if its change of motion depends wholly on impressed forces, then it will follow that the change of motion must be proportioned to the impressed force, and take place in the direction in which the force acts. And this is precisely what the second law positively affirms. Thus it appears that the first and second laws of motion are merely the positive and negative aspects of the same fundamental principle of the extended world.

But this fundamental principle is an all-pervasive one. We have already seen that every force-center is necessarily related to every other force-center; that, in fact, each force-center is in its full significance an infinitely extended sphere, which again but indicates the concrete aspect of continuity in force manifested as "matter."

This same conception indeed is otherwise expressed in the universal law of gravitation which declares in effect that every body is concretely related to every other body. Every body or force-center, then, acts on every other body or force-center. So that no single body in all the universe is or can be free for a moment from the action of an immeasurable complex of impressed forces.

And this shows that the first law of motion is not only negative, but that, taken literally, it presupposes the case of a body not acted upon by external forces. That is, taken literally, the first law of motion presupposes a case that can never, by any possibility, be verified, or even realized. "Every body continues in its state of rest, etc., *unless* compelled by impressed forces to change that state." But every body is perpetually subjected to the action of impressed forces. Hence a state of "rest" is wholly impossible for any body whatever. So, too, a state of "uniform motion in a straight line" is equally impossible for any body whatever, for the reason that the impressed forces must have the effect to constantly produce changes in the motion of the body. Thus, at the surface of the earth, a falling body may *seem* to the observer to move in a straight line. But the observer has only to reflect that the earth itself is revolving on its own axis, to be convinced that the real movement of the falling body has the direction of a curve. And when he reflects further that the earth is moving in its orbit at the rate of nine miles or more each second, he can but see that the curve described by a falling body is a very complex one, the complexity becoming incalculable when the movement of the solar system through space is taken into the account.

So, too, the velocity of the falling body, simply with reference to the earth, is approximately calculable as a rate at any given moment, the increment being virtually the same within narrow limits. Add to this the constantly varying velocity of the falling body in its association with the orbital motion of the earth, and the problem becomes highly complex, while, with the inclusion of the unknown velocity of the solar system through space, the problem of the velocity of the falling body, of course, becomes altogether insoluble.

But more and more it comes to light that motion, whether in respect of direction or of velocity, is a result that can arise only from the *mutual action* of forces upon each other. A force can really act, or become an "impressed force," on no other condition than that of overcoming resistance. This we have seen to be involved in the very nature of force. And when it is declared, in the law of gravity, that every body attracts every other body, it is declared, in effect, that between every two bodies there is a mutual attraction. Or, since every center of force lays hold on every other center of force, it may be otherwise said that every force-center attracts and is attracted by, repels and is repelled by, every other force-center in the entire range of the extended world.

Each force-center, then, to repeat once more, is a veritable center of the physical universe, and as such acts upon and is in turn reacted upon by every other force-center. So that, in the cases of falling bodies just named, it is evident that there is one factor which we have wholly overlooked, and that is the fact that while any given body is falling toward the earth, the earth is also falling toward that body. And if the variations thus introduced into its movements are too minute for even the most refined infinitesimal calculus to seize and measure, that does not render them any the less real.

The relation of attraction, with its manifestation of *mutual* approach, is not less real, as between the merest mote on the one hand, and the earth's mass on the other, than between the earth and the moon, or between the units composing a group known as a double star, where such relation, as exhibited in the revolution of the bodies round each other, is so immeasurably more conspicuous. By a "scientific" fiction, we attribute all the motion to one of the bodies and assume that the other is wholly unaffected by the relation.

It is, indeed, true that in the case of "falling bodies" this does not affect the accuracy of the results, so far as external measurement is concerned. But it cannot fail to vitiate the results more or less seriously, so far as really scientific thinking is concerned. At the least, the notes of caution in this respect ought to be unfailingly given in text-books of physics, and ought to be far more strongly emphasized than is the case where they are given at all—at least, if a text-book is to be an instrumentality in mental discipline, and not merely a means toward percentages in examination.

Finally, before leaving the consideration of the second law of motion, let us note the ultimate implication of the parallelogram of forces as illustrative of that law.

The case is sufficiently familiar. Any two forces acting (let us here suppose) from different directions, and not in the same straight line, upon one and the same body or force-center, will each produce the same amount of motion in the body, and in the same direction, as if it alone acted upon the body. Thus, by compounding the two motions, we may find at what point the body will be at the end of any given time.

If, again, the body be acted upon by any number of forces, the resultant of any two may be found, then this resultant may be compounded with a third, and this resultant with a fourth, and so on until the resultant of all the forces has been ascertained.

If, finally, the forces are infinitely multiple, as must be the case in the total round of force-centers in the physical universe, then the forces acting from all directions upon the body *must balance each other.*

And this will be the more readily admitted if we remember what has been more than once repeated, that force really acts or can act only in overcoming opposition—it being now necessary to add the explanatory clause—"or in balancing opposite phases of force."

Such must be the conclusion from the second law of motion. And it is really to this conclusion that Newton gave utterance in his statement of the

THIRD LAW OF MOTION.

In this law it is declared that "to every action there is always an equal and contrary reaction; or, the mutual actions of any two bodies are always equal and oppositely directed."

Of course, the most elementary case to which this law would apply would be that of the action and reaction, or, as the second part of the law significantly expresses it, the *mutual actions* between two bodies. This second part is, indeed, manifestly offered, not as an addition to, but rather as an interpretation of, the first part.

But the full significance of this third law is to be apprehended only when it is regarded in connection with the second law in its widest range of meaning. We have just seen that the second law, rightly understood, already anticipates the mutual actions of force affirmed in the third law, and that it points out, through the illustrative parallelogram of forces, this further vitally important point: that the whole truth of the motion of any body, whether mote or star, is to be known only by compounding into one all the forces impressed upon such body.

Let us now further recall the fact that in the very nature of force, as the essence of matter, there can be no such thing as an isolated body in all the universe, but, rather, that every body, or force-center, is necessarily related concretely with every other body or force-center—"bodies" being but the discrete phases of "force" or "energy," which again is the name given to the physically continuous; that is, to the reality which occupies space. Then, holding these several points together in our minds, it must become evident that the third law of motion is applicable equally to any and every group of bodies, to the most complex as well as to the simplest case of physical relations manifested in the mutual actions of bodies. That is, the third law of motion is applicable to the total sum of actions and reactions, or of mutual actions constituting the physical universe as a whole.

Here, indeed, we come upon that universal relation of every body to every other body, to which Newton gave definition in the law of gravity, and which we shall have occasion to consider more fully in a succeeding chapter.

Glancing now once more at the three laws of motion, their organic relation to each other becomes strikingly manifest. The *first* law expresses *negatively* the fundamental characteristic of the external world, declaring it to be a world of inertia—a world in which there is no spontaneous action, and, hence, a world in which motion can only occur through external impulse; that is, through "impressed forces."

The *second* law expresses *positively* the externality of the physical world by declaring that whatever motion a body possesses it has received from without; its motion is always in the direction of, and is directly proportioned to, the *impressed forces*.

But the union of these two phases shows also that, after all, no body is moved wholly by external or impressed forces. For the body can in reality be acted upon only in so far as it itself presents to the action a corresponding force of reaction.

Thus, finally, the *third* law declares in effect *absolutely* that the externality of nature is, in truth, a completely reflexive externality. The total round of nature presents us with an externality which already bears within it the factor of internality. It may be true that no body is able, apart from other bodies, to change its own state. But there is manifestly a vital, indestructible relationship between body and body, such that change is ceaselessly effected in every body.

Chemistry, indeed, knows nothing of actions but only of *re*actions. It is as if one were to say: "The 'atom,' the isolated body, can indeed change its state in no other way than through impressed forces, but in the totality of bodies there is a principle initiative of change. The totality alone is truly active. Particular aspects of the totality are manifested only as reactions, or as mutually balancing phases of the total action."

It turns out, then, that these three laws are but the three successively deepening phases of a rational conception of the fundamental energy which constitutes the physical world. Or, we may say: just as the three fundamental *laws of thought* all coalesce into the one primordial law of *self-harmony*, so the three fundamental *laws of motion* in the material world all coalesce into the one primordial law of *equilibrium*.

What is ultimately implied in this equilibrium will appear as we proceed.

CHAPTER XIII.

ENERGY AS ADEQUATE CAUSE OF MOTION.

HERE, then, we have a further development of the world as a self-measured whole. Each particular phase can only act as it is in turn acted upon, and the reaction is always precisely equal to the action. Every force-center, then, may be said to have its own action reflected back to itself.

At the same time, the thorough-going externality of the forces of nature is manifest in the fact that in every phase of activity either side may be regarded indifferently as action or as reaction; though this, too, has its deep-reaching suggestion that all action is equally reaction, and that all reaction is itself a phase of the total initiative, or spontaneous action.

In fact, as has already become evident, it is only through a balancing of action and reaction that force can be force at all. The centripetal and the centrifugal modes of force cannot exist, save in complete interfusion. And, let us repeat, force can be force at all only through acting. A force that does not act is not a force. And force can act only as a strain against an opposing phase of force.

Evidently, then, the totality of "forces" in the universe must be completely self-balanced. Equilibrium is the only possible condition in which the totality of energy can be conceived as existing.

At first view, indeed, this would seem to involve the absolute impossibility of motion. And it is not to be disguised, that even from the standpoint we have here reached the existence of motion must once more seem to be something fairly inexplicable; and this for the reason that in itself matter is wholly destitute of the principle of motion—a reason quite different from and far more valid than any of those given in the Zenonian dialectic. Doubtless, however, we may shortly be able to advance to a standpoint from which the contradiction will be seen to be not without its reasonable solution.

Meanwhile we may tentatively insist upon the necessary interrelation between attraction and repulsion, as at least possibly variable *locally*. Indeed, as appeared in our investigation concerning this interrelation, there must be, as its necessary outcome, an infinitude of force-centers throughout space.

So, also, each of these force-centers must still be related to—that is, must extend out so as to include and thus lay hold upon—every other force-center. But this can only mean that the given force-center is in reality nothing else than the *focus of a force-sphere* extending indefinitely outward on all sides and hence becoming more and more attenuated in proportion to the distance from the center.

The degree of action and reaction between any two force-spheres must then depend upon the distance between their centers. More precisely, such interaction, in its direct and most important phase, can take place only through a single direction, joining their centers. And further, each sphere, so far as its action on the other is concerned, may be considered to terminate in a circumference whose radius is the distance between the centers of the spheres.

Since, then, each of the bodies or force-centers occupies only a small portion of the circumference of the force-sphere into which the other center expands, it is evident that the interaction between the spheres will not only depend upon the distance between the centers, but will conform to the law of the relation between the surfaces of spheres; namely, the law that those surfaces are to each other as the squares of their radii.

Of course, then, so far as mere distance is considered as the determining condition, the attraction or repulsion between two force-centers at any given distance will be four times as great, for example, as that between two other equal centers separated from each other by twice that distance. Each force-sphere must, besides, act from its center or focus outward in all directions on all other force-spheres, in accordance with this law.

Thus we arrive at one of the two fundamental phases of what since Newton's time has been accepted in the scientific world as the universal law of gravitation.

The other phase, involving *mass*, however, remains to be accounted for. And here it is to be remembered that force or energy is the substance of things. It has also developed that the action of force must necessarily result in the differentiation of force-spheres at all points throughout space.

And yet this setting up or development of force-spheres is but the stress of balanced phases of force, which, so far as can be seen from our present standpoint, must, as has been said, prevent instead of producing motion. In short, upon the pre-supposition of mere "physical" force motion must forever remain inexplicable. According to that standpoint, all action is and can be only from without. No single change in any body in all the universe can take place save through *impressed forces;* that is, forces acting upon the body from without. And it only needs that this law be resolutely followed round in all its applications to see that as no portion of the extended world contains within itself as such any initial principle of motion, so it is absolutely necessary to look beyond the merely physical phase of the universe to find that principle. A system of merely "impressed forces" could, as we have already seen, only result in absolute equilibrium, excluding motion absolutely.

This, it need hardly be added, Newton saw with perfect clearness, and accordingly assumed a non-physical cause of motion.

And yet it is not to be overlooked that if the principle of motion is not within, neither can it be beyond the physical universe. For, were that principle wholly beyond or outside the extended world, it could indeed have no relation to that world. Or, if such relation be allowed to be possible, it must at least leave the extended world in a state of inertia, indifference, or passivity.

So much, indeed, Newton's third law of motion really implies. And yet, as was pointed out on a former page, the " passive " is that which is acted upon, is that which *receives action.* But, in this very fact of receiving action, the "passive" necessarily also proves to be active. For it can receive action only through itself reacting. Nay, as we have already seen, action and reaction are but complementary phases of every possible action in which either phase may equally be considered as action or as reaction, and hence, as both action and reaction.

Or, otherwise stated, the active can exert its action upon the passive only in so far as the passive reacts upon the active. And in receiving the reaction of the passive the active itself proves to be necessarily also passive.

This much, let us repeat, is already contained implicitly in the laws of motion.

The conception of a merely passive world, then, proves to be self-contradictory, just as, on the other hand, a purely active world, from which passivity is excluded, is seen to be impossible. We can only conclude, therefore, that a real world must involve both these characteristics as the necessary complementary phases of its very existence.

And this amounts to the same as if we were to say: *The concrete totality of the world or universe is a necessarily self-related totality.* For, as a totality, and *the* totality, it can indeed be related to nothing else than just itself. All its relations of activity are relations of self-activity. As active, it can act only upon itself, while as passive it can only receive its own activity.

The totality of "forces" in the universe is, therefore, from its very nature, a self-active or spontaneous energy, and as such, contains within itself the principle and cause of all movement.

And yet, while this principle is involved in the merely physical universe, the principle itself proves to evolve, through its own activity, something more than a merely physical universe; and the something-more is precisely the explicit aspect of this principle of spontaneity itself. It is, in other words, a self-unfolding principle, which presents phases reaching wholly beyond (in the sense of being absolutely superior to) the realm of the merely physical.

It becomes increasingly evident, then, that, while we must indeed look within, we must also and equally look beyond the extended world, if we would discover the true principle of actual movement in that world. And this is, in a manner, confirmed by the significant change that has recently come over physical science in its use of certain terms.

When Mr. Spencer wrote his *"First Principles,"* the expression, "conservation of force," was in fashion. Since then this expression has been modified, by common consent, so as to put the word *energy* in place of the word *force*.

In this substitution there is manifest a distinct advance from a relatively more to a relatively less mechanical view of nature. For not only is the element of spontaneity and personality implied in the popular use of the term "energy," as opposed to the phase of mechanical necessity implied in the term "force;" but the use of the term energy itself takes us back inevitably to Aristotle's use of the same term (ἐνέργεια) as the name for that ultimate unit of power to the activity of which he traces all modes of reality, and which he ultimately names the *Absolute, Divine Spirit*.

Another indication of the feeling among scientists that the mechanical view is inadequate and that a term expressive of spontaneity is required in describing the ultimate unit of power is furnished in a suggestion by Professor Huxley, which was followed by Mr. Spencer.

The latter found the expression, "conservation of force," objectionable because it "implies a conserver and an act of conservation;" which would seem to mean that the expression implies that force is conserved by an agency apart from force. Accordingly, at Professor Huxley's suggestion, Mr. Spencer* substituted the expression, "persistence of force," for "conservation of force."

But the persistence of force (or energy, as we are now to say) surely implies that the ultimate unit is self-active; that its very persistence is a manifestation of spontaneity. In other words, the expression, "persistence of energy," is preferable to the expression, "conservation of energy," only because it brings very near to the surface the conception that the process of the conservation of energy involves the immeasurably significant characteristic of *self*-conservation. It is thus, and thus alone, that it does or can "persist."

It is this view of a self-active, self-conserved energy that opens the way to an adequate explanation of motion. And now, having obtained a first assured view of a principle adequate to explain to the reason what to the senses is the unquestionable fact of motion, let us return to the question of the accepted law of universal gravitation.

* See note to heading of Chapter VI. of "*First Principles.*"

CHAPTER XIV.

THE LAW OF UNIVERSAL GRAVITATION.

THE spontaneous World-Energy, as necessarily related to itself alone, cannot move as a whole. That is, there can be no change of space-relation for the total physical universe. For, as a unit, even if finite, it presents the conditions of a single, absolutely isolated "body" in space, which, as we have seen, could not be said to be either in motion or at rest.

On the other hand, as a totality limited only by itself, it is essentially infinite. And if this be understood to include space-relations (as it must so far as the totality is extended), it is, in dimensions, co-extensive with space itself—to which, indeed, as we have already seen, there is nothing reasonable to oppose.

But though the World-Energy as an infinite whole cannot move or change place, yet as self-active energy it cannot fail to produce, through its own self-activity, infinite movement within itself. Not only must the stress of the opposed modes of force result in the development of an infinitude of mutually inclusive force-spheres; but it must also result in the aggregation of the foci or nuclei of such force-spheres. For the very first phase of the movement of the force-centers must increase the distances between some and diminish the distances between others, thus increasing the tension on one side and diminishing it on the other. That is, with decrease in distance the gravitative strain must become intensified between centers approaching each other, just as, on the other hand, with increase in distance the strain between those receding from each other must undergo corresponding diminution.

Thus there must arise aggregations of force-centers within certain regions surrounded by relatively vacant fields of space. And this conclusion will appear the more substantial as in the further course of our argument we find increasing reason for believing the World-Energy to be guided in its activity by a consistent method; or, in other words, in so far as we find reason to regard the World-Energy as itself an infinite, self-conscious process.

But again these force-centers or nuclei of force are but the more condensed portions of indefinitely extended spheres. There is, therefore, a tension of force constituting each of these separately, and at the same time relating each through its indefinitely diffused substance to all other centers.

In every single force-center, then, we already have the simplest relation of force constituting matter. And this nucleus of an indefinitely extended, infinitely diffused force-sphere is just that part which, through the very fact of its being such nucleus or focus of force, presents most resistance to the action of external force.

It is this nucleus, then, that constitutes the "atom" which thus proves to be something very far different from the once popular atom, consisting of a simple, isolated, infinitely hard, infinitely small, absolutely bounded piece of some incomprehensible something wholly apart from force, and which thus had no possible office to perform in the economy of the universe. On the contrary, it is the primal element—that is, the most elementary phase of existence—and from the aggregation of such the whole extended world is constituted. It is to be still more explicitly stated, too, that any given "atom" is merely a more or less momentary unit arising through the ceaseless process of the World-Energy, and that such unit must inevitably be dissolved and rediffused through the same perpetual Process. Thus not only is matter infinitely divisible in the merely abstract metaphysical sense. It is also forever undergoing infinite division in the "concrete" physical sense. Here, too, it may be remarked by the way, we get a glimpse of such truth as there is in the doctrine of emanation and absorption; though, doubtless, in a symbolical sense, that doctrine has a much higher significance than this merely physical one of the emanating atoms.

It may help to make clearer what is here meant by a force-center, or nucleus of a force-sphere to say, by way of rough illustration, that the earth itself, with its relatively solid nucleus, and liquid (oceanic) exterior, extended indefinitely into space by the envelope of atmosphere, shading imperceptibly into the "ether," is but a gigantic atom pursuing its complex motions in the vast molecule of the solar system. In other words, the atom is here conceived to be but the minute and relatively dense core of a sphere of force, infinitely extended indeed, but also attenuated more and more in proportion to the distance from its center.

And here let us remark, by the way, that we have in what precedes the rational explanation of "action at a distance." The "explanation," indeed, explains it out of existence. There is and can be no such thing as action at a distance. A thing acts only "where it is;" and to Carlyle's query: "Where is it?" the proper answer is: *Everywhere*.

Of course it is not everywhere in the grosser forms which directly affect our senses. On the contrary, as must be manifest in what has already been said, it is only the infinitesimal nucleus of a force-sphere that enters into intimate combination with other nuclei, resulting in the building up of "bodies" sufficiently dense and unyielding to definitely impress the senses.

Every one familiar with the action of a magnet must see at once what is here meant. With the magnet there is so-called "action at a distance," and this is rendered visible by the visible effect; for example, on iron filings, the action taking place, even with a feeble magnet, through thick plate glass. So also the effect of such action becomes visible through magnetic induction and all its peculiarities.

Instead, however, of "action at a distance" in such cases, the explanation to be given on the theory here developed must rather be: That the force-spheres of whose nuclei the magnet is constituted are, in their very nature, as themselves constituted by the interaction of attraction and repulsion, *elastic* and therefore subject to condensation and rarefaction in greater or less degree, according as the more immediate conditions of the nuclei change; and that the magnetization of a piece of iron or steel consists in the special condensation—temporarily in the iron, "permanently" in the steel—of the portions of the force-spheres more immediately surrounding the nuclei, and thus, while not adding to the body as visible or ponderable, yet increases its force-tension sufficiently to visibly affect through short distances other portions of matter of like characteristics.

And this seems the more reasonable as an explanation as the force is found to be under the same law as gravitation with regard to distance—that is, the magnetic attraction or repulsion is inversely as the square of the distance.

But this, it may be repeated, is in the present place merely incidental. What must be held firmly in mind here is, first, the action of force producing aggregations of force-centers, and, secondly, the significance of such aggregations.

As each force-center is essentially an "atom," and as "bodies" are built up from such "atoms," it is evident that the quantity of matter within a given body will depend precisely upon the number of force-centers constituting the body. But the quantity of matter in a body is called its mass.

Evidently, then, so far as the universal law of gravitation declares that every body attracts every other body with a force whose magnitude is directly as the product of their masses, it is but formulating one of the necessary relations between groups of force-centers. For each force-center, independently of the others in the same group, must attract every force-center in the group constituting the distant body, and would do so precisely in the same way and in the same degree were it widely separated from the other members of its own group. Hence, with each additional force-center in any given body, such body, as a whole, must exert a still greater force of attraction upon every other body.

At the same time, it should not be forgotten that the attractions are exerted, not between the masses as such, but only between the ultimate force-centers constituting the masses. And, finally, since the qualitative differences in matter arise from the complexity of grouping of force-centers, it is evident that the different "kinds" of matter could have no effect whatever upon the intensity of the gravitative pull between any two force-centers.

Here, again, then, our theory, in the free course of its development, presents a simple, natural explanation of what has long since been experimentally shown to be the fact—namely, that gravitation is invariably proportional to the *quantity* of matter, and is not in the slightest degree influenced by the *kind* of matter.

The experiments of Newton rendered this conclusion highly probable, while the more elaborate and delicate experiments of the German astronomer Bessel, in the earlier part of the present century, gave it such complete confirmation as to leave no further room for doubt.*

We have, then, arrived at a rational account of the fact generalized in the first part of the universal law of gravitation, as that law is usually stated, though it is now evident that its more adequate explanation must be sought through the second part of the law, as may be seen from the law as stated in full. "Every particle of matter in the universe attracts every other particle with a force, whose direction is that of the line joining the two, and whose magnitude is directly as the product of their masses, and inversely as the square of their distance from

* See Whewell, "*Hist. of Inductive Sciences*," 3d (N. Y.) Ed., I., 549.

each other."* This brings us to the consideration of momentum.

*See Thomson and Tait, "*Elements of Natural Philosophy*," 2d Ed., I., 167.

CHAPTER XV.

MOMENTUM.

WE have next to trace out the necessary implications or corollaries of the law of gravity. And, first, let it be remembered that the attraction is between the ultimate force-centers severally, and not between aggregated masses, as such.

At the same time, the mass itself is nothing else than an aggregation of force-centers, and the attractive force exerted by a given body must therefore be directly and exactly proportional to its mass.

Between any two bodies, or aggregations of force-centers, then, there will be a constant strain, tending to bring the bodies nearer to each other with a force proportional to the product of the masses of the two. That is, there will be a constant pull between each force-center in the one body, and every force-center in the other.

It is to such strain, indeed, that we have already traced the primary aggregation of force-centers into single masses. And it is evident that the continuance of the strain between the force-centers of any one of these already formed groups, and the force-centers of any other group, is but the continuation of the same tendency. The motion due to the strain, therefore, can but result in further aggregation through the meeting and coalescence of such groups into larger ones.

But the motion produced in these cases, according to the second law, must be proportional to the impressed force, and must take place in the direction of the line in which the force acts; that is, in the direction of the line joining the mutually attracting groups of force-centers. And not only so, but in tracing the development of the conditions of the action of force, we have seen that, as indicated in the formulation of the universal law of gravity, the force impressed upon each other by the approaching groups must increase with the decrease of the distance between them—must ever be inversely proportional to the square of that distance.

But, again, the motion is proportional to the impressed force. And we have now to inquire whether this impressed force, and consequent motion, is the same, or different, for the two bodies.

To this the answer must be that either can act upon the other only so far as it is acted upon by the other. The action is necessarily mutual; or, the action and reaction between them must be equal, as well as in opposite directions. Hence, the quantity of force impressed by the greater mass upon the less is precisely the same as that impressed by the less upon the greater. And when we recall the fact that the distance separating them is at any moment but one and the same distance, it is evident that the force of gravity which the one body exerts or "impresses" upon any other body must necessarily be precisely the same as that exerted or impressed by the second upon the first. Indeed, the gravitative strain exerted by the two bodies upon each other constitutes but *one indivisible relation* between the attracting bodies.

Since, then, the quantity of force impressed by and upon each body, in the case of any gravitating pair, is precisely the same whatever the relative mass, it follows, necessarily, that the two bodies will each acquire, through their mutual action, precisely the same quantity of motion as the other. And yet, it is not to be forgotten that the quantity of motion depends directly and essentially upon the quantity of matter.

It is here, indeed, that we find *time* entering in a definite, quantitative way, into consideration as an essential element of motion. We saw at an earlier stage of our inquiry, that motion is a *change* of space-relations. But change necessarily implies succession. Hence, motion can take place only as a continuous modification of space-relation between bodies.

Fundamentally, however, the space-relations exist between the ultimate force-centers. We have, indeed, already traced the law of variation of that order of space-relations directly constituted by the force of gravity. It is required now, especially, to trace the law of change of space-relations as relations of distance; for this is conspicuously the class of space-relations whose change constitutes motion.

Note now, again, that all space-relations, whether of distance or of direction, are primarily relations between ultimate force-centers; whence it follows that the quantity of change in those relations will necessarily depend directly upon the number of force-centers involved in the change. The greater the number of force-centers— that is, the greater the quantity of "matter," the space-relations of which undergo change—the greater must be the quantity of that change. In other words, the greater will be the quantity of motion.

It is evident, then, that while in every respect the actual force impressed upon each other by two gravitating bodies, must be the same for the one as for the other, the quantity of resultant motion of each must be directly dependent upon, and precisely proportional to the mass of the body. The greater the mass, the greater the quantity of motion; the less the mass, the less the quantity of motion.

Nevertheless, as we have but just seen, the second law of motion declares, what proved on investigation to be necessarily true, that change of motion is precisely proportional to the impressed force. Evidently, then, the mass of a body is not the sole factor of motion.

Indeed, it has just been shown that, since decrease of distance between gravitating bodies intensifies the force impressed by each upon the other, and since the motion is always proportional to the impressed force, the quantity of motion necessarily varies with the distance. But the variation here is a variation in the rate of approach. Each of the bodies must approach the other with a regularly increasing velocity. And yet, it has been shown that the force impressed by each body upon the other is precisely the same in quantity as that impressed upon it by the other. In short the "impressed force" is a *relation* in which each acts and is acted upon in precisely the same degree.

The same quantity of force, then, is, in the one case, impressed upon a greater mass, in the other case upon a less mass. But, where there is less mass, there is also less resistance to change of motion. In this respect, then, the less mass will yield more readily to the mutual attraction than will the greater mass. The less mass will, therefore, acquire the greater velocity. And its velocity at any given moment must be precisely as much greater than that of the greater body as its mass is less than that of the greater.

It is now evident, that while the greater body has precisely as much *greater* quantity of motion than has the less body, as its mass exceeds the mass of the less, when we regard the quantity of motion from the side of the number of force-centers moved; it has, when we consider the quantity of motion from the side of velocity, as much *less* motion than the smaller body, as its mass exceeds the mass of the smaller body.

It is clear, then, that the total quantity of motion is compounded of the quantity of motion dependent upon the number of force-centers moved, on the one hand, with the quantity of motion dependent upon velocity, on the other hand.

We thus arrive at the definition of *momentum*, as equal to the product of the mass into the velocity. In other words, momentum is merely the technical term expressive of quantity of motion in this compound sense. And this the usual works on physics declare it to be.

Having, then, traced the conditions determining the quantity of motion in any body, we have next to follow the actual motion and ascertain its essential phases. And since, at the outset, any change in the motion of any given body must take place in the direction of the line in which the impressed force acts, the motion of any two bodies attracting each other, must be in the direction of a straight line connecting them. Each body must, therefore, move or "fall" directly toward the other, so far as the two bodies are considered merely with reference to one another.

What we have next to do, then, is to watch the development of the essential phases of this "fall."

CHAPTER XVI.

LAWS OF FALLING BODIES.

IT has already been shown that the actual quantity of motion of two bodies approaching each other in consequence of their mutual gravitation must be the same in the one body as in the other, no matter what the actual difference in their masses may be. We have already, therefore, ascertained the fundamental law of falling bodies; so that what follows can be but the rendering explicit of what is already implied in this primary law.

Indeed, there has already become explicit this much: That mass and velocity are the necessary reciprocal factors of the total quantity of motion of any and every body. If, therefore, in any pair of bodies gravitating toward each other, the one has twice the mass of the other, it will at any given moment in their approach toward each other have acquired but half the velocity of that other, and at the end of any given time will have passed through but half the distance traversed by the other body in the same time. In case they meet, it is evident that the double mass will have traversed one-third the original distance of separation, while the smaller mass will have traversed the remaining two-thirds. If the masses are to each other as one to one thousand, the less will approach the greater with a velocity a thousand fold that with which the greater will approach the less, and in case they continue their approach undisturbed until they meet the greater body will have traversed but one thousandth of the originally intervening space, while the remaining nine hundred and ninety-nine thousandths will have been traversed by the smaller body.

In short, the greater the difference between the masses of the two bodies, the less significant relatively becomes the velocity of the greater body, so far as the mere question of quantity of space traversed in the approach between the two is concerned; though it is never to be forgotten that the total *quantity of motion* of the one body is precisely the same as that of the other, and that in this sense the "fall" of the greater body toward the less is exactly equal to the "fall" of the less toward the greater.

But, let us repeat, the attractions are between the ultimate force-centers and between them alone. Through the same distance, therefore, the attraction between any two such force-centers must ever be the same; and since the total quantity of motion is proportional to the impressed force, it is evident that any two force-centers must, so far as their mutual attraction is not masked by external forces, traverse any given space between them in precisely the same time, whether they act singly or in groups. For, suppose a group of ten particles or force-centers on one side, and a group of five on the other. Each of the ten particles in the one group will attract and be attracted by each of the five particles in the other group precisely in the same way and precisely with the same result as if each particle on either side were completely dissociated from the other particles of its group. In other words, *the fall together of two bodies through any given space will take place in precisely the same time, whatever the masses of those bodies may be.*

This may be regarded as the second universal law of falling bodies. And it will be noticed that it develops directly from the second law of motion.

It is evidently a necessary inference from this that velocity, properly speaking, is the rate of approach of two bodies toward each other, and that it is only when the mass of the one body becomes infinitesimal, as compared with the mass of the other, that it is even approximately correct to refer the velocity solely to the smaller body.

But, again, as the distance between the approaching bodies grows less, the force of attraction between them becomes greater. It is evident, therefore, that, since the force not only acts continuously, but also with continuously increasing intensity, *the increase in the rate of approach of any two bodies, due to their own mutual attraction, will be by a ratio whose value must constantly increase, and must at any given moment be equal to that which would have resulted from the action of a constant force, through the given time, compounded with that produced by the increased action of the force for the same time.*

From the fundamental conditions of motion, it appears then that, in the *first* place, the mutual attraction of any two bodies results in each acquiring in any given time precisely the same quantity of motion as the other, regardless of mass; *secondly,* that the meeting of any two bodies through any given distance, in consequence of their mutual attraction, will take place in precisely the same time, regardless of mass, though the portion of the total distance at first separating them traversed by either body will be inversely as its relative mass; and, *thirdly*, that the velocity or ratio of approach of the two bodies toward each other is a compound, constantly increasing ratio which is wholly independent of mass.

These are the fundamental phases of the motion of bodies, so far as they are considered merely from the side of their mutual attraction. And it is important to notice that these three phases of motion are not merely three different phases of relation between mass and velocity,— for that would be merely to substitute one term for another,—but also, and especially, it is important to notice that they are three stages in the *progressive subordination of mass as a factor of motion.*

And this serves to remind us again that mass and velocity are reciprocal factors in the quantity of motion. It is the "inert" mass that draws to itself the detached and lightly moving force-sphere, though the "inert mass" is itself made up of precisely similar force-spheres. That which is relatively without velocity appears to impart velocity, and that which is relatively without mass gains increase of power through its added velocity.

The latter statement may indeed seem, at first view, to be a gratuitous one, so far as the course of our argument thus far can give justification. But we have only to refer to the first law of motion as the law of inertia to see that the justification is already implicit there. A body can no more stop its own motion than it can put itself in motion. And to overcome its motion requires precisely the same amount of force as that expended in giving it the motion it possesses. The quantity of motion a body possesses is, therefore, an exact measure at once of the force that has been impressed upon it in giving it motion, and of the force that would be required to bring it to rest.

The moving body itself, then, is a factor which, combined with velocity, constitutes a realized force; and the greater the velocity the greater the force, so long as the mass of the body remains unchanged.

But, again, velocity is a product, the formal factors of which are space and time. In other words, velocity is the unity of time and space relations. Evidently also, as a factor of force, velocity has greater value in proportion as the time-element is diminished and the space-element is increased. Thus the kinetic energy of a given body or mass increases, not in the same degree as the velocity of such mass increases, but in a ratio corresponding to the *square* of the velocity.

Here, then, a new phase of force develops, *the force of motion itself*. For momentum, or quantity of motion, is the product of mass and velocity, and a moving body is nothing else than a certain mass possessing a certain velocity. Motion, therefore, is not something apart from force. It is just force itself in realized form.

Let us next recall the fact, already developed, that the abstract phases of attraction and repulsion are but mere vague pull and push in the realm of "matter." And let us also recall the further fact that has come to light in the course of our inquiry: that it could be only through the spontaneous element of self-activity necessarily implied in the totality of the World-Energy, as self-measured, that aggregations of force-centers could take place at all.

Putting these two facts together, it is evident that not only is motion inevitable as a state of all bodies, but that all such motion must be unified into a perfectly consistent system.

In the aggregations of force-centers into masses, then, we see the same tendency as that which, at a more advanced stage, cannot fail to produce still larger aggregations. Masses attracting one another must move toward one another, and this with increasing velocity, both from the continuous action of the mutual attraction between them, and also from the increasing intensity of the gravitative pull, as the distance separating them diminishes.

Thus masses, which are but groups of force-centers, come to have velocity as such. And this combination of masses and velocities is the development of that phase of force technically known as "molar motion," and which, regarded simply as energy, is called kinetic energy.

It is true that, in popular language, motion is distinguished from bodies. Thus bodies are said to be "in motion." And it must doubtless be something of a shock to the ordinary consciousness to be assured that bodies are "in motion" only in the sense that they are themselves one of the necessary factors of motion. And yet this is universally recognized, at least in words, in the treatises dealing with this subject.

As to the decrease of molar motion, and the special phase of energy which it embodies, this is effected either gradually, in which case there is friction or compression; or suddenly, in which case there is .percussion. But these may be better considered in connection with their effects under the subject of heat.

It is to be observed that our consideration of the laws of falling bodies has confined us to the simplest cases of molar motion. We have abstracted or withdrawn our thought from all action of force save that between two bodies mutually attracting each other.

In such case, the resultant motion must, of course, be literally in the direction of the straight line joining the bodies; and this could not but terminate in the meeting and fusion of the two bodies unless their inherent elasticity should be of such degree as to cause their rebound from one another, to be once more drawn together and again rebound, and so on *ad infinitum*.

On the other hand, however, the recognition of the truth of the universality of the law of gravitation recalls us to a consciousness of the very abstract, incomplete, and therefore, thus far, untrue representation which we have as yet formed of the actual relation of body to body in space.

Nevertheless, it can hardly be denied that we have proceeded consistently with the second law of motion in finding the resultant of two directions of the action of force. So that the representation we have thus far formed is doubtless "untrue" only in the sense of being inadequate.

What remains to be done, then, in this respect is that we shall proceed to the further step of finding the resultant of a third direction of the action of force with the resultant already obtained, and thus gain a clue by which we may approach the conception of something like a complete system of forces—the system itself being in perfect equilibrium, while the bodies comprised in the system are in ceaseless motion.

It will be found, too, that actual motion can never be in a straight line, but rather that it must ever be in curved directions. It is to the consideration of such motion, then, that the next chapter will be devoted.

CHAPTER XVII.

CURVILINEAR MOTION.

SUPPOSE three equal bodies at the vertices of an equilateral triangle. Their mutual attraction upon one another must result in their traveling each along a straight line, to a point within the triangle equally distant from the several vertices. Each, without moving directly toward either of the others, yet moves in such direction as to meet them both by the shortest line.

If, however, we take a more complex case, we shall have a very different result. Even three unequal bodies, and the more if not symmetrically grouped, must present a wholly new set of relations. So intricate, indeed, are the relations thus presented that "the problem of the three bodies" is one upon which, as Whewell assures us, mathematicians have long exercised their highest powers.*

The precise quantitative determinations of this and other complex quantitative problems we must, indeed, leave to the mathematicians. All that will be necessary for our present purpose will be to trace the qualititative characteristics of the motion arising in such case as that which is actually presented in the concrete world. And for the sake of simplicity, let us assume the concrete case of the relations existing between the earth, the sun and the moon, severally.

* "*History of the Inductive Sciences*," 3d (N. Y.) Ed., I., 367.

These are three masses gravitating toward each other. Assume the present distances of these bodies severally from each other. Assume, also, that the line joining the earth and the moon is approximately at right angles with that joining the earth and the sun—assumptions which, on the nebular hypothesis, are entirely justifiable.

Upon these assumptions we have to ask: What will be the result of their mutual attractions?

We know, from what has already preceded, that each will approach the other; that the earth and the sun will move toward each other; that the earth and the moon will move toward each other; and, finally, that the moon and the sun will move toward each other. In each couple, too, it is evident that the *quantity* of motion of each body will be precisely equal to that of the other body. But the body having the less mass will, therefore, necessarily acquire the greater velocity. Hence the sun, as vastly the greatest mass, will acquire relatively very slight velocity as toward either the earth or the moon.

Leaving out of account, then, the velocity of the sun, as a quantity relatively so small that it may be neglected without vitiating the result qualitatively considered, we may trace the motion of earth and moon toward the sun and toward each other.

And first, let us note that the distance between the earth and the moon is so small, as compared with their distance from the sun, that the intensity of gravity, as between them, is necessarily correspondingly greater than that between either of them and the sun. Whence the velocity of approach between earth and moon must be far greater than the velocity of their approach toward the sun. And the greatest velocity of all, here as elsewhere, must belong to the body having least mass.

The *attractions* will all necessarily be exerted along straight lines. For gravitation, as we have seen, is an essential property of the bodies themselves, and whatever their relative positions, it is necessarily a direct connection of the one with the other.

We may remark, by the way, too, that this (taken in connection with what has already been said concerning the really indefinite extension of even the smallest "bodies") is a simple and natural explanation of the otherwise mysterious fact that gravity "acts" instantaneously through immeasurable distances. Gravity is not itself a special form or kind of matter; nor is it, like light or heat or electricity, a special mode of motion requiring time for its propagation through space. On the contrary, it is *there* always and everywhere in space as itself a necessary aspect or mode of "whatever can occupy space."

The *movements*, nevertheless, must be along highly complex curves. For both earth and moon approach the sun at the same time they approach each other. The earth will be drawn, by the moon's attraction, out of the straight line joining its original position with the sun. Meanwhile, the moon itself, as possessing relatively so little mass, will acquire a much greater velocity. And the direction of its movement will be toward the earth in greater degree than toward the sun. At the same time, the earth, as possessing so little mass relatively to the sun, will acquire a velocity mainly in the direction of the sun.

Thus earth and moon must acquire momentum each in a curved direction. And the momentum of the moon, consisting in so large a degree of velocity, will carry the moon quite over so as, approximately, to reach the line originally extending between earth and sun.

Meanwhile the earth must have moved toward the sun, but must, also, have been drawn aside from a straight line joining its original position with the sun by the force impressed upon it by the moon's mass. Whence it must result that the earth will speedily reach a point exactly between sun and moon.

Just at this point, so far as the attraction between earth and moon affects the earth, it will tend to draw the earth away from the sun; or, in other words, it will tend to diminish the earth's velocity toward the sun. On the other hand, the moon will now be drawn in one direction by the combined attraction of both earth and sun. Hence, its velocity must be increased at the same time that it rapidly changes the direction of its motion.

Again, the acquired momentum of the earth must carry it still further aside from the original line joining it with the sun; so that by the time the moon has come to follow the new direction of the impressed forces, the attraction between itself and the earth will tend to carry it again beyond the earth in the opposite direction.

But now, the powerful impulse it has received from the combined action upon it of earth and sun, must not only carry it past the earth, but must also direct its movement along a path lying between earth and sun. And yet, the increased intensity of gravitation between earth and moon, from their nearer approach must result in a rapid change of direction in the moon's motion, and with this result; that the moon must now again cross the earth's path, but this time in advance of the earth itself.

Thus the moon will once more reach a position, relatively to the other bodies, similar to that in which we first found it.

Evidently, it needs but to pursue this series of movements—which anyone can figure to himself on paper if he finds it difficult to follow otherwise—to see that in their fall toward the sun the earth and moon must inevitably pursue a curved direction of great complexity, and that they must in this complex movement inevitably fall *past* the sun.

At the same time, it is to be remembered that the fall is real. There is, up to a given point, constant decrease in distance between these two bodies and the sun. And that point will inevitably be determined by the relation between two phases of force—the centripetal and the centrifugal. So long as the former is greater than the latter, the approach will continue. The moment the latter comes to predominate over the former, that moment the movement toward the center (sun) will be transformed into a movement away from the center.

What constitutes centrifugal force? The answer has in reality already been given. The mutual attractions of three or more bodies must result in a complex movement on the part of each body; the distances passed over by the several bodies being inversely proportional to their masses. And as the multiple attractions render impossible the direct approach of any one body toward any other, the total resultant is the curvilinear movement of all.

But, again, as we have seen, a mass in motion presents a case of actual energy—energy of motion. And since this energy of motion is directed, not in a straight line toward the center, but in a curved line about the center, it is evident that what began as a tendency toward the center has developed into a tendency away from the center. It is this latter tendency that is properly termed centrifugal force.

And, now, let us note that the nearer the smaller bodies approach the central one the greater becomes their velocity, and, hence, the greater becomes their energy of motion. But since this increasing energy of motion is directed in a curve about the center, it must (the bodies being of the given relative mass) attain at length a degree of intensity that is not merely sufficient to balance the tendency toward the center, but which will be even sufficient to overbalance the centripetal tendency and thus actually carry the lesser masses away from the center.

At the same time the gravitative strain or tendency toward the center is a continuously impressed force. And at the maximum point reached in its intensity (which is, of course, at the moment of nearest approach of the bodies to the center) the gravitative strain is adequate to overcome the heightened degree of the energy of motion (here developed as centrifugal force) acquired by the revolving bodies so far as to cause a rapid change in the direction of their motion.

Thus, while they do indeed pass the center, it is not until, with their extreme velocity, they have passed so far around it as to make a swift retrograde movement toward the distant point from which their fall began. Their fall toward the sun was a process of accumulating energy by which they were able to resist actually falling into the central body, and by which also they are now seen to actually "fall" away from that body.

Centripetal force is direct attraction. Centrifugal force is energy of motion, due to attraction, but having a tangential direction, this tangential direction itself being due to the complexity of gravitative relation inherent in the group of the assumed three bodies.

It ought to be remarked, finally, that the movement away from the central body on the part of the smaller masses necessarily takes place in opposition to the attraction between them and the central body. Hence, their velocity must now diminish until, their centrifugal force becoming less than the force of attraction between them and the central body, they gradually return upon their path of approach toward the central body, to repeat the same round.

It is easy to see, too, from the relations of force here developed, that the path of a smaller body revolving about a larger one must approximate an ellipse, and that, as was discovered by Kepler, the radius vector must describe equal areas in equal times.

Such, it seems perfectly safe to assume, is the nature of all curvilinear motion, and hence of all motion whatever, throughout space. It may be rendered incalculably complex by multiple attractions. But in every case the perturbations in the movements of the heavenly bodies are but the further illustration of the same law of relation necessarily applying as between all the force-centers of the material universe, as has been repeatedly and brilliantly shown in the course of the development of astronomical science.

Not only are all those force-centers related one to another, but a number of them, grouped together with a special degree of intimacy, constitute a complex system through their own mutual relations. The many are inevitably resolved into the one; or, the many are necessarily interrelated, and through their interrelation they necessarily constitute one.

On the other hand, it is equally evident that the many moving bodies in space, with all the phenomena of their existence, constitute but the manifold outer modes of the all-inclusive, perfectly self-balanced and self-active World-Energy, the primal *one*, which is the source of all reality.

We have traced, in brief, the essential characteristics of molar motion. We have next to inquire what are the fundamental phases of molecular motion.

CHAPTER XVIII.

MOLECULAR MOTION.

OUR inquiry thus far leads manifestly to the conclusion that all motion, whether molar or molecular, must necessarily follow the same laws. Or, more precisely, all motion, whether molar or molecular, is ever the manifestation of the same primal relations existing between the force-centers of the real world in space, whether those force-centers be considered as simple or as aggregated into more or less extended groups.

On the other hand, we have already seen that, along with increased complexity of grouping of force-centers, there develops also increased intensity of strain, which further results in the bringing into realization of new and richer qualitative characteristics.

It is this development which takes place more especially in the sphere of molecular motion.

The grouping itself, indeed, is due to the mutual attractions between the simplest force-centers; so that all attraction may be regarded as ultimately atomic. But the more closely these centers are gathered, the more intense becomes the strain between them. That is, the more strongly does the mutual attraction between any two centers oppose the realization of the qualitative result that would otherwise naturally follow from the attraction between either of these two and any other center.

Thus, the force-centers of a given group come to acquire more and more rigid relations, one with another, until they at length take on a definite form, and offer greater or less resistance to any and all forces tending to change that form. That is, what primarily is but lax gravitative energy, becomes more and more intense, until at length it develops into cohesive force.

But now, when there comes to be applied to such rigid aggregate of force-centers another group of force-relations sufficient to overcome its cohesion, then the molecular strain is developed to a correspondingly high degree. But whether the applied force bears the character of compression, or of percussion, it is in either case due to, or is a form of, gravitative energy or attraction. And if the application takes place suddenly—that is, if the quantity of force in action be mainly intensive—then the motion imparted to the molecules of the given body will be so great that their impact upon one another must have the effect to widen the distances between them in greater or less degree, and thus to correspondingly increase the volume of the groups as a whole.

The result of the attraction, then, in such case, is, first, percussion of one body against another, and through this the sudden enhancement of the motion of the force-centers constituting the bodies, so that the bodies themselves increase in volume through the energy thus imparted to their molecules. That is, molar motion, due to gravity, results in percussion of the moving bodies, which in turn gives rise to molecular motion, and this again results in increased intensity of percussion of molecules, causing the expansion of the bodies.

A phase of force drawing bodies together is thus seen to develop into a phase of force driving the constituent portions of those bodies asunder. Nay, the bodies themselves, so far as they are elastic, rebound; and the expansion of the body as a whole is but the increased intensity of rebound of the molecules of the body, estimated in the increased extension or volume of the body as a whole.

But whether the impact and rebound be between large bodies (*moles*), or between small bodies (*molecules*), in either case precisely the same principle applies; and the thing to especially notice just at this point is that the manifestation of force is perpetually *dual*. Concentration, we are accustomed to say, is due to attraction, while expansion is due to repulsion. But we must repeat that, as here shown in brief, and as proven more extendedly in preceding chapters, the tendency toward concentration itself involves the tendency toward expansion, just as the tendency toward expansion involves the tendency toward concentration. Attraction and repulsion are reciprocal phases of every manifestation of force; and their interrelation, as exhibited in the particles of any given mass, great or small, is precisely what we are accustomed to call the "elasticity" of that mass. That is, elasticity is a molecular property of bodies; and it should not be forgotten that this property is nothing else than an essential relation or interplay between attraction and repulsion, as the two necessary, and mutually inclusive, properties of all matter.

Finally, since the same principles determine motion, whether molar or molecular—the difference between these two classes of motion being, as just seen, arbitrarily assumed rather than actually existent—and, since motion may be imparted or transferred from one body to another, the balance between attraction and repulsion within any given quantity of matter must be constantly undergoing change, and, as a consequence, the volume of any and every body must as constantly undergo variation.

Let us trace, briefly, some of the consequences of this evident fact of the interrelation between attraction and repulsion. And, first, let us note the special characteristics of

a.—HEAT.

That phase of molecular motion specially manifest in the expansion of bodies, is now named Heat. It is affirmed as a general law in physics that heat expands all bodies. That is, heat is declared to be a mode of repulsion. Thus, the degree of expansion which a given volume of a selected substance undergoes, serves as the measure of intensity of heat.

In reality the expansion is a measure of the increase of one phase of force, as compared with another, in a given quantity of matter. So that heat, as measured by a thermometer, may be said to be the varying degrees in the intensity of repulsion relatively to attraction; just as weight, far from being identical with gravity, is in reality the measure of the excess of centripetal over centrifugal force.

It is also worthy of notice, that the "exceptions" to the law that heat expands all bodies, are found to be no exceptions. They are, in fact, due to crystallization. We have already had occasion to notice that the complexity of grouping of particles follows upon the complexity of relation between attraction and repulsion. To this it is now to be added that the grouping of particles known as crystallization, takes place for each of the crystallizable substances at a single definitely fixed temperature of the substance, *provided always that the pressure is the same.* That is, for every crystallizable substance, the process of crystallization can take place, only upon the establishment of a definite fixed relation between attraction and repulsion within the substance. With any excess of repulsion above that point, the crystals dissolve if already formed, or refuse to form if the substance is in the liquid state.

Crystallization, then, is a special phase of the solidification of bodies, a process which takes place only upon the reduction of the repulsion between their particles to such degree as to leave the attraction predominant, and thus allow the particles to cohere in fixed relations. These fixed relations again constitute a tendency to break up a larger mass into a multitude of smaller masses. Within the larger mass certain groups of particles combine into relatively small masses of perfectly definite shape; the shape being fixed for each particular kind of crystallizable matter. Thus the larger mass is differentiated into a multitude of smaller masses, which yet cohere in irregular groupings, leaving *unoccupied spaces between them,* and thus thrusting the boundaries of the entire mass outward on all sides. Thus, while the matter in cooling to or below the point of crystallization becomes more dense, and really occupies less space, yet the bulk of the entire mass is increased; or, in crystallizing, the body "expands," but without really contradicting the law that loss of heat is accompanied by loss of actual volume.

Another point of interest to be noticed in this connection, is found in the discussions of physicists concerning the "*absolute zero.*" Calculation once made of the loss of volume for each degree of reduction of temperature in a given mass of air, it is easy to determine the absolute zero point, on the presumption that the ratio of loss of volume to each degree of diminishing temperature will *continue unchanged.*

Of course this ratio would *not* remain unchanged. But the point of interest for us here is the fact that theoretically the absolute zero of temperature falls precisely where the given quantity of matter has also reached the *zero of volume.* That is, as was intimated on a former page, *where there is absolute zero of temperature, there is absolute non-existence of matter.* And, indeed, one might naturally enough infer that since "heat" is a state or phase of "matter," there can be complete absence of heat only where there is complete absence of matter.

It may also be remarked, that so far as this speculation of the scientists is of any real value, it serves to confirm our previously attained conclusion, that repulsion—of which heat is merely a mode—is an absolutely essential phase of matter. This, indeed, is the real meaning of that other speculation to the effect that if the action of gravity were wholly unchecked, it would reduce the material universe to a mathematical point. On the other hand, as we have already seen, gravitation itself would be impossible apart from repulsion, as its opposing or complementary mode of force. Or, as previously shown, the very action of gravity must, of necessity, develop within itself the opposite mode of force. Whence it may be said that, though we may in a certain degree *imagine* the action of gravity apart from repulsion, yet it is impossible to conceive such action in the sense of *thinking* it.

There is, besides, no little significance for our present purpose in the fact that, in modern science, heat is treated throughout as exclusively a mode of repulsion. The entire discussion of the subject proceeds upon, and is but a development of, the proposition that "heat expands all bodies." The chief topics regarding the action of heat are: Expansion; change of state; relation between tension and density of vapors.

Finally, as regards the distribution of heat, it need only be said that conduction of heat is simply the progressive transfer of the energy of motion from particle to particle in a series; while convection begins in conduction, which, in turn, brings about a difference in specific gravity in the fluid medium, the result being currents *conveying* the energy of motion (whence *convection* currents) and distributing that energy by contact—that is, by conduction again. So, also, radiation itself appears to be but a modified form of conduction, and the more when we recognize that all "bodies" are in reality indefinitely extended, and, hence, mutually inclusive.

But let us now pass to the consideration of another mode of molecular energy, which is also intimately related to heat.

b.—CHEMICAL ACTION.

We have already noticed that molecular combination depends upon the varying degrees of relation between attraction and repulsion. We have just seen that crystallization depends upon a definite fixed relation between these two modes of energy for each particular substance; and in former pages reasons were shown for concluding that the chemical elements themselves must have had their origin in the cumulative strain incident to the gradual radiation of heat from a given diffuse, gaseous mass, the mass gradually condensing into the solid state through the constant action of gravity; this phase of force itself, indeed, becoming more and more intense the farther the condensation advanced.

Modern chemistry itself points definitely and emphatically in the same direction. All chemical compounds are separable into their elements through the action of heat. Chemical combination is the result of attraction, here named "affinity," while heat is a mode of repulsion. Above a certain degree of intensity, therefore, heat must serve as an absolute bar to the formation of any known chemical compound.

As far as observation goes, then, the qualitative differences of matter are seen to be completely dependent upon the relation between the intensive and the extensive phases of energy in a given realm. Quality is, in truth, the intensive phase of matter developed through a preponderance of the intensive phase of energy. That is, it is a perfectly logical inference from the principle thus far developed that the so-called chemical elements are themselves simply so many phases of matter that have been differentiated from a practically homogeneous, nebulous mass, through the gradual transition of the total quantity of energy immediately constituting that mass from a predominantly extensive to a predominantly intensive phase.

The same laws, then, must hold in chemistry as in physics. And it is a noteworthy fact that the latest researches in chemical science tend to verify this conclusion also. Nay, at least one work—Berthelot's remarkable and extended treatise, entitled, "*Essai de Mécanique Chimique*"—is devoted to the presentation of the evidences tending to establish the identity of chemical forces with the other natural forces.*

But the general action of these phases of energy cannot fail to develop specialized, local strains within the mass of matter thus undergoing reduction in spacial extent, on the one hand, and differentiation of qualitative content on the other. And it is evident that the investigation of these specialized local strains must result in the development of a new branch or branches of science.

Historically, indeed, such investigation has resulted in the development of two distinct branches of purely physical science; the one being chemistry itself, the other being electricity. And it is especially worthy of notice that both the phases of energy, whose special modes are traced in these two sciences, are most intimately related to the still more complex modes of energy manifested in life.

It is to a brief consideration of the central characteristics of electricity that we have now to turn.

*In his conclusion he says: "Ainsi, les énergies chimiques se trouvent nettement caractérisées et mises en opposition avec les autres énergies naturelles: les unes et les autres obéissent également aux lois de la mécanique rationelle." II., 754.

c.—ELECTRICITY AND MAGNETISM.

In crystallization, the molecules of certain kinds of matter are seen, under favoring conditions of relation between attraction and repulsion, to undergo arrangement, so as to constitute definite geometrical solids. These solid forms possess, too, in most cases, a relatively stable equilibrium.

Another class of strains, however, is induced by the sudden cooling of a mass of molten matter—for example, glass or iron—to the solid state. The Prince Rupert drop is a well-known and striking example of extremely unstable equilibrium, produced by the sudden chilling of a small mass of molten glass, so that the surface becomes solid, while the interior is still in a more or less liquid or viscous state. When the whole has become solid, the interior and exterior strains are imperfectly balanced, the density of the central part being less than that of the outer, since an outer rigid shell was formed over an inner nucleus that was still molten, and which, in its solidification, has tended to shrink away from the outer rigid shell. Hence, the slightest break in the exterior portion at once makes way for the complete disruption of the entire mass.

It is well known, also, that cast car-wheels and edge-tools, when chilled rapidly, possess the same peculiar characteristic of "brittleness." And this, it can scarcely be doubted, is due in reality to the unequally distributed strain characterizing the Prince Rupert's drop, rather than to the additional "hardness" produced by the sudden cooling; for, in truth, the "hardness" must, by the very conditions of rapid cooling, be confined mainly to the superficial portions of the chilled mass.

We have now to remark that electrification would seem to be a similar case of unstable molecular equilibrium in this far: that it is found to be a special molecular condition, which very few kinds of matter will retain during any at all extended portion of time. The evanescent character of electric disturbance, too, is, when considered in connection with the Prince Rupert's drop, confirmatory of the usual statement of physicists that such disturbance is confined to the superficial portions of the electrified bodies.

It is only when the disturbance penetrates through the entire mass that it assumes a relatively permanent character; and then the electrified body becomes a *"magnet."* In confirmation of this, it is scarcely necessary to do more than refer to the beautiful experiments with the solenoid, by which a current of electricity is shown to possess all the essential properties of a magnet.

It is interesting to note, too, that a bar of iron resting within the solenoid while a current of electricity passes through it, becomes a temporary magnet, while a steel bar, under like conditions, becomes a "permanent" magnet. And this, too, has its important suggestion. For steel is simply a more dense state of iron. That is, relatively to steel, iron is "soft," or fluid. The attraction between particle and particle is less intense. The relation between particle and particle is less rigid. The relation between particle and particle in steel, then, is less easily disturbed. Hence, when a new relation is established, it tends, in its turn, to persist. And this is especially the case when the new relation between particle and particle becomes, in a measure, organic, or, as it is usually expressed, "polarized."

Thus electricity (and, therefore, magnetism) consists of a special, local molecular strain, opposing the ordinary cohesion of particles. It may, too, become sufficiently intense to quite overcome the cohesion, and thus to fuse, or even vaporize, a solid mass. It thus performs the same office as heat—is, indeed, in such case, said to be transmuted into heat. And not only so, but, just as heat is a mode of molecular motion, transferable from one portion of matter to another, so electricity is also only a varied mode of molecular motion, capable of transmission.

If, indeed, we take into account the relations involved in its development, it becomes evident that, in reality, electricity cannot but be in perpetual process of development and transmission into other phases of force wherever there is matter. True, it is not merely or mainly a phase of molecular repulsion, like heat; nor of molecular attraction, like chemical affinity. On the contrary it constantly exhibits both these phases of energy in its activity, and is thus a specially complex phase of molecular energy.

Electricity is, indeed, described as of two kinds— "statical" and "dynamical." The former is said to be developed by friction, the latter by chemical action. But friction involves adhesion, which is an approach to molecular attraction; while chemical action is a separation and recombining of "atoms," in which there is necessarily involved molecular friction. Here, again, then, we find ourselves face to face with the identity in kind of molecular and mechanical energy, while the two "kinds" of electricity are seen to be but two phases or degrees of one and the same kind.

But we have further to note that all strains producing flexure or compression—in short, any change whatever, whether "mechanical" or "chemical," in the configuration, or volume, or state, of any given mass of matter—must be attended with a greater or less degree of molecular friction, resulting in "electrification," as well as in change of temperature. In short, electricity is evidently a phase of all matter, and a phase no less essential than is heat or gravitation.

At the same time, it must not be overlooked that in still another way the complexity of electric energy is evident. For in its manifestations there are ever found to be two phases possessing opposite characteristics, and to which are given the designations respectively of "positive" and "negative." It is to be observed, however, that the law which these manifestations are found to follow brings out a peculiar result. The law is that "like electricities repel and unlike electricities attract." But this can, in reality, mean nothing else than that positive electricity is negative toward positive, and positive toward negative electricity; while negative electricity is positive toward positive, and negative toward negative.

And not only so, but the designation of the one rather than the other as positive is found to be purely arbitrary. Either is equally positive and equally negative. Each is therefore both positive and negative.

This is a specially significant phase of relation in force, to which we shall have occasion to return.

Finally, we must not fail to note, further, that electricity not only exhibits this two-fold character as electricity, but that its activity constantly develops into both heat and chemical change, just as, on the contrary, both heat and chemical change are accompanied by electrical excitation.

In an important sense, then, electricity may be regarded as the higher unity in which heat and chemical action—molecular repulsion and molecular (or "atomic") attraction—combine, the result being, indeed, a state of very unstable equilibrium. And this corresponds to the general law in nature that the more complex the physical unit the more is it susceptible to dissolution.

It will be observed that, up to this point, in dealing with "molecular motion," we have had to do with facts that belong definitely to the external or physical world. We come now to consider those phases of molecular motion which are very closely intermingled with factors pertaining to the inner world of mind. This fact gives to the study of those phases a special interest at the same time that it adds greatly to the possibility of error in the results.

The special phases referred to are

d.—LIGHT AND SOUND.

As a physical fact, strictly considered, light is inseparable from radiant heat. And radiant heat is predominantly repulsion—a central throbbing that communicates motion outward radially to and through the surrounding medium.

Nevertheless, this transmission of motion from the center outward by means of vibrations in a medium involves something more than mere *outward* impulse. Both center and medium must be highly elastic if any movement is to be actually transmitted. For the outward thrust of every single particle from the center of radiation already, and necessarily, involves a tension which can exist only through the inseparable union of attraction and repulsion.

The vibration, besides, is not merely an outward thrust, but is also and equally a rebound. In other words, vibrations can take place only in an elastic medium. And elasticity is nothing else than the interfusion of molecular attraction and repulsion. Thus the undulatory theory of heat, light and electricity, only brings into greater clearness the extreme simplicity of the physical world.

So, too, this simplicity of the physical world becomes still more impressive when we further consider the familiar fact, that like light, sound too, as an outer physical fact, is nothing else than vibratory motion in an elastic medium. It would indeed be only to repeat what has been said of the former, were we to state the fundamental characteristics of the latter.

There are, of course, important qualitative differences in the media, as well as quantitative differences in the vibrations which take place in these media. No doubt, too, that the complexity of grouping of the particles incident to the vibrations, in the one case, is greater than in the other. But, after all has been said, the fundamental fact remains that sound and light, considered simply as physical facts apart from their effects in sensation, are alike modes of vibratory motion and nothing more.

In truth, what we commonly call "light" and "sound" are *subjective creations of our own*, which we spontaneously attribute to the physical world as if they pertained to that world and were among its inherent properties.

It is necessary to reflect quite deliberately upon the subject before one is able to form to himself a clear and even approximately adequate conception of the extent to which he is himself the creator of the world in the midst of which he lives. He must first become thoroughly conscious of the infinite variety that is given to the "external" world by color and sound, taste and smell. He must then dwell upon, until he realizes the full force of, the proofs that these have absolutely no existence save in sensation. Then, and only then, can he adequately appreciate the barrenness and utter poverty of the merely physical world. Then, and only then, can he rightly appreciate the fact that the world in space, apart from those "attributes" which in no wise belong to it, but which are literally *given* it by the contemplating mind, is in reality nothing more than the balancing of complementary phases of energy developing into "material," but constantly changing forms, characterized chiefly by their mutual exclusion—their pure *externality*.

That, in truth, is all that is real of the "outer world." Elasticity—the interfusion of attraction and repulsion in varying degrees, resulting in perpetual vibration, in perpetually recurring condensations and rarefactions—here, indeed, is the essence of the *external conditions* of sensation; but this is far from constituting the *internal fact* of sensation. This internal fact of sensation is an act of the mind. The stimulus leading to this act is found in the outer vibrations; but the act of sensation, together with its product, known as an "image," these are inner, subjective facts. Even the "image," involving all there is of color, or of sound, or of odor, or of flavor, is not a possession of the mind, as something separate or separable from the mind. Rather, it is itself a state of the mind, a factor inwoven with the very existence of the mind.

That color, and sound, and odor, and flavor are purely subjective is, indeed, a fact recognized and acknowledged as a matter of course, even by the most thorough-going empiricists.

And now, all this being the case, it serves to suggest the possibility that even that portion of the outer world which we must still regard as quite external to and independent of *us*, is still itself nothing else than the outer manifestation of the inner, spontaneous energy of a higher, and, indeed, highest, consciousness. This would doubtless prove to be the most adequate term of the world, a term infinitely concrete, the vital principle of all things.

But so far as the present argument extends, this must as yet be regarded as conjectural. What has developed all along, what the most recent developments of physical science point to with special clearness and emphasis, is the conception that the world in space is a sum-total of energy; that everywhere there is indestructible unity of relation; that the total complex of relations extends infinitely in all directions, and thus that the sum-total of energy is an indivisible, self-balanced whole. Even the modes of molecular motion are seen to be nothing else than the various phases of the manifestations whose essence is the infinitely varied inter-play of attraction and repulsion as the primary and necessarily complementary phases of the one all-pervading and all-constituting energy. And now that we have come to recognize the identity in nature of all the phenomena of the outer world, and have found the theory to be entirely reasonable that all these phenomena are due to the varying degrees of complexity of the activity of the one primal energy, we may next proceed to inquire more precisely what are the necessary implications as to the essential, innermost property of this one primal energy.

CHAPTER XIX.

CORRELATION OF FORCES AND CONSERVATION OF ENERGY.

THE doctrine of correlation of forces, now so generally known and accepted, will require but brief reference in this place. And so much the less need it be here dwelt upon, as the whole course of our argument thus far has been chiefly a statement of that doctrine in its more universal form. All possible phases of force have been shown to be necessarily interrelated, and even interfused, so that in reality the exclusive occupancy of a given field by one single phase of force would be wholly impossible. Force, to be force at all, must be complex. At every point where force is, there it is as *active;* and in its activity it must involve strains and counter-strains productive of constant changes in the intensity of molecular energy, which changes become manifest as heat, or chemical action, or electric (or magnetic) polarization; or rather in all these it becomes manifest simultaneously in varying degree. Not merely percussion, but also compression—both due to attraction—give rise to heat, which is itself a mode of repulsion. And in general we find everywhere complete confirmation of the third law of motion—that "to every action there is always an equal and contrary reaction."

But this law, in thus presenting the two-fold nature of force, also declares implicitly that either phase may be regarded as either action or as reaction. And this is in effect to regard each phase as both action and reaction. So that the theory of the correlation of forces seems already announced in germ in this law. Given certain conditions, a definite quantity of heat will in its consumption develop a corresponding definite quantity of electricity. But just as well the case may be reversed and a given definite quantity of electricity may be expended and have for its product a corresponding definite quantity of heat. And yet, in either case, the force expended cannot even be conceived as existing otherwise than as in action, and hence as meeting an equal quantity of force in reaction. And in these cases the force in reaction must evidently be molecular or atomic attraction. The percussion of world colliding with world must develop sufficient heat to reduce both to the nebulous state. And that compression is productive of heat is sufficiently known from familiar facts, and is strikingly illustrated from the estimated quantity of heat developed by the strain toward the center in case of all large masses—the heat of the sun being, as Helmholz suggests, kept up by this means.

In short this interrelation, let us repeat, is manifest everywhere in nature, and the whole physical universe is but its perpetual realization and illustration.

But, allowing this to be the case, there appears one grave difficulty, as we are assured by those who insist that "science" must above all things be "exact." And the grave difficulty is this: The energy of the system may "run down" to a dead level, so that all motion, all development, all change, all life, must forever cease.

"The principle of degradation," says Balfour Stewart, "would appear to hold throughout; and if we regard not mere matter, but useful energy, we are driven to contemplate the death of the universe."*

Assuredly this would be a deplorable outcome—especially as it could scarcely be hoped that there would be any survivors to mourn the loss of the "useful energy." In any case we seem here to arrive from the opposite direction, at the same difficulty as that which presented itself at a previous stage of our inquiry. The difficulty is that of discovering an adequate principle of motion.

On its first presenting itself the difficulty was to find a principle that could initiate motion. It now appears under the form of an unavailing search for a principle adequate to maintain motion. What if the really hopeless search should prove to be for a principle or "force" adequate to the putting an end to motion?—seeing that "rest" is altogether inconceivable as a state of matter.

It would seem that we might formulate our need thus: "Wanted:—a sufficient reason alike for the birth and for the death of the universe." Meanwhile the undeniable and assuring fact of the universe itself, as here and now actually existent and throbbing with vitality manifested in motion, offers itself pending the settlement of such questions as whether in truth the "universe' ever was really born, or whether it will ever indeed die—whether, if its birth can really be even conjecturally dated, we can ever hope to estimate out of what possible conditions of chaos or mere void it

---

* "*Elementary Lessons in Physics,*" p. 375, and similarly at the close of his work on the "*Conservation of Energy.*"

came into being; or if its death be indeed a fore-doomed fact, whether it may not after all be that it will undergo self-cremation and, supreme Phœnix as it would then be, evolve a new "universe" of at least equal splendor, from its own infinite nebulosity,—for "ashes" assuredly there could then be none.

Fortunately a way out of this grave difficulty seems already provided. It may be that the inevitable and seemingly final "dissipation of energy" is but a phase of the wider process known as the conservation of energy.

This doctrine affirms in what is now accepted as an axiom of science that the total quantity of energy in the universe remains and must continue to remain unchanged. Energy can neither be brought into existence nor put out of existence. To bring energy into existence must pre-suppose the existence of energy. And, as the energy previously existing could act only through the reaction of that upon which it acts, the energy brought into existence must have already been in existence.

Energy, then, is not merely something existing, not merely something indestructible, it is evidently also something uncreated, something the creation of which is inconceivable. But if energy cannot be created, then all energy now existing must always have been in existence. So, too, on the other hand it must require energy to destroy energy. And the destroying energy must be greater than that destroyed. Nay, as we have already seen, there are not many energies, but only one all-inclusive energy. And evidently this total unit of energy could not destroy itself in any degree. For in acting upon itself it could only bring itself into equilibrium;

and, indeed, this appears to be what is really meant by the theory of the dissipation of energy.

Is this equilibrium necessarily an equilibrium of death, or could there possibly be for the universe just as well an equilibrium of life?

Implicitly, at least, the answer to this question has already been given. The totality of energy remains forever unchanged. As energy, it is changelessly active. "To every action there is always an equal and opposite reaction." Hence, the totality of energy *must always have been in equilibrium*. For its activity could only be within and upon itself; and, since the activity of the one unchanging energy must be changelessly the same, including the aspect of reaction, then the total product must likewise be changelessly the same.

Evidently, unless energy persists in all its relations, there is thus far, on the one hand, a failure of the persistence of energy itself; while, on the other hand, a failure of energy to persist in all its relations necessarily implies that the correlation of the various phases of energy is, after all, not complete. In which case there would be absolute lines of separation in the total energy; whence, in reality, there must be many mutually exclusive forces. And this is the same as saying that the doctrine of the correlation of forces is no more than a fiction.

In short, the conclusion that the energy of the universe is undergoing degradation, or that it is in any way in a process of running down to a dead level of rigid equilibrium, would seem to have been drawn from premises which were no doubt perfectly "exact," but which, there is reason to believe, were insufficient in their scope. In the first place, the conclusion is based upon mathematical calculation. That is, it is a (relatively) quantitatively determined result. But the universe, as a whole, the total "quantity" of energy, is by no means quantifiable in the sense of being expressible in terms of any human calculus. It is, as has already been shown, measurable only by itself.

Doubtless the quantitatively determined results which scientists have attained may be approximately correct as regards finite portions of the universe—the solar system, for example—where the process of the "running down" of energy may very well be considered as in actual progress. As already intimated, this running down of energy in finite portions of the universe is manifestly a necessary phase of the total process of the conservation of energy.

Nor can it reasonably be doubted that it is precisely here that the depressing pessimistic (or is it really uplifting-optimistic?) conclusion is reached as to the approaching "death" of the "universe." For, after all, it is fairly evident that the estimates respecting the dissipation of energy have reference only to "our" universe in contrast with another universe, or even with innumerable other *universes*—to which it would seem that any speculations of exact science can have no reference.

But any such local running down of energy necessarily implies a previous process of running *up*. It is impossible that a body should fall unless it has been previously raised to the height from which it falls.

Equally impossible is it, because really repeating the same thing, that the solar system should have resulted from the falling together of a nebula, unless the matter composing it had been previously expanded or "raised" to the vastly distant spaces occupied by the nebula.

And doubtless the energy that was capable of bringing about these conditions of potential energy primarily will be perennially equal to this and all other tasks which it pertains to its nature to perform. For the total quantity of energy must forever remain undiminished according to any rational interpretation of the doctrine of the conservation or persistence of energy.

And this doctrine, when reflected upon and fairly understood, is seen to be, if not self-evident, at least clear and consistent; while the contrary of this doctrine is plainly self-contradictory, and, hence, "unthinkable." So forcibly, indeed, does the truth of this doctrine of the persistence of energy appeal to Mr. Spencer, that he declares it to be "the sole truth, which transcends experience by underlying it."* And so, too, it would seem, it must appeal to all minds; though it is of the utmost importance to bring into explicit statement the significance that is only latent in the formulation usually given to this truth.

And, first, it is essential to fully appreciate

a.—THE ABSOLUTE UNITY OF ENERGY

We have already seen that force or energy is necessarily complex or manifold; that at every point in space there is a focus of force, and that the force thus focused consists necessarily of the interfusion of attractions and repulsions. It is in this far that force appears especially as manifold.

On the other hand, the doctrine of the correlation of forces points clearly to the conclusion that, after all, force is, strictly speaking, a single totality having manifold

* "*First Principles*," (N. Y. Ed.), p. 192.

modes. So that now scientists no longer speak of *forces*, but only of *modes of force.*

And this view follows necessarily from the very nature of force. Precisely the same reasoning applies to the total sum of force or energy as applied to a single focus. To be force at all, it must present all the fundamental characteristics of force throughout its whole extent. Otherwise there would be, as already shown, not only distinct phases or modes of force, but absolutely different, and hence forever mutually exclusive forces.

This, however, could only be through the development of each force as absolute repulsion, since, physically, absolute exclusion can mean nothing else than absolute repulsion. But thus all would possess the same characteristic. Whence they would hold themselves as absolutely different, one from another, through an identical characteristic. They are absolutely different through their absolute identity.

And not only so, but each, as absolute repulsion or differencing power, must exert its repulsion within itself, as well as toward other forces. Otherwise it would be unable to resist their pressure and must be reduced to no-dimension. In other words, it would undergo annihilation. And this process must go forward until but one force remained. Hence, if many forces exist, it can be only by and through the absolute self-repulsion of each.

But in this case, each, by its own absolute self-repulsion, must expand infinitely, and thus not merely thrust itself against, but also thrust itself through the contiguous forces. The very power by which one force would be able to exclude from itself another force, and thus give rise to many forces, is thus found to be equally a power by which the one force must inevitably penetrate the other throughout its whole extent, and ultimately *in*clude it as well.

That which excludes also includes. The external is ultimately the internal. The conception that there are mutually exclusive forces proves self-contradictory. There is ultimately but one force or energy, which includes all, and is, at the same time, the "all" which is included. *It is a self-including, self-contained total.*

It thus turns out that energy is not merely an indivisible total, but that it is the very *substance of all reality.* For, as energy, it is substance, and as active, it can find its object only in substance. This substance, too, which is the object of the activity of energy, must itself also be a phase of energy, since it can be acted upon only by reacting; and, in reacting, it necessarily proves to be energy.

There can, besides, be but one substance. For, were there two, these could be distinguished or maintained as separate only through the possession, by the one, of characteristics which the other lacked, and through lacking what the other has. But thus, again, these two "substances" would prove to be mutually dependent, and hence, but complementary phases of one total substance.*

Thus, from whatever side we view it, energy is seen to be an absolutely indivisible, all-inclusive unit. And yet, as that which contains and also that which is contained, the total energy, or substance, is different from itself, and hence, self-*ex*clusion, as well as self-*in*clusion. All the relations that are possible to it, indeed, are relations of

---

*Compare Spinoza: "*Ethics*," Part I., Propositions I. to VIII., incl.

itself to itself. For, beyond the self-contained total, there is absolutely *nothing* with which that total could possibly sustain any relation whatever. It is itself the sum of all reality, the one positive *fact*, the all-inclusive *deed*.

But this one positive fact, or all-inclusive deed, is thus an infinite, or perfectly self-inclusive process. And this process is that of

b.—THE DIFFERENTIATION OF ENERGY.

The totality of force or energy, then, is a self-identical Unit, but a unit whose very self-identity necessarily involves its own infinite self-difference or self-negation.

As self-identical it is in truth self-affirming. But self-affirmation is in reality just the process of *self-realization*. It is the unfolding into reality of its own essential characteristics, qualitative and quantitative. Hence the self-realization of the total energy is a genuine process or practical activity; which activity, it has been shown, and must now be constantly borne in mind, is and can be nothing else than an activity upon itself. It is at once actor, and that which is acted upon.

Its self-realization, then, as the process of unfolding into reality those characteristics, both qualitative and quantitative, which essentially belong to it, is a process of unfolding within itself distinctions or mutually exclusive differences. That is, the self-identical World-Energy in the very process of its self-realization becomes self-different.

But differentiation is negation, and self-differentiation is self-negation. At the same time, the process of self-realization on the part of the World-Energy just consists in its self-differentiation. Thus alone can it determine itself in the sense of rendering itself concrete, actual. Hence, in affirming itself the World-Energy negates itself in a twofold sense. First, it negates its own identity so far as that may be regarded as a blank, abstract identity. Secondly, it unfolds negation as a necessary factor of its own concrete identity in so far as the phases of its own self-differentiation or self-determination present the characteristic of mutual exclusion. Here, indeed, there is brought to light the true meaning of the dictum, *omnis determinatio est negatio;* a meaning, however, which Spinoza himself seems not to have fully apprehended as belonging thereto.

A glance through what immediately precedes will make it evident that in our discussion of the doctrine of the conservation of energy, we are already approaching the question of the nature of cause. It is to the direct discussion of this that we have now to turn.

CHAPTER XX.

DOCTRINE OF CAUSE.

THE very conception of motion necessarily implies initial impulse. This is the principle underlying the laws of motion. And the impossibility of motion or change of motion taking place otherwise than through an initial impulse, is itself but a special case of that wider law that no event can take place without a cause.

Considered as involved in time-relations, the event must follow the cause. Such is the ordinary view. A bullet is fired from a gun. At the end of a second it strikes a bird in the air. The bird falls dead to the ground. The elastic force of the explosive is the cause of the velocity of the bullet. The velocity of the bullet, combined with its mass, is the cause of the bird's death. The action of gravity is the cause of the bird's fall. The explosion seems to occur before the velocity of the ball; the accumulation of velocity by the ball occurs before the death of the bird. But a moment's reflection shows that the action of gravity was not only prior to, but was also simultaneous with, the bird's fall. A little further reflection will bring to light the fact that the expansive force of the explosive is nothing else than the energy of molecular motion, which, when transferred to the ball, becomes the energy of molar motion. That is, the momentum of the ball is really the same force as that of the explosive whose energy has been transformed into that of the moving mass of the ball.

It is true the force acts through time. But it is equally true that the effect produced by the progressively developed force is unfolded in precisely the same gradual way, so that the force considered as cause is not precedent to, but simultaneous with, the various phases of the complex effect produced—disturbance of the air, killing of the bird, etc.

It is worth noticing, too, that the example chosen presents the two phases of force commonly called "constant" and "impulsive" forces. Gravity is a "constant" force. The explosion of gun-powder is an "impulsive" force. The doctrine of the correlation of forces, however, shows that this distinction is in reality the same as that between continuous and discrete quantity, which we have already considered. Indeed, physicists themselves treat this distinction as a fiction, when, for the sake of convenience, they consider a continuous force as made up of minute impulsive forces; which seems a little like reducing everything to infinitesimals preliminary to omitting the inconvenient parts. Though, of course, it must be admitted that in any of the "exact" sciences, quantity is scarcely manageable, otherwise than in its discrete aspect.

With a moment's reflection, however, it is evident that in all cases the exertion of force through time must be constant, that is, continuous. At the same time it is not less true that the known correlation of the various phases of force shows with equal plainness that force is at the same time impulsive. A constant force is not merely made up of a series of independent impulses. It gives impulse because it is constant. And the changes produced depend upon the conditions both in the cause and in the effect.

But thus it would seem that, after all, the "cause" is not confined to one side merely. Not only does the vapor of the explosive press outward against the ball; the ball presses back upon the vapor. Not only does the moving ball cause vibrations in the air; the friction between the air and the ball has the effect to raise the temperature of both the air and the ball. Not only does the ball rend the tissues of the bird; the resisting tissues of the bird diminish the velocity of the ball. There is ever action *and reaction*. Each phase is cause and each phase is effect. In other words, cause and effect are but the reciprocal aspects in every event which takes place, and hence are simultaneous rather than successive.

The relation between cause and effect is, nevertheless, commonly presented as one of succession. A as cause is followed by b as effect; b by c; c by d, etc. But here two causes at least alternate with effect as the characteristic of the same term, though b as cause is related only to c, while as effect it is related only to a. In this way causality is extended into an infinite series—c is the cause of d, d of e, * * * x of y, *ad infinitum*. In such infinite series, however, the phase of cause utterly vanishes, a on its part being likewise an effect of a cause which again is effect, and so on forever.

Here again we have all reduced to the infinitesimal degree and then spread out so that the limit is lost to view, whence it is supposed we have reached a solution of our difficulty. But far from any correlation of forces, we have here really no force at all—only the fleeting shadows of mutually exclusive forces, all which vanish into an infinite series of "effects" without cause.

The only possible real cause is one which is not itself the effect of something external to itself. It must be sufficient to itself, capable of acting from its own impulse. It must be self-moving, self-realizing, and in this sense *self-cause.*

And yet care must still be taken to avoid narrowing and distorting this view of cause. Cause thus conceived evidently transcends time. Self-complete, it must be completely self-active. Related only to itself, it must receive all its own activity. It is then completely self-receptive. Infinitely active and infinitely passive or receptive of its own act, it shows itself to be an eternal process, forever realized in all its perfection. It is infinite cause and infinite effect in absolute interfusion, and hence is the all-inclusive, absolutely self-complete One.

This may be rendered still more evident by a consideration of the four phases of cause known since Aristotle's time as the *"Four Causes."* It is intended here to state their rational significance and relation rather than to restate historical views concerning them.

Material Cause is the matter, or substance, or essence of which anything and all things are constituted. Nothing can exist otherwise than as involving "matter" in the sense of essence or substance. Hence in so far as the existence of things is dependent on matter, matter must be regarded as *"cause."* And yet matter as such is mere blank, self-identical substance, characterless and formless. It is mere passivity, bare potentiality. Nothing can arise from it alone. Its potentiality can never be realized save through some agency capable of differentiating it, reducing it to *form.*

Thus material cause proves to be but one of several necessary phases of cause.

And first a *formal cause* is demanded. "Matter" is impotent, a mere abstract identity. A complementary formative principle is also necessary. In the first place, too, this formative principle would seem to be something quite external to the "matter;" in which case it applies itself to the matter, gives it form, but still remains separate from it. But form apart from matter is also a substanceless abstraction.

Thus, taken in isolation, it is evident that just as material cause is a mere abstract, possible matter, so formal cause is a mere abstract possibility of form. On the other hand, in its concrete significance matter necessarily presupposes form just as form presupposes matter. Matter or substance can exist only so far as it takes on form, only so far as it has specific character. Form is possible only so far as it is the system through which matter gives evidence of its reality.

But this is not all; for the very potentiality, alike of matter or substance and of form or system, presupposes also a *potency* through which that potentiality becomes actuality.

Thus an *efficient cause* or working, realizing energy is necessarily implied in the conception either of material or of formal cause. And here again we might suppose the efficient cause to be independent of the other two. Yet to be really *efficient* it must possess substantial reality. Nor must it merely *possess* such reality; it must *be* that reality. The working energy or efficient cause, then, is itself already the essence or substance of things. Separated from that substance it would be unreal and non-efficient. Or, allowing it to possess reality and potency apart from the material cause its very reality would prove it to be already its own substance, and hence its own material cause. So, also, allowing the material cause to have reality apart from efficient cause, it must then be an independent, self-realizing potency and therefore its own efficient cause.

Clearly, also, efficient cause could really be such only by being completely consistent with itself, only by embodying a perfect method. But the self-consistency of its activity is the development into reality of cause in its character of formal cause. Hence, while matter and form mutually presuppose one another, their realized unity is found in efficient cause, which is at once its own matter or substance and its own form or method, as well as the concrete potency which fuses these phases into a vital unity at the same time that it brings them into perfect realization.

Evidently, then, these three "causes" are the absolutely necessary, because complementary, phases of the one true, vital *cause*. Each phase necessarily presupposes or implies the others; and that not as external the one to the other. On the contrary each is found to necessarily involve the others within itself. Matter cannot be matter without being also both form and efficient formative principle. Form cannot even be form without being also the vital energy constituting the matter which thus spontaneously unfolds into form, while the potency of efficient cause, as just seen, cannot prove itself to be potency save by unfolding as vital, self-forming (that is, self-differentiating) matter.

Thus we reach the conception of cause as absolutely self-complete. As efficient, self-forming matter, it is an absolutely self-dependent unit. Nothing beyond it is required for its perfection. That is, it is self-cause, and as such is necessarily an eternal process, forever complete in itself. Nothing can be conceived as existing beyond it or apart from it. It is the vital sum of all reality; the absolute, self-forming substance; the supreme truth, or *final cause*.

But this vital, self-differentiating unity, while it is seen to be the final cause in the sense of ultimate perfection, is just as clearly the *primal* cause in the sense that everything necessarily presupposes the existence of the perfect cause. In, and through that, all things necessarily have their being. Apart from it they are not merely *as* nothing; rather, apart from it, they must literally *be* nothing.

As final cause it is infinite *act*, and hence, absolute actuality, it is the infinite, eternal *Unit* which as such is "without variableness or shadow of turning." In it potentiality and reality absolutely coincide. As a whole it cannot change. It is, therefore, not subject to time, which is nothing else than the abstract form of change. Time is in this total, but the total itself cannot be in time. It is the perfect *World-Energy*, and as such all possible phases of change are produced *within* it, while *of* it there can be no change. The changing proves to be a phase of the changeless, and therefore time proves to be a mode of the timeless, just as the measurable in another way proved to be merely a phase of the measureless.

The self-active, self-realizing World-Energy is, then, the spontaneous, efficient and sufficient cause of all movement. It is that for which we have from the first been seeking. It is the final cause which is seen to be in itself its own infinite substance, the spontaneous, eternal process of balanced evolution and involution.

It is the absolutely persistent force or *self-conserved Energy* in which all modes of force are realized and perfectly correlated. Whence the "dissipation of energy," in the sense of an ultimately "dead universe" as the outcome, is impossible.

CHAPTER XXI.

CREATOR AND CREATION.

IT turns out, then, that the World-Energy is a self-active, self-sufficing, self-differentiating Unit, which is at once cause and effect. It is the Universe or Cosmos itself, now seen to be an infinitely vital totality. It is the concrete identity of the world and its Creator. That is, Creator and creation are the complementary aspects of the self-existent, self-unfolding World-Energy, in its changeless perfection.

Let us now inquire, briefly, how this conception comports with accepted views of the creation of the world.

It is usually objected to any form of the monistic view that the Creator must necessarily be superior to creation. The objection is based upon the assumption that the created world is the realm of the finite and imperfect, while the Creator must necessarily be regarded as infinite and perfect—in substance, Plato's view.

To this it may be, and has been, answered that if we hold the finite and the infinite asunder we represent to ourselves an infinite which is contrasted with the finite, and which thus stands in opposition to the finite. But in such case the infinite is itself limited by the finite; whence it proves in reality to be itself finite.

So, also, when we contrast the Creator, as independent and perfect, with creation, as the dependent and imperfect, we represent to ourselves a "Great Artificer" standing above, and thus apart from his work. He himself is the efficient cause of the world. That upon which He works is the material cause.

In this (usual) view, then, these two phases of cause, which we have already seen to be inseparable, are held asunder, thus reducing Creator and creation alike to mere abstractions. And not only so, but in this view creation is figured as taking place in time. In which case the Creator is at times active, and again, at other times, inactive. He is then not only separate from the world of his own creation, for the substance of which he must draw upon a pre-existent, and hence unaccounted for "matter," but he is also not continuously the same with himself, though the perfect must unquestionably be regarded as "yesterday, to-day and forever the same."

Thus, it appears that the effort to exalt the Creator by contrasting him with, as separate from, his creation, proves really to involve the very opposite result from that which was intended. For it makes him appear as dependent upon something lying quite beyond himself as the material without which he must be powerless to unfold a world in space.

There remains the conception of what we may call *absolute creation*. It is the conception that the world has been created from *nothing*. And this, though often looked upon as self-refuting, really contains in germ, the one really adequate view. For if the world was, or rather *is* created from nothing, then in reality the Creator brings the world into being by and through and from his own absolute perfection. That is, he requires *nothing beyond himself as infinite creative energy* to enable him to unfold the infinitely extended, infinitely varied world of finitude and change.

"Creation from nothing," then really means: Creation through the pure self-activity of the absolute First Cause. And the First Cause, let us repeat, is the one absolute energy, the very nature of which consists in its complete, perpetually self-equal *activity*. So, also, its activity is exerted solely and necessarily upon itself. Its activity is absolute self-activity and self-receiving activity.

Once more, then, the First Cause as absolute energy is an eternal, self-realizing process, and Creation is but the eternal self-realization of the Creator. The universe, or cosmos, is nothing else than the self-externalization of the great First Cause. Whence, that Cause is the truth and substance of the world—the one sole reality and infinite actuality.

CHAPTER XXII.

THE WORLD-ENERGY AS SPIRIT.

WE have seen that the World-Energy is identical with the First Cause. And the various phases of cause are, therefore, involved in it. We are now to inquire what further is implied in this conception.

And, first, we are to remember that our investigation thus far has brought us to recognize the World-Energy as the absolute, self-sufficing totality of existence. All its relations are necessarily self-relations. For there is absolutely nothing beyond or outside of it to which it could possibly be related. Thus, what we have now to do, is to investigate the fundamental phases of this round of self-relation which is necessarily involved in the total World-Energy as the absolute First Cause. And once more we are to follow the course of development in the logical order of the unfolding of these phases of self-realization, remembering that, for the World-Energy, those phases are necessarily and absolutely co-existent; any appearance of succession in time for it being incident wholly to the fact that we ourselves are under time-conditions, and must, therefore, view the phases of the World-Energy one after another. This we must do, indeed, even in our examination of a piece of mechanism or of art, though the total work is there before us as a whole from the beginning of our study of its various phases. So, in our investigation of the World-Energy itself—the process is not the merely fanciful one of evolving that object from our own inner consciousness, as thoughtless wit, or witless thought, would have it. On the contrary, it is the process of developing our inner consciousness itself so that it shall be progressively more and more in harmony with, by which process we shall come to have a more and more adequate view of, the World-Energy in its completeness as the one primal, eternal FACT. It is the progressive "adjustment of inner relations to outer relations" which constitutes life in the highest sense.

With this as our object, then, we will set out again from the simplest phase as the logical "first" in this culminating stage of our investigation. That is, we are not to set aside the results of our investigation thus far. Rather, we are to take those results, henceforth, as so much that is proven, and which may therefore be assumed as assured data from which further conclusions may be legitimately drawn.

And the central result we have thus far reached is, let us repeat, the conception of the total universe as the absolutely indivisible totality of existence, and yet, as presenting two necessary and complementary aspects. Regarded concretely, it is the World-Energy as self-active—that is, it is infinite activity, and at the same time infinite receptivity. It is infinite Cause and at the same time infinite Effect. It is at once Creator and creation.

a.—UNITY OF THE WORLD-ENERGY.

The phase which here presents itself with special impressiveness, is that of the absolute unity of the

World-Energy. This has, indeed, already come into view under the phase of the unity of substance. What now develops, however, is the fact that the World-Energy as such presents the character of vital reality. It is essentially a total of activity, and of self-activity; whereas substance appears rather as inert, relatively passive.

As the vital sum of reality, then, the World-Energy bears the aspect of absolute *potentiality*. All that is, or is to be, alike with all that has been, could only be, or have promise of being, or have actually been, through the activity of the World-Energy. That is the absolute presupposition of all things. All things are, or could be, only as phases or modes of the World-Energy.

Viewed as potentiality, however, the World-Energy appears especially as a self-equal, self-poised unit. It is the vital *One*, forever equal to itself. It is the *universal* of infinite extent. Self-comprised, it comprises all. Self-related, it involves all relation within itself.

But again, as self-related totality and, therefore, as involving all relation within itself, it is the potentiality of all distinction, differentiation, particularization. Thus *particularity* is no less distinctively a mark of the total World-Energy than is *universality*.

At the same time this self-multiplying unity remains forever One; multiplicity being but the form or mode of the potentiality of the One.* So, again, as self-particularizing universal, it must forever remain indivisible; for the very setting up of particularity within it, is solely the result of its own act as One. Its indivisible unity is emphasized precisely through its own self-particular-

---

*See the dialectic of the "*One and the Many*" in this abstract phase as developed in Plato's Parmenides.

ization, which is ever and absolutely its own process of concretely relating itself to itself.

Thus as self-particularizing (that is, self-differentiating) universal the World-Energy is seen to be the one absolutely self-poised *Individual*.

Universality, particularity and individuality prove, then, to be the complementary, mutually inclusive, absolutely interfused phases of the one total World-Energy. Each necessarily implies and in its own unfolding is found already to contain the others as vital elements or phases of itself.

Special attention, indeed, should be given to this fact. These three phases are the logical or rational, and hence necessary, phases of the World-Energy; and they are necessarily *co-existent* phases. To be World-Energy at all it must be *individual*, and prove itself to be such through its own *self-particularization* as the one absolutely active *universal*.

But to regard the World-Energy as potentiality merely is still to form a very abstract, inadequate conception of it. Potentiality merely as such must itself be impossible. The potential cannot be even potential save through a *potency* capable of bringing about the full realization of what is potential. Hence the potentiality could not possibly precede the potency in *time;* though it is, of course, "first" in logical order, or in point of simplicity, and thus may well be first in the *chronological* order of *our investigation*. And in the multiform aspects of the finite world, in the world of change, all particular phases of existence undergo development and decay, and, in so doing, undergo a series of logical transitions in time; and the chronological order is here found to coincide with the logical. The world of finite things presents in *chronological order* the *logical relations* which must of necessity be *co-existent* in the absolute, self-equal process which the World-Energy itself forever *is*.

It is to be remarked now that the self-equality of the World-Energy, when considered specially with reference to its potentiality—that is, when considered abstractly— leads to the conception of a moveless *equilibrium;* * and this easily passes into the anthropomorphic conception of *repose*. Whence all early forms of religion present in one or another way the conception of the Divine as "taking rest." This appears in the familiar description of creation, as presented in the Hebrew scriptures. The Divine is seen in council, deliberating; then as creatively active for a period; following which comes a period of repose.

Here the deliberation or thought of the Divinity is represented as passing in time. A plan is considered, developed, matured, and *then* put into execution; this latter phase of predominant activity also being one which unfolds through a period of time. Finally, the Divinity, having *completed* His work, desists from labor and relapses into a state of relaxation and repose—the abstract self-equality of potentiality, of passive equilibrium and self-satisfaction.

Here, indeed, we find the three fundamental phases of spirit imaged to us, but in such way as to represent those phases to us as not merely each variable in degree, but also as separable from one another. God here appears first as predominantly a *thinking* agency; then as predominantly a creating agency, or as *will;* then as predominantly a self-poised, passive unity of self-satisfaction

---

* A further stage in the development of that equilibrium which we have already seen to be the logical outcome of the Laws of Motion.

or *feeling*. That is, God is here represented under the image of a man, and as exhibiting the limitations of a finite, changeable being. And such must inevitably be the result whenever the Divinity is conceived under imagery, however lofty and dignified the imagery may be.

Another remarkable representation of the Supreme Power appears in the Hindu conception of creation. Here Brahm is indeed conceived as universal substance; and yet so imaged as that passivity and activity are assumed to be completely separable states of that substance. Thus, during immeasurable *kalpas,* or ages of ages, Brahm may remain wholly quiescent, all being, all reality absorbed and merged in his unity, which then presents absolutely no distinctions. At length, however, the repose of Brahm is brought to an end. Then begins a new and likewise enormously extended period, characterized by the activity of Brahm—the self-unfolding of his substance into a world of infinitely varied reality. And yet this is destined to be at last reabsorbed into the substance whence it emanated. Thus, as having no true, abiding existence, the world of finite forms is declared to be naught but *maya,* or illusion.

Thus to the Hindu, more literally perhaps than to the average modern Christian, "the world is all a fleeting show, for man's illusion given."

Nevertheless, there is a profound difference also underlying the outer similarity. In the Hindu view, the external world appears at first as a world of reality and permanence. It comes, however, to be recognized as in a state of perpetual change and dissolution. Yet the fact that change itself would be impossible otherwise than as a phase of the permanent does not wholly escape them.

Rather, the Permanent itself comes to impress them as the one primordial fact.

At the same time, the habit of the Hindu mind has ever been to "think" in the forms of the imagination; and its sense of the infinite can find no expression save in excessively exaggerated imagery, in which, of necessity, the infinite is ever represented as *one among other objects* of thought. Whence the endless mystification and straining after what must, of course, forever remain unattainable through the modes of the imagination. Greatest of possible symbols it is, doubtless—that of Brahm, the one enduring reality, putting forth infinite emanations from his own substance through measureless æons; and yet, again, when those æons have passed, reabsorbing all back into himself as substance, pure and simple—the ONE in which all multiplicity is absolutely canceled, and which thus reposes in its absolutely distinctionless potentiality for again other measureless æons. Mightiest of symbols; but a symbol, a mere image it remains.

On the other hand, the popular Christian conception—which is mainly identical with the Hebrew—is that of God as complete and completely active as infinite Spirit, apart from the outer physical world, which is "as nothing" compared with Him, or even with the spiritual interests of man himself. Thus, with the Hindus, the physical world is illusory, because it appears to have a real, abiding existence, and yet is in reality a mere temporary, and, hence, illusory, manifestation of the Divine essence. On the other hand, with the Hebrews and Christians generally the physical world is illusory partly as appearing to possess greater importance than it has in reality, but especially because, as the world of change,. it is a wholly vanishing world; nay, even illusory in the deadliest sense, as being the special medium of the anti-divine;* a view which, in spite of the advances in science, still lingers in its crudest form in many an unexpected corner.

Such imperfect conceptions inevitably accompany the unthinking representation of the Divine as a being limited in space and in time, and hence subject to change. To the mere phantasy there is no contradiction in the conception of limited space, nor in the vision of creation as having a beginning in time. Similarly, the phantasy finds no difficulty in picturing to itself a God who at one time is engaged in reflection, at another is occupied with the work of constructing a world, and at another is simply taking His ease.

It is only with the maturing of reason that the contradictions involved in such a view are brought to light; just as it is only by being made to pass through the dialectic of mutual cancellation that those contradictions give place in the mind to the complete, self-consistent view of the World-Energy as its own infinite, self-measured substance, one and unchanging, at once the all-including potentiality and the all-producing potency; hence the absolute, eternally self-equal PROCESS OF CREATION.

b.—THE WORLD-ENERGY AS SELF-UNFOLDING SYSTEM.

Such process of creation, however, is possible only as an absolutely fixed system. For, otherwise, it would be

---

* Wherein appears also an Eranian element familiar enough with those acquainted with the *Zend Avesta*.

a self-contradictory process, which is as much as to say that it would be no process.

In its very nature, too, as the sum and substance of all reality, it is, necessarily, a completely self-active, self-unfolding system. And, not only so, but a system is in its very nature a method; that is, an expression of thought. In other words, an absolutely self-unfolding system must of necessity be an expression of absolutely self-consistent thought.

Thus, the World-Energy is seen to be a process, unfolding as a perfect system, which system is but the explicit development of absolute thought. But thought thus unfolded in a perfect system is already the realization of *consciousness* in its absolute form of *self*-consciousness. This is the very core of spontaniety; and without spontaneity there could be no First Cause, no World-Energy, no *process* at all.

Thus, it appears that the World-Energy is in truth a self-knowing process, the perfect system, the spontaneous development of which is now to be the special object of our inquiry.

And, in this connection, we have first to remark, that the process of self-realization on the part of the World-Energy is first of all a process of self-*revelation*. For the World-Energy, as spontaneous process, is at once product and producer, while as self-conscious process it is at once knowing subject and known object. And, further, as absolutely conscious process it must eternally recognize and absolutely comprehend that process. It is absolutely self-knowing and, hence, is an absolute process of self-revelation. It would thus seem that Thought is the central truth and essence of the world.

But, secondly, it is to be noted that, as shown in the introduction to the present essay, the test of the adequacy of thought is that of self-consistency. This is recognized everywhere. In natural science that is accepted as the most reasonable hypothesis which brings into harmony the greatest number and variety of facts and relations—not indeed by setting aside or abstracting from the contradictions involved in those facts and relations, but rather by reconciling such contradictions and showing them to be, in reality, nothing else than elements of the concrete harmony of the world of nature. That is, the thought of man struggles perpetually to bring itself into harmony with the system of the world. And the specially conspicuous instances of success attending this struggle, are announced and accepted as "great discoveries." And the "discoveries" are nothing else than stages in the growing consciousness of man that the world of nature, the world which on first view seems to be an external and alien world to man, is yet a world whose very essence is to be traced in a faultless system, in a concrete unfolding of absolutely complete, self-consistent thought.

It appears, then, that the secret of man's ability to "think out" the "laws" of nature is precisely this: That the "laws" of nature are nothing else than special aspects of the perfect method, the absolutely complete, self-consistent thought of the World-Energy. So that, in his successful efforts to comprehend nature, man is simply adjusting his own thought to the thought which unfolds itself in nature. It is, in truth, just the thought or method of the World-Energy, and that alone, that man can really *think*.

And the boundless confidence which man has in the absolute perfection of the system of thought unfolded in the world or universe as a whole, is shown in the fact that he unhesitatingly accepts that system as the ultimate standard by which the validity of his own thought is to be measured. One "fact" is declared to be worth more than a thousand theories only in the sense, and in so far as, the theories are proven to lack validity by failing to harmonize themselves with the great system of facts constituting the world or universe. Thus the "fact" is taken (perhaps unconsciously) in its true sense of deed, act, *actuality*, genuine thought unfolded in concrete form, and hence as an essentially valid, indestructible phase — nay, as the very essence — of the world-system.

Thus the great thinkers of the world are they who have most adequately comprehended and most consistently given expression to the thought which constitutes the world-system. For this reason are they the typical discoverers, though the whole human race has participated in the explorations, and aided by its whole cumulative power in the effort to bring to light the indivisible totality and perfect self-consistency of Thought. And this entire struggle, let us remind ourselves again, is in reality nothing else than the struggle for self-development on the part of human thought itself.

We have now, thirdly, to remark that there is no difference in essence or type between the thought of man and the thought unfolded in the activity of the World-Energy. The one real difference consists in this: That the latter is the absolutely actual and complete system of thought forever self-realized in the universe or cosmos as a whole, while the former is the same ideal system of thought progressively undergoing realization in and through and for each individual man in time. Hence in proportion as man is successful in his efforts to discover the essential characteristics of the Thought of the World he discovers at the same time and in the same fact the true nature of his own thought. And the discovery consists in this: That his own thought is in its essential or true nature identical with the great world-system as the perfection of Thought. Both are of one and the same ideal type, of one and the same nature, and indeed it is inconceivable that they should be different. For, as already indicated, to conceive them as different must be to conceive the modes of activity of each, in order to know them as different. But thus, in conceiving the modes of activity of each, one must think in the modes of each; and this would be to include in one's own thought the modes of a consciousness assumed as different from one's own. And yet this must be a contradiction in terms, since whatever modes of consciousness I can really include in my own thought are by that very fact already proved to be modes of my own consciousness as well.

Thus, then, the perpetual self-revelation of the world-process is not merely a revelation of itself to *itself*, but also a revelation of itself to all beings having power to recognize that revelation. And the revelation in any given case is real precisely in proportion to the degree in which the power to comprehend the revelation is unfolded on the part of the receiving mind.

The whole universe, physical and spiritual, is therefore the eternally accomplished fact of Revelation, while on his part man is ever progressively unfolding his own power to comprehend the revelation. For this reason, too, men have ever tended to look upon Revelation itself as progressively unfolding. In other words, the tendency has ever been to make the mistake of attributing to the changelessly perfect Thought which is forever unfolded in the world those changes in time which in reality take place only in the unfolding consciousness of man himself.

And now we are the better prepared to recognize that in his efforts to construct a system of thought man is not really engaged in the idle task of evolving from his own inner consciousness a phantasmal creation, pleasing possibly to himself, but having no vital reality or relation to the actual world. On the contrary, he is engaged in the effort to discover the characteristics of thought which are universal and necessary, regardless of his own special phantasies. In other words, he is engaged in the effort to trace out on the one hand the fundamental characteristics of thought in its universal nature, as constituting the very essence of the world as a whole, and on the other hand to discover his own fundamental relation thereto. The outcome of all which is the infinitely important discovery, as we have seen, that thought as such is one in nature, realized in changeless completeness and perfection in the Cosmos, and also in perpetual process of realization in man himself.

Nothing, then, is "unknowable"—precisely *nothing*. The "unknowable" is the non-existent. The universe, or Cosmos, in its very nature is Intelligence in absolute manifestation—an open revelation to all beings capable of asking questions and receiving answers.

The one true system of Thought is the actual System of the World; and, conversely, the system of the world is the one absolutely complete system of Thought. For, as we have seen, thought is the truth of the world, and the world but the concrete form of thought. Hence, while pedants play with words and trifle with thought in the name of that logic which is said to deal solely with the *forms of thought,* and to have nothing to do with the *truth of things,* people who deal with things as the embodiment of truth clearly recognize the existence of a "logic of events," and shape their lives in accordance with the inexorable order of reason, which they designate under that name.

Now the true "logic of events" is just the absolute system of thought constituting the vitality of the total world. And this system, explicitly stated, would exhibit the true logic wherein the universal and necessary relations of thought as such are traced out. It is upon precisely this task, indeed, that the greatest thinkers of the world have exerted their best powers. Aristotle's work in this direction, it is well known, was done with such thoroughness as to remain unrivaled for two thousand years.

And yet he emphasized the formal aspect so far as to afford somewhat plausible excuse for the development of this phase in a spirit wholly foreign to his own, and with an excess of pedantic trifling that brought, as it could not fail to bring, contempt upon the very name of logic.

It was Kant who gave irresistible impulse toward the restoration of vitality to this science, and Hegel who organized it on a wholly new basis, so that, under his hand, it appears as the outlines of the genuine, vital system of thought as such both in its subjective and in its objective phases. The *"Logic"** of Hegel, it is not too much to say, is the most thorough-going, consistent and adequate presentation of the fundamental categories of thought in their vital, organic relations that has yet been given to the world. Nor is it likely to be surpassed for, it may be, centuries to come. In any case, it must prove increasingly indispensable to thinkers from generation to generation as a fundamental link in the historical development of human reason.

Its method is already working into the thought of the time, though it be silently or with but guarded acknowledgment in perhaps the greater part as yet, and is destined to exert a more and more profound influence as time goes on. That it is a book exceedingly difficult to really read there can be no question. For impatient, flippant people, doubtless the only practicable way to dispose of the work must ever remain the one usually adopted by them in disposing of any and every really serious book, namely, that of casting it aside with the contemptuous air of one who has already grown too wise to spend time over such vagaries.

For really serious students, however, the work must become increasingly accessible through the gradual increase in familiarity with its method that must follow upon the multiplication of works imbued with its spirit. Even works only superficially Hegelian must conduce to this end. And the "evolution philosophy" itself, with whatever of self-contradictory one-sidedness and materialistic tendencies, giving it the appearance of irreconcilable antagonism to the "absolute idealism" of

---

* The *"Logik"* of Hegel, as the reader may know, is in three volumes. The Logic of the "*Encyclopedia*" is a compendium of the larger work, and is now well known through Professor Wallace's excellent translation.

Hegel, is, after all, a magnificent *imaging* of the self-evolution of the world-energy; though for that "philosophy," indeed, the process vanishes hopelessly in the inane void of the "unknowable." On the other hand, in the Hegelian philosophy, as also in that of Aristotle, this self-evolution of the World-Energy is shown to be the eternal process of the self-realization of the absolute, divine Spirit.

It is toward this conclusion, too, as I attempt to show in the present argument, that the central conceptions of modern science also really point. Antagonism between real science and real philosophy there is and can be none. Philosophers need only to attentively consider the actual results of science to discover in them practical illustrations of the fundamental conceptions of philosophy; while scientists need only to familiarize themselves with the central principles of the much-decried "speculative philosophy" to find in them the clue to the complete harmonizing and unification of the results of science.

It is true that Hegel's "*Naturphilosophie*" is a most unfortunate "application" of his admirable dialectic method. Its arbitrary fetches are such that no scientist of the present day could read it with any degree of patience. This, indeed, proves Hegel's deficiency on the side of empirical science. But the *Logic* of Hegel, nevertheless, remains as one of the completest and most symmetrical of all the monuments constructed by the energy of human reason. If it affords no clue by which one may learn how to evolve the facts of nature from his own inner consciousness, it at least affords a clue by which those facts, once they have been brought to light by actual observation, may be recognized as constituting necessary phases in one consistent, abiding whole.

Surely genuine seekers after truth might well afford to adopt as their motto: "With malice toward none; with charity for all."

But let us turn again to and pursue the main line of our investigation. And we have now to notice that thought simply as thought is necessarily abstract. But, as already seen, the World-Energy is the one all-inclusive, absolutely concrete fact. Hence the method of the World-Energy as the complete system of thought can be comprehended in its truth only as a completely self-realizing method. But, again, such completely self-realizing method cannot but be completely conscious of itself. That is, it cannot but be a spiritual unit, and the one absolute Spirit.

It is to the central aspects of this process of the self-realization of thought that we have next to turn our attention.

c.—SELF-AFFIRMATION OF THOUGHT AS CONCRETE EXISTENCE.

Thought affirms itself as real. It is the one immediate, undeniable reality. To deny thought is to affirm thought. For denial is itself an act of thinking. Thus absolute negation is absolute affirmation.

At the same time, and equally, in its own self-affirmation thought also proves itself to contain negation as one of its essential factors. Thought is the power which makes affirmation; and yet, at the same time, it is that which is affirmed. Its self-affirmation is then in the first place a self-division, and since self-affirmation belongs to the very nature of thought this self-division which makes its appearance in the nature of spiritual existence as such is seen to be a *primal characteristic.* It inheres in the very form of self-affirmation, which again is a fundamental, distinguishing characteristic of spirit.

Thus, in affirming or realizing itself, the World-Energy as spirit must perpetually bring about its own self-separation or self-differentiation. Otherwise it must be, and remain a pure, abstract identity, which in truth is nothing else than pure nonentity. To be real and actual the World-Energy must constantly unfold negation within itself in the sense of developing infinitely manifold differences or specific qualities which again are the positive characteristics through which its nature is affirmed as concrete self-activity.

As actuality, then, and above all as the primal actuality and truth of the world, spirit must, from its very nature, unfold itself as just this process of absolute self-negation or self-differentiation. Its process of self-determination or systematic self-realization is just the process of its own self-negation. "All determination is negation," as Spinoza has it.

But thus negation again proves to be equally affirmation. It is the process by which the World-Energy as the one absolute spirit unfolds itself into infinitely manifold reality. As a concrete individual its reality is exhibited through its own self-particularization. The One parts itself into Many.

But also, as just indicated, the One realizes itself in the many. Hence the many have their reality only in the one. They are its modes, the phases of its realization. And, more precisely, the One as the inherent, formative principle proves its truth, its concrete actuality, through the multiplicity of realized *forms* involved in its own infinitely complex nature.

These particularized phases, again, in the very fact that they are such, show themselves to possess, in and for themselves, no real independence, nor even existence. They are ever only modes, vanishing phases of the one indivisible Spirit, which thus proves to be the one all-inclusive *Individual*. But the individual which is all-inclusive is by that very fact also *universal;* and as that universal in which all particularity is contained in vital, organic union it is precisely the one *individual Spirit* now seen to be *universal* through its own spontaneous self-differentiation or *self-particularization*.

While, therefore, the World-Energy negates its own abstract unity by self-separation into infinite manifoldness and particularity of existing and mutually exclusive forms, it also negates this very negation in the fact of showing itself to be the one sole substance of these infinitely manifold forms, thus binding them forever into one through what seem to be relations only of one to another, but which are seen to be in reality the system of the infinite self-relation of the all-creating One. All possible phases of multiplicity forever in process of coming forth from the one are equally in perpetual process of returning into the one in the sense of vanishing into the one universal substance. This is the central truth in that magnificent symbol of emanation and absorption. And it fairly represents the truth so far as the merely physical forms of existence are concerned, save that true science now recognizes that the vanishing of any given form is not its merging into the one universal Substance with the utter loss of all form or character. On the contrary, one form vanishes only as another arises. And the dissolution of one structure goes hand in hand with the integration of equally definite, though it may be more or less complex, forms.

It is thus alone, indeed, that change involving the existence of finite things is possible. But it is also precisely through this absolute interfusion of the positive and the negative phases of its activity that the World-Energy as spirit proves itself to be the genuine, concrete Infinite. By the positive exertion of itself as energy, it negates absolutely the abstract phase of infinitude implied in its mere self-identity, while through the fact of its perpétually self-emphasizing individuality as the truth of all multiplicity it negates the (logically) first negation, and shows itself to be possessed of true infinitude in the form of absolute, infinitely manifold self-reference or self-relation. Its self-affirmation is its self-negation. But its self-negation is its self-differentiation or self-realization, the process of unfolding its absolute, self-sufficing wholeness and self-dependence.

As self-particularized universality, and hence as absolutely concrete individuality, the absolute Spirit (which we have found the World-Energy to be) is, as we have just seen, absolutely self-sufficing, and hence spontaneous. It is a self-realizing system. It is thus in its very nature absolutely self-consistent. Its self-negation is such only in the sense of self-differentiation or self-realization. It is absolute self-affirmation.

But this it can be only as involving consciousness; for this is the very essence and truth of self-relation. As a perfect, self-realizing system, whose fundamental characteristic of spontaneity is in truth consciousness, then, the World-Energy as spirit is the absolute process of Reason unfolding itself into an infinite self-ordered world.

But even so the absolute self-consistency of this process seems to impose upon it a restraint. It *must* be so and not otherwise. It is, then, in its very perfection and self-consistency, the perfect expression of *necessity*. Absolute Reason is absolute Necessity. Only as changeless self-consistency, hence only as necessity, is it possible that reason should realize itself. And unrealized reason would of course not be reason, or *be* at all.

But thus Necessity as the fixed order and self-consistency of Reason is the indispensable basis of the realization of reason. And yet reason realized is without obstruction. For Reason is the essence and soul of all Reality. Whence it can be opposed by nothing but itself. But its own self-opposition is nothing else than the true equilibrium of its own self-consistency. It is thus, therefore, spontaneous and absolutely free. For Necessity, as we have seen, is nothing else than the changeless law of the self-consistency of Reason. In other words necessity, in so far as it has any positive meaning, is of the very essence of freedom, just as, on the other hand, freedom is the concrete truth of necessity. Necessity is the unalterable method of which Freedom is the actual fulfilment.*

d.—THE WORLD-ENERGY AS SELF-REALIZING REASON OR AS WILL.

On arriving at the conception of the World-Energy as spirit, the simplest phase of that conception was the first

---

* Here we arrive at the highest conception of equilibrium as foreshadowed in the *Laws of Motion.*

to formulate itself in our minds. On first view spirit seems a vague universality. It bears the contradictory aspect of an *abstract reality*. It appears abstract in so far as it is understood only in the vague sense of something exclusively supersensuous. It appears real so far as it presents the characteristics of a spontaneous power.

Now this spontaneity is precisely the characteristic which constitutes the *internality* of spirit. It is subjectivity; and it is this in the first place as infinite concentration within itself. In this sense spirit seems wholly non-material and to be merely a spontaneous power acting from without upon matter. It is infinite *impulse*, a wish or even mere vague presentiment.

And yet the internality of spirit is but one of its two necessarily complementary aspects or phases. The internal cannot be simply and solely internal. The subjective cannot be merely subjective. The internal in its very nature already involves external reference. The "internal" must be meaningless unless it be the internal of an "external." And this outward reference is precisely the measure of the reality of the internal.

Spirit, then, as being spontaneous energy, is essentially a self-externalizing internality. As subjective it proves to be self-objectifying. It makes itself its own object; or rather, as with each step of our inquiry it becomes ever clearer, the World-Energy as Spirit is the one infinite Subject for which there is and can be no other object than just itself.

The first phase of this self-externalization or self-objectifying of spirit which our developing consciousness seizes is, nevertheless, still a relatively abstract one. It is the phase in which spirit appears as unfolded in a *sys-*

tem. It is merely *formal* objectivity. And this formal objectivity first proves its completeness as the abstract system of *thought.* In this system, too, we have seen the fundamental characteristic to be that of absolute self-consistency. It is the spontaneity of spirit that proves to be in its highest term absolute Reason.

But this system of thought as merely formal is still predominantly subjective. In it spirit is as yet seen only as virtually or potentially objective. And, as we have seen, the truth of spirit, even as subjective, is measured absolutely by the degree in which it develops itself into substantial objectivity. The internal, let us repeat, is wholly without meaning save so far as there is a completely corresponding external. Nay, the internal, so far as it is real, already bears within itself its own complementary externality.

The World-Energy as spirit, then, proves once more to be not merely infinite internality as impulse, not merely infinite subjectivity as thought, but also absolutely spontaneous energy as infinitely self-realizing reason, or WILL. Through these three complementary phases the World-Energy as spirit unfolds itself as the infinite, unchanging, completely self-conscious process which constitutes the absolutely perfect personality of God. They are the three fundamental and absolutely correlated modes of the World-Energy now seen to be in its final analysis an absolutely spiritual energy.*

It is in the spontaneity of this divine World-Energy, then, that we discover at last the secret of all motion,

---

*A brief consideration of the Christian doctrine of the Trinity is withheld from this place and will appear in a succeeding volume under the title: "*God and Man.*" Of course the intimation given in the text is altogether inadequate in this respect.

and along with this the perfect assurance of the absolute and eternal conservation of energy in the full perfection of its vitality. The absolute equilibrium of energy looked to by physicists as in *process of culmination* is in reality an *eternally accomplished fact*. And the equilibrium, instead of being realized in a "dead universe," is seen to have its perpetual fulfilment in the infinite vitality of the divinely constituted Cosmos.

For in its truth the one possible equilibrium for the universe or cosmos is nothing else than the absolute self-poise of the divine World-Energy itself.

The central conception at which we have arrived in our investigation thus far, then, is this: That the truth of matter is force or energy; that the truth of energy is spirit, and that the truth of spirit is absolute Personality. God, then, is not a mysterious being apart from the world. On the contrary, He is the sole truth and self-unfolding Reality of the world. Hence, it is to be concluded that there is no "material" world apart from the spiritual. The truth is that the so-called material universe is but the out-putting, the utterance or outerance, the external mode, of the divine, spontaneous energy of Spirit. The world in space is nothing else than the external aspect of the world as Thought. It is the absolute Subject self-objectified. There is no reality but God. What we habitually call the "universe" is nothing else than the outer modes of his existence.

Thus, once more, does it appear that the laws of Thought are equally the laws of things, for things are but the objective forms or modes of Thought.

CHAPTER XXIII.

FUNDAMENTAL MODES OF MANIFESTATION OF THE WORLD-ENERGY AS SPIRIT.

WE have seen that the World-Energy is necessarily a self-consistent, self-unfolding *system*. We have now to indicate the chief fundamental phases involved in the process of actualization of that system. We have, indeed, already traced in outline the proofs that the World-Energy is the ultimate potentiality; and, as such, the primal *potency*. Nevertheless, it still hovers before our view rather as an abstract system than as a concrete totality.

And yet, that the World-Energy must be such concrete totality is evident from the fact (as previously indicated) that potentiality itself necessarily implies or presupposes the existence of a *potency* wholly equal to the realization of such potentiality. And the potency itself can be such only as active energy unfolding itself into concrete realization.

That realization, too, must in the nature of the case be complete so far as the potency is complete. The potency *is* only so far as it is actively unfolded. Hence, the realization of the totality of existence *as totality* must forever *be*. It cannot possibly become or enter into existence, out of non-existence, nor could it ever have been in process of becoming. Though all becoming is involved in it, it could never itself have been involved in becoming.

To remind ourselves of this betimes is of the greater moment, as neglect of the distinction is almost certain to involve us in the confusion of assuming the identity of two radically distinct orders of relation. The one is the logical order, the other the chronological. It is one of the conditions of human thought that it can only trace out successively the various degrees in the logical order of relations necessarily unfolded in the concrete totality of the World-Energy. And we are led on almost inevitably to assume that this chronological order in the development of our own consciousness of the world or universe as a whole coincides with a chronological order in the development of the universe itself. In other words, we mistake the becoming or process of development in our own consciousness for the becoming of the total sum of Reality. And this false impression is strengthened by our observation of the chronological order of development in which we see all finite things to be involved. And yet this is to assume that, just as our consciousness of the nature of creation unfolds in time, so creation itself must have unfolded in time. Whereas, to repeat once more, though change, and time as the form of change, are involved in the total creation, yet creation itself is not involved in time and change. In the concrete, changeless Totality of things all possible phases of change are forever present, and thus time as merely the abstract form of change is completely subordinated and merged in, as nothing else than one of the modes of, the eternal Whole.

Similarly, as shown in the introductory chapter, space

is the mere abstract form of externality. So far as spirit externalizes itself, so far it must adapt itself to or make use of space-relations; or rather, the truth is, that in externalizing itself, spirit gives rise to space-relations.

On the other hand, spirit, as such, possesses modes of activity wholly independent of space-relations. When thought concentrates upon itself and investigates its own more complex properties and powers, it is thus far engaged in a process that has no reference to space at all. Whence space, equally with time, proves to be but a subordinate mode of the spirit's activity. Only the less adequate phases of spirit present themselves in the externality of the world in space; though these phases, of course, belong none the less essentially to the complete realization of Spirit as the truth of the world.

To these phases we now turn with the purpose of indicating the fundamental relations involved in them. And first in regarding the World-Energy as simple potency, we seize upon the characteristic of universality involved in that energy, and hold fast to that characteristic as its truth.

As potency, however, it must act. And as universal potency, it must specialize, or differentiate, or determine itself in particular forms of reality. But this particularization or differentiation is necessarily a self-separation—a *self-repulsion*. The universal Potency gives proof of itself as such by *externalizing* itself. That is, the simplest phase of its self-realization is that of externality, that of space-filling forms.

But as universal, the potency is not a special, limited, particular fact. On the contrary, as universal potency, it is primarily, in its simplest relation to space, *everywhere present*. Whence its self-externalization does not consist in its expanding itself outward from some special center in space until it becomes indefinitely diffused through space. It does not go out into space from some *where* that is yet *not in space*. Rather its logically first (that is, simplest) relation to space is its universal occupancy of space. Its *externalization* consists in its unfolding special forms of existence from its own internality; that is, from its own subjectivity or spontaneity. And primarily subjectivity or spontaneity is Spirit in that sphere of relations which is wholly independent of space-relations, and hence, thus far cannot be rightly thought of as located in, or in any way related to, space at all. Thus internality is here a term equivalent to subjectivity or spontaneity. And this is in strict truth its *only* meaning. As ordinarily applied, it represents a vanishing, wholly illusive element. For, as regards space-related objects, it is only necessary to penetrate to the internal in them in order to prove that "internal" to be wholly external; and this to infinity.

The internal, then, is not the infinite energy of the universe focused in some point in space (and *hence nonexistent*) but rather it is the essence or truth of things, the spontaneity of spirit, the logically first phase of the realization of which, as just indicated, is the universal occupancy of space. The world of internality or of thought unfolds itself, in its own less adequate phases, as the world of externality or the world of things in space.

The self-externalization of the Absolute as Spirit, then, presents the infinitely extended as its (logically) first phase. The internal in its self-realization proves to be also external. The absolute Subject in its own self-externalization makes itself absolute *object*. The internal and the external, subject and object, are in their ultimate and absolute significance complementary and completely interfused phases of the one infinite fact, the one eternal deed, the absolute actuality of the divine Reason forever revealed to Intelligence, whether creating or created, in the infinite process of the universe.

Thus, the universal Potency as self-objectifying thought fills infinite space and everywhere meets only with itself. Its self-externalization is thus at the same time a return to and collision with itself. And the tremor of this collision is the logically first (or simplest) phase of the infinite heart-beat of the universe. It is *centrality* infinitely diffused, and hence, everywhere present. As has often been said, the circumference of the universe is nowhere; its center is everywhere.

It is from this infinite diffusion of centrality that infinitely manifold lines of differentiation result. Thus the universal Potency specializes itself into endlessly varied particular forms. That is, particular forms arise only as the manifestation of the universal Potency; and it is at once evident that each form is adequate only to the partial manifestation of the universal Potency, which must therefore continue itself and complete its own manifestation through still other forms.

The Universal is thus far indifferent to the perpetuation of this or that particular form. Rather, as the continuous Reality of which the particular forms are but the discrete phases, its activity must result in the fusing of form with form. In other words, the dissolution of one series of forms is involved in the integration of others. Each particular form as inadequate to the complete expression or manifestation of the universal Potency is riven within itself, dissolves and passes into other phases of the manifestation of that Potency.

Thus the universal Potency, as the *unchanging Totality*, gives rise through its own activity to *ceaseless change*. Hence, it might be said that the one changeless fact is the infinitely complex fact of change. And this is doubtless what Aristotle meant by the phrase: "The unmoved mover of the world."

The particularized form is, within its limits, a manifestation, an utterance or outerance of the inner universality of the World-Energy. It is an object. But with its limitations it is an object among other objects. All these objects are, however, but the discrete phases of the universal or continuous totality. They are thus far in a state of likeness and equilibrium or rest as toward each other. They bear toward each other, therefore, a twofold relation, a relation at once positive and negative. As imperfect but mutually complementary phases of the manifestation of the totality they attract and tend towards fusion, the actual accomplishment of which must involve the dissolution of each and every existing form. But each is at the same time in some measure the actual manifestation of the universal potency or World-Energy. And this is the ground of its existence, more or less prolonged, as a distinct and seemingly independent unit. It is precisely as the manifestation or present realization of the universal potency, indeed, that these particularized forms possess the power of self-preservation even momentarily. And this power is developed as cohesion within the given unit on the one hand, and on the other as resistance to and hence exclusion of other units.

In one respect then, this relation of mutual exclusion is one of independence and *individuality* on the part of the particularized phases of the universal potency. So that even with the least adequate phase of its development, individuality shows itself to be the vital fusion of universality and particularity.

In another respect, however, it appears here as something determined or given explicit existence through external agencies. So that, while in its character of an explicit realization or manifestation of the universal potency it possesses validity and independence; yet as being only a partial, inadequate realization of that potency, it proves to be wanting in validity and hence to be quite dependent.

Such is the contradiction inherent at every stage in the finite individual. The contradiction varies in degree and yet never wholly disappears.

It is essential to note further, indeed, that with the initial stage in which we are here considering it, individuality is rather a premonition than a realization; though as being the incipient stage of realization, it is especially important that it should be observed and properly characterized. Indeed, individuality can be properly understood only by tracing the dialectic of its development from that stage where it is indistinguishable from mere particularity as a simple mode of universality to that stage in which it is seen to be the concrete and absolute fulfilment of universality in its total significance as the divine individual, the "absolute, divine Spirit," as Aristotle named it.

A particularized phase of the universal potency, then, so far as it has attained to the semblance of individuality and independence, already presents itself as a definite object. But such object is already concentrated upon itself and presents the semblance of internality which here is *centrality*. The object gathers or collects itself about its own center. At the same time, as being but a partial manifestation of the total energizing principle it is necessarily related through that principle to other manifestations thereof—that is, to other objects. What the one object lacks the other possesses. They are therefore complementary phases of the same totality. Hence, each not only collects itself about its own center but also, in its complementary reference to other objects, finds its center also in each one of them and in turn proves to be a center for each and all other objects.

Thus, *centrality* is seen to be the primary form assumed by the phase of *unity* throughout the total development of the universal potency or World-Energy. It is thus, too, that sphericity presents itself as the natural, necessary form in the primary aggregations of matter.

But the World-Energy as Reason must in its self-objectification take on all rational forms. Whence, in the first place, the development of the other and more complex regular solids through the process of crystallization.

In all these phases of aggregation, however, it is to be observed that there is change of external form without marked alteration of internal character. Hence, the process is thus far apparently altogether external and *mechanical.*

And yet, the characteristic of externality presents a still further significant phase already incidentally noticed. It is this: Each particular object as being but a partial, one-sided manifestation of the universal potency exhibits a relation of dependence upon other objects. Each lacks what another has, and has what the other lacks. And precisely for this reason must their fused union approximate toward an equilibrated total.

This is exhibited qualitatively in the tension toward such fusion as that arising from what is usually known under the name *affinity*. It is evident that the resultant or product of affinity must present characteristics radically different from those exhibited in either of the one-sided phases or "elements" between which the affinity exists.

It is well worth noting, too, that the very fact of affinity with all its complexity of development completely negates the assumption that the "elements" are "simple." And, not only so, but in their manifold combinations these "elements" become wholly unrecognizable. The truth is, indeed, that it is only in their compounds that the elements attain their full realization. Their "affinity" for each other, so long as they are held asunder, is their potentiality. The compound formed by their combination is that potentiality developed to real potency. And to form some approximate conception of the marvelously complex potentiality of the so-called elements, one need only trace out the multiple and extremely varied oxides; or glance through a volume giving the amazingly manifold series of known carbon compounds, and then reflect that in no two cases is the "affinity"—the action and reaction—of precisely the same degree, and hence that in no two cases are the resultants of precisely the same character.

And here we have a premonition or even elementary phase of *spontaneity* developing in the space-world. The internal shows itself to be ever spontaneously developing itself to externality. Similarly the external, as being itself but the outer phase of the internal, proves to be completely pervaded with or characterized by internality. Affinity shows itself to be primarily the tension toward union between two oppositely characterized elements. And the affinity of these for each other gives them the appearance of exhibiting choice or preference. For while they show tension for or toward one another, they prove themselves to be, at least relatively, indifferent toward other elements.

True, this is only formal and even mechanical choice. And in this fact, indeed, is shown the fundamental identity (that is, identity in *kind*) of chemical action with mechanical action. At the same time the preference does here present itself; though it is also to be observed that this is the most external phase of recognizable internality beyond that of centrality in general. The principle of "chemism" appears with far profounder import in sexual tension, even as this is manifest in the vegetable kingdom, and still more in the animal kingdom; while its most elevated sphere of manifestation, where it is revealed as genuine internality, is found in the love and friendship existing between pure and noble minds. At the same time, no really thoughtful mind would for a moment allow the abstract identity here apparent, under the form of continuity of principle, to obscure the enormous difference in degree requiring in the higher sphere quite other categories than that of "chemism," or mere "affinity."

Indeed, this leads quite out of the sphere of externality and dependence and brings us face to face with the internal and spontaneous. And the question very properly arises whether we have not here the real solution of the question of "final causes."

The answer to this question in its universal character was reached, indeed, at an earlier stage of our inquiry, when the general question of causality was under consideration. Here, however, the question presents itself as to the adaptation of means to ends, as exhibited in the physical world.

First of all, it is evident that the results arrived at in nature, show plan or method, and therefore, purpose. This cannot be reasonably denied. But that plan and purpose are imposed upon nature by some power external to nature is a view which the whole course of the preceding argument tends absolutely to refute. Nature, or the external world, is, as we have seen, nothing else than the externalization or outerance of the internal world which is otherwise to be named Spirit. The purposing, planning Intelligence, proofs of the activity of which appear at every turn, is precisely the inner, vital principle which, instead of applying itself upon a world of externality already at hand, unfolds *itself* in a world of externality which is thus nothing else than Spirit thus far self-realized in the forms of the space-world.

The plan of the world, the "established order" which Mr. Spencer recognizes as a necessary phase of the totality of existence, is nothing else than the perfect method of the divine Spirit, whose eternal activity exhibits, necessarily, the two absolutely balanced and complementary phases of involution and evolution—of an infinite internality which is forever completely unfolded in the infinitely manifold world-in-space.

Whence, once more, the universe can never grow old nor decay. The absolute, eternal process, of which the "universe" itself is but the outer form and revelation, preserves the whole in perennial vigor, transforming death into life, and decay into renewed youth. For the Process which preserves is itself the Whole which is preserved.

Evidently, too, in this all-comprising process the "plan" could not be first deliberated upon and then put in execution—the "world" being formed and then left to fulfil the complex divine Purpose, running on by mere "physical" energy until it fulfils the plan, runs down and collapses into nonentity or mere wastes of equilibrated but "useless" energy. On the contrary, if the foregoing argument has led to any result, it is that creation is the eternal vital fact or deed; that the divine Spirit is the truth and sole substance of the world, and that, apart from this, there is absolutely nothing. Were the divine Energy for a moment to cease its activity, the world must that instant vanish utterly.

On the other hand, the divine Spirit itself, as absolute energy, bears in its own nature the absolute necessity of activity. For energy is real only as active. The very law of the conservation of energy presupposes this. Thus God is everywhere revealed before our eyes. And if we fail to behold Him it is because we are blind, and not because He is hidden. The pantheism of antiquity, in which all is God, is replaced by the pantheism of Christianity, in which God is all and (therefore) in all.

Des Cartes was right in saying that the same power

required to create a world is also necessary to its preservation. For "creation" and "preservation" are but different names for one and the same eternal deed. Thus, all "final causes" coalesce into the one eternal purpose of the self-realization of the divine Reason. So that once more the Final Cause is simply the absolute method by which the Primal Cause forever works, and in its consistent working preserves its own absolute equilibrium at the same time that it creatively preserves its own eternally complete self-realization.

All "causes" then, are but the partially understood phases of the one absolute self-cause, or self-existent Substance, as Spinoza defines it. This is the true teleological principal which has been coming into more and more explicit utterance throughout the present discussion.

There remains to be considered the process of the development of life as one of the fundamental modes of manifestation of the World-Energy as spirit. But to this we must devote a separate chapter.

CHAPTER XXIV.

EVOLUTION OF LIFE-FORMS.

IT has been shown that the sole sufficient cause of all movement and of all reality is to be found in the spontaneity of the absolute divine Spirit. We have also seen that as spontaneity the divine Spirit is absolute internality or subjectivity.

But subjectivity and internality are themselves one-sided terms. Neither can have any meaning save in connection with its correlative. The inner apart from the outer, the subjective apart from the objective, could be nothing else than a pure abstraction of our own finite thought. At the present stage of our inquiry all this has grown familiar. The subjective, in its ultimate significance, is now understood to be the energizing principle which is ever unfolding itself into all forms of objective reality.

This principle, then, is itself absolute Vitality; and, as such, it must from its very nature unfold into all phases of reality belonging thereto. As already seen, it involves within its own nature the necessity of self-externalization in the mechanical and chemical relations of the world in space. The first phase of recoil from this merely outward tendency is seen in centrality, the second in affinity, or chemism in its wider acceptation. We now come to inquire what must be the next fundamental stage.

Centrality in the world of external forms, let us remember, is energy directed toward a given point. It is itself, therefore, a tendency toward the annulment of the extended. For the strain toward the center manifest in the external is in reality a tendency toward the annulment of externality. And this is but to state in its dialectic form the conception often repeated that, were attraction to act without restraint, it must concentrate all matter in a point. In other words, it must reduce the extended to the non-extended.

The abstractness of such view is thus rendered apparent. In all genuine reality there is necessarily action and reaction. Either phase without the other, as already sufficiently shown, must be wholly impossible.

At the same time centrality, however abstract a characteristic when taken simply by itself, is still an essential phase of every specialized unit. In its simplest form it is *external internality*. The parts of an extended unit are grouped *around* the center. They are therefore side by side with and thus external to the center; whence, conversely, the center, considered in relation to the parts singly, is also external to them.

Thus the purely physical center has, after all, no true internality—of which, as already remarked, the world in space, as such, affords absolutely no genuine instance. And yet, at the same time, the center of an object in space shows the first phase of tendency in the external toward internality; though in the object, as physical object merely, the tendency must of course remain unrealized.

In affinity, on the other hand, the external already exhibits a true phase of internality. The elements entering into a compound have not merely served as centers for one another while remaining external and qualitatively indifferent to each other. On the contrary, they have become completely fused. Each thus becomes internal to the other, while yet it remains external. Hence, their fused unity presents the realized possibilities of both within the range of their mutual relation, and the compound thus appears as something wholly new in its qualitative character.*

And yet even here the new relation is no sooner established than activity, as producing further change of relation between the elements thus combined, falls into abeyance; or rather, it remains only as preserving the balance of relations, and so resisting further change. What has been accomplished appears to be nothing else than the production of a state of indifference or equilibrium— a mere dead result (typical, it would seem, of a prospectively "dead universe"). And one begins once more to inquire with not unnatural concern, whether, indeed, such dead result is, after all, the ultimatum of the results to be produced by the spontaneous energy of the primal cause of things.

But here it is to be observed again that this spontaneous energy is, from its very nature, incessant in its activity; from which fact it could hardly be inferred that a mere dead result is ever to follow. Besides, the permanence of the chemical compound in any given case is largely a question of *relative* affinity. Let another element appear, having for either of those in the compound an affinity stronger than that between those of which the

---

* As already intimated, we can really *know* an element only by tracing it through all its relations, as actually exhibited in the compounds formed by its union with other elements.

compound is constituted, and at once the compound is reduced, and another and different one is formed.

Thus the internality exhibited in affinity is still characterized by externality. The two phases seem ever to be held asunder—whence internality is found to be thus far external to externality. And we have seen that the truth of internality is in its own continuous unfolding of itself into externality. The internal is to become external, not by being violently held in isolation from the external, but through its own free, ceaseless self-evolution into external forms.

But this fusion of the internal and the external in a *continuous process* is *life*. The object possessing life exhibits centrality and also affinity; but both these are definitely subordinated in the life-process constituting the living object itself.

More precisely, centrality, in the very process of its subordination, undergoes development into higher form; for it now appears not so much as an abstract "within" respecting the mere space-relations of the "body" through which life is manifested, but rather as the spontaneity or inner impulse which appears in each and every part of every living body. And this impulse, as the spontaneous effort toward self-preservation, is manifestly also *affinity*, now appearing under the form of a *continuous process*. Even here it is worth noticing that the term "affinity" no longer suffices. The more complex aspect of the process requires its own special category; and the one here appropriate is the familiar name, "assimilation." Whence centrality and affinity prove not merely to belong to the dead externality of "mere matter," but also to have their place in the realm of life as phases of one and the same process—the process of life itself.

It is evident, then, that the same activity of the one all-comprising World-Energy, according to the degree of complexity of that activity, gives rise alike to "atoms," to "molecules," to crystalline forms, and to the "*zöon*," or object possessing life. If "matter" means "substance," and if substance in turn means the divine World-Energy, then matter does indeed contain the "promise and potency" of all life, terrestrial or other. Similarly, the question whether the true theory of the origin of life is that of "Biogenesis," or that of "Abiogenesis," is evidently based upon a complete misconception of the nature of the case. Life can assuredly come only from the living. But the "living" is primarily the World-Energy itself as absolute Vitality. Thus following next upon centrality and affinity, the elementary forms of life are found to constitute but the next grade in advance of the simplest developments of the characteristic of internality or spontaneity, as that characteristic is ever unfolding in the forms of the world in space. Evidently, therefore, they belong to the (logically) first stages of the return movement from externality to internality in the total process of creative activity, which the World-Energy forever constitutes. For the external itself—the whole of space-filling reality—as we must constantly remind ourselves, is nothing else than the internal self-externalized—the spontaneous continually expanding itself into the inert, only to gather itself once more through endlessly varying degrees into spontaneity again.

Abiogenesis in the literal sense of the term is absurd, seeing that aside from life and its manifestations there is absolutely *nothing*. Out of so-called inanimate nature doubtless life does constantly arise. But this must ever presuppose the World-Energy as the total divine Life-Process which gives itself outer manifestation through all the forms of nature. Doubtless spontaneous generation does perpetually take place in the sense that everywhere through all the universe the mechanical and chemical relations of energy in the physical aspect of existence grade insensibly into, and in their higher ranges of complexity constitute, the relations of energy which are known under the name of physical life.

But this conception of life coming from the not-living must forever remain infinitely self-contradictory, unless it is explicitly recognized that physical force, as such, is absolutely unthinkable otherwise than as the external mode of the internal, spontaneous World-Energy which constitutes the truth of all reality, and which, in its highest aspect, is the one absolute, divine Spirit.* We cannot too often remind ourselves of the absolute unity and continuity of the total world or universe in all its modes. This is one fundamental aspect. The other and complementary aspect is that of the infinite multiplicity

*The beginner in philosophy is apt to stumble over the word "thinkable" because he confounds *thinking* with *imagining*. In reality one can *think* only the consistent, the rational. He can *imagine* any monstrosity. One can really think only relations, and truly think only rational relations. To think adequately is to think groups of relations as constituting totalities, and ultimately, to think the universe as the absolute totality of all relations. Though I must hasten to add, for the comfort of readers likely to be shocked by such expressions, that by the phrase: "to think the universe," I mean no more than this: To so far pursue in thought the nature of relation as to recognize the necessity of all relations being comprised in a Totality which is organic in its very constitution—a Totality which is active and whose activity is in accordance with an "established order." This, I must also add, may be, and is, done in degrees of adequacy widely different. Need it be still further added that the genuine thinker will be constantly advancing to greater degrees of adequacy in his estimate of this Totality?

and variety into which this absolute unity unfolds itself. The continuous, let us repeat, does not exclude the discrete. On the contrary, the discrete is a necessary mode of the continuous. Hence, physical energy, chemical energy, vital force or energy, and the energy of reason or of will, are all only so many modes, so many degrees, in and of one and the same total, divine World-Energy.

And now let us observe that in the physical aggregation about a center, in the chemical compound, and in the living unit, we have in each case alike a limited unit. But there is this difference, that in the first class of units, so far as they are regarded as mere aggregations of the extended, division may be carried to any degree without change in the character of the unit; while in the second class mechanical division with the same result may be carried as far as the "molecule," but can be carried no further without changing the character of the unit; and finally, in the third class division means in general the death of the living being, which is a result quite different from the mere division itself. In the first case any given quantity of matter is a totality wholly indifferent to division (though even here a crystal proves an exception as, doubtless, ultimately does every "particle" of matter). In the second case a given quantity of matter, so far from being an indifferent totality, is known to have a perfectly definite limit, beyond which, if division is carried, the character of the unit is radically changed. In the third case any division threatens the existence of the unit.

And yet here a most significant exception presents itself. The living being, as we have seen, is itself a *process*. Here, indeed, is found the radical distinction between the organic and the inorganic unit. The latter is also constituted by a process. But in order that the unit may be preserved, the process through which it came into existence must cease. This is conspicuously true in case either of a crystal or of a chemical compound. On the other hand, the organic unit, instead of being preserved, is at once destroyed by the cessation of the process by which it came into existence as an organic unit. The functions which constitute it as a living unit must continue without interruption in order to preserve its existence as a living unit. Thus its parts are in more or less pronounced degree members or organs, each of which has a necessary function in the total complex process which the animal itself may alike be said to constitute and to be constituted by. Hence the removal of any of its members so far deranges the process, or stops the process altogether. And in any case the severed member, in the very fact of its severance, at once loses the characteristic process of life and speedily dissolves into merely mechanical and chemical units. Thus the division of the living unit results necessarily in death, partial or total. Death is, indeed, an aspect necessarily involved in life. And it is so in this way: The functional efficiency of this or that portion of matter included in the organism ceases. By that fact such portion becomes separated from the organism, and in its separation loses its organic character. That is, it "dies." And this "dying" of parts within the organism must continue so long as the organism continues to live; that is, so long as it continues to be an organism.

The apparent exceptions which the cases of gemmation, and especially of fission, offer to the rule that division of the organism means death in whole or in part, occur only in the less complex forms of life, where the life-principle itself is still diffuse, and hence presents the characteristic of externality in so marked a degree that division of the form does not of necessity result in the destruction of vitality in either of the separated parts. Different from this in degree, rather than in kind, is the separation of the germ, as well as of the offspring, from the parent in the higher forms of life.

Again, the internality of life is, as we have indicated, in the first place mere impulse. The specialized living being is a limited unit. It is therefore dependent, and stands in necessary relations with the specialized objects of the external world, in the midst of which it exists. But as itself a process, and as at the same time dependent upon the world-process surrounding and including it, the living unit must constantly adjust itself to its environment. And its impulse toward such adjustment is the phase of spontaneity or subjectivity which it has unfolded.

At the same time, this characteristic of spontaneity presents also a passive phase. It is the relatively automatic response which the living being makes to the exertion upon it, in any way, of force from without. This is the quality of "sensitiveness" or "irritability," which is exhibited in self-preservation—the struggle for immediate existence on the part of the individual—and in reproduction, whereby the existence of the species is secured. The degree in which the life of even the higher orders of animals is limited to these relatively mechanical aspects, is far beyond what seems commonly supposed. It can hardly be doubted, by one who carefully considers the subject, that the "intelligence" of the lower animals is enormously overestimated, as is also their sensibility. The facts brought to light in biological investigations appear to justify, in great measure, the Cartesian view that the animal organism is an automaton.

It is to be noted further, indeed, that the living unit as thus far considered is merely one example of a particular type or species. As such it is essentially limited in its possibilities of development. And this implies that all the various phases of growth involved in its nature must be completed within a limited period. Whence it appears that the destiny of such living unit is to fulfil the total round of functions of which it is capable, and, even in so doing, to bring to an end its own separate existence.

And yet, though from its very nature, the individual living (animal) unit must undergo dissolution, it is evident, on the other hand, that the very process constituting such unit also involves its own perpetuation as type or species. Though the individual dies, the species survives.

Such is the general conclusion respecting the physically constituted living unit. We have next to inquire a little more in detail as to the process of development of such living units.

CHAPTER XXV.

FURTHER CONSIDERATIONS AS TO THE EVOLUTION OF LIFE-FORMS.

FROM what has developed thus far, it would seem that "origin" is a word which can have meaning only locally. The total World-Energy is a process which is perfect, eternal, unchanging. As such, all possible change, including the complementary aspects of beginning and ceasing, is perpetually involved in the World-Energy. Creation, in its totality, is the one eternal Fact. It is in the manifold aspects of Creation that change appears. And since time is the form of change, it is only in the manifold aspects of Creation that time has any reality.

Evidently, too, it is the aspect of change that must be the first to appeal to finite minds.* Hence it is that in all cosmogonies Creation has been figured as taking place in time, and, therefore, as having a beginning. Even Mr. Spencer represents Evolution as a time-process, and only guardedly indicates that were it possible to really conceive the "Unknowable" in its totality, it could be conceived only as eternal.

Of course, if one has made an open profession of the religion of agnosticism, he must, if he would be at all

---

* "Mind," as such, is infinite in its very nature. Each individual created mind is finite in respect of the degree in which it has realized this infinite ideal nature common to all minds.

consistent, make at least occasional confession that there really are limits to his present actual knowledge; though it is not so easy to see why he should feel bound to assert as something already certainly known that there are absolute barriers beyond which knowledge can never go. It may be further remarked that if agnosticism means simply that no human being is at any given moment omniscient, doubtless all except the insane are, have always been, and must ever be agnostics.

It is a curious fact, too, that agnosticism itself does not prevent some of its votaries from taking up and attempting to solve certain problems sometimes declared to be insoluble. Among these is the problem of the origin of life. And attempts in this direction have been made in quite characteristic fashion; that is, by observation and experiment. Serious, ingeniously planned, and prolonged work has been performed in the laboratory with the hope of artificially producing, if not a *homunculus*, at least a *protogenes*.

Thus far, however, from all experimenters (except, perhaps, one or two suspected of being more eager than painstaking) there comes the somewhat disheartening report that no really positive results have been attained. And the reports are the more disheartening since organic matter has been presupposed (that is, it has been actually present) in these very experiments.

Not, indeed, that there have been no encouraging signs. On the contrary, more and more complex compounds have been built up, and these approach more and more nearly to, not merely organic, but even to really organized matter.

It is important to observe, too, that the very nature of the experiments seems to suggest a doubt as to whether it is at all likely that there should ever be perfectly reproduced in a test-tube the entire complex of conditions precedent to the transition of inorganic into organic matter, even though such conditions actually exist in nature as a whole. It is also worthy of note that even apparent success on the part of the experimenter must evidently be, if not neutralized, at least greatly discredited, by the fact that he has made use of organic matter in his very attempt to demonstrate the development of the organic from the inorganic. On the other hand, it is equally evident that failure on the part of the experimenter can never prove that the actual transition of inorganic into organic matter is impossible in nature. Until man can manipulate nature as a whole in his experiments, he can never be justified in making empirically grounded assertions as to what is impossible in nature as a whole.

At the same time, as the whole argument of the present volume has tended to show, all nature is nothing else than the manifold expression of the World-Energy as Spirit. That is, Nature as a whole is but the outer, organic aspect of the perfect Thought. Only as such can it be rightly understood; that is, *understood* at all.

But, now, what follows? Nothing less, it seems to me, than the complete reconciliation (already pointed out) of the two opposing views as to the origin of life. Biogenesis, the theory that life can come only from the living, finds its full justification in the fact that all nature is instinct with the Life of the World-Energy—

is, in fact, as we have seen, nothing else than the outer, organic aspect of that Life. From which it is evident that the difference between organic and inorganic matter is merely one of degree. Thus the theory of Abiogenesis, the theory that life may come from the not-living, is itself but a special aspect of Biogenesis in the wider sense of the latter term.

There is, then, nothing contradictory in the thought that organisms not only arose, but are forever arising, out of "inorganic" matter. For inorganic matter itself, when seen in its vital relation within the Universe as a whole, consists of nothing else than the more elementary of the infinitely manifold thought-forms constituting the Universe. Looked at in this way, it is evident that nature tends inevitably to unfold into the more adequate thought-forms which we know as organisms. Thus we arrive at what may be called an organic view of nature as constituting the elementary phase of the vital, and, in its total range, forever self-equal process of creation. Whence it would seem that the transition of inorganic into organic matter is itself a ceaseless aspect of the eternal process of Creation. Doubtless in the evolution of each planet, where the conditions rendering life possible are reached at all, there is a definite moment * of transition from not-living matter to living matter; while at the same time, in the creative process as a whole, that "moment" is eternalized in the ceaseless evolution of worlds.

Instead, therefore, of resenting the work of such men as Spencer, and Darwin and Haeckel, and angrily declaring them to be undermining all grounds of faith while

---

* The "moment" being continuous so long as the conditions favorable to such transition continue to be the same anywhere on the given planet.

engaged in the mad effort to run down an *ignis fatuus,* it would seem wiser to note what there is of truth in their work, and to gladly accept it as opening up to us a wider view of creation as the infinitely complex, but absolutely organic Process of the self-revelation of the divine World-Energy. If these men have themselves stopped short of seeing the full significance of their own discoveries, that surely is no ground for withholding our glad and grateful acceptance of the aspects of truth which those discoveries unfold. So far, indeed, from proving that the conception of creation is a false conception, their work really turns out to be on the contrary an improved calculus, enabling us to attain a clearer and more adequate estimate of the infinite range and faultless method of creation.

Crude in many ways, doubtless, this improved calculus still is. The discoverer is such precisely through his attainment to a new attitude as toward the Truth. He is in part, but not wholly, prepared to receive the stronger and more varied light with which this new attitude of his brings him face to face. Hence is it that while his vision is extended and clarified to a degree more or less marvelous to his contemporaries, it is afterward seen that with this sudden access of light he was also partly or wholly blinded to certain aspects of the general truth which he was the first to clearly recognize in its larger characteristics.

The discoverers in the special field of Evolution could not be expected to prove exceptions to this general rule. Intent mainly upon the empirical evidences of the actual evolution of the earth and of the organic forms inhabiting the earth, it is hardly surprising that for a time at least the question of the ultimate Cause involved in the process of evolution should seem to them too remote and shadowy to have in it the promise of any positive solution; though, as we have seen, Mr. Spencer is too much a philosopher to stop short of at least an intimation of the fact that there lies in the human mind the necessity of considering and attempting to solve that ultimate problem.

Darwin, on the other hand, deliberately held aloof from this problem; and it can hardly be doubted that in this he did wisely. He had attempted a special task which must tax to the utmost even his exceptional powers for a lifetime. And this task could be performed while yet the larger problem was relatively in abeyance. Nevertheless, so long as the larger problem of Evolution in its universal aspects remained but partly resolved, or was left out of account in the consideration of the special problem of organic evolution, this latter problem itself could not but prove insoluble in its most elementary as well as in its most complex phases. Variation in typical forms might be accounted for while yet the beginnings of life, as well as the culminating aspects of life, still remained to all appearance inexplicable.

And yet it is this fact, as it seems to me, which more than any other has caused the Darwinian theory to be persistently regarded by many as something purely hypothetical and even fanciful, in spite of the overwhelming accummulation of empirical evidence showing that specific types have always been unstable, and that there has been actual transition of inferior types into superior types through continued variations,— these variations being due in ever-increasing degree to the spontaneity of function in the organism, though primarily such function must have received its definiteness of direction from the "environment."

What is of special significance here is, that so long as the environment was regarded as merely an aggregate of physical forces, it was impossible to avoid a feeling that somehow the difficulty which presented itself in face of the new view respecting the origin of Life, and even of the variations of structure and of function in organisms, had received little more than a mythical treatment. It is, in fact, only when we come to regard the physical world as itself but the outer mode of the spiritual, only when we come to regard "things" as nothing more nor less than the expression of thought (aspects, that is, of the perfect Thought which constitutes the Method of Creation), that the "environment" assumes a really intelligible character.* For then in any given case the "environment" itself must appear to us as nothing else and nothing less than a more or less complex phase in the concrete unfolding of the divine creative Energy, conformity to the Method of which means increased adequacy of life; antagonism with which means and can only mean degradation of life; continued antagonism with which can mean nothing less than final extinction; that is, the utter dissolution of the organism as organism.

It is in and through the World-Energy, then, that whatever of Life we know or can ever hope to know must have its origin. In other words, Life comes from the living and, from this point of view, it can come from nothing else.

* In fact, we can really *think* nothing else than *thought*. And when we think out the "laws of nature," those laws are by that very fact proven to be nothing else than modes of thought.

But doubtless also any living unit can originate only in conformity with the Method of the World-Energy, a Method which has already been shown in the present volume to be the Method of Reason. It is, in fact, no other than that Method of which scientists have for a long time been so industriously and successfully tracing out the rudimentary aspects under the name of the "Laws of Nature." It is that Method the logical order of which is vaguely intimated in the now hackneyed phrase, "from the simple to the complex." In other words, the Method of the World-Energy presents itself to us as the absolute Method of Evolution, in which creation takes place with unfailing logical sequence. Everywhere there is absolute order, unbending law. Any degree of complexity in a given unit, whether organic or inorganic, necessarily presupposes that such unit has come to be what it is only by a progressive development, the stages of which have a fixed order. And such unit can attain to any further degree of complexity only by passing through a further series of stages equally unalterable in their serial relation. Nature leaps no chasms, only because "Nature" is but the outer manifestation of Reason. And just as Nature is the outer form of Reason, so Reason is the inner substance, the vital principle of Nature. It is to the Totality of which these are the complementary aspects that I have applied the term World-Energy, and by which I mean: the one Substance, the primal Cause, the *Logos*, "without which was not anything made that hath been made."

But if Nature is to be regarded as but the more elementary aspect of the *Word*; that is, the outer form or expression, of the *Logos* or divine Reason, then there is nothing to forbid, rather there is everything to encourage, the view that each more complex species of organism arose by development from a less complex species, and this in turn from a species still less complex, and so on until we reach the limit of simplicity in the organic world and discover it to be a primal type of units without specialized organs, and distinguished from inorganic matter only in possessing the characteristics of "irritability" and "contractility." And by "irritability" we can scarcely understand anything else to be meant than the most rudimentary phase of the inner quality of self-movement; while "contractility" can hardly mean anything else than the most rudimentary phase of the outer expression of self-movement, or life.

Nor can we, as it seems to me, without ceasing to really think, resist the further logical conclusion that just as all more complex organisms on each inhabited sphere must have descended from a primal type of units that, though organic, were yet not organized; so these latter units themselves arose out of the most complex phase of inorganic matter; which in turn must have developed from the commingling of still simpler elements in the laboratory of nature—however impossible it may be to verify all this in a test-tube.

Thus it appears that we may, with equal truth, declare both that Life comes from the living, and that it comes from the not-living. For, while on the one hand, the particular units of the inorganic world which come to be aggregated into an organism are not themselves living units, yet, on the other hand, it is never to be forgotten that they have no existence save as modes of manifestation of the Life of the total World-Energy. Looked at in its merely physical aspects, this is doubtless a purely mechanical view of nature;* while, on the other hand, we are equally justified in saying that "in our study of natural objects we are approaching the thoughts of the Creator, reading his conceptions, interpreting a system that is his and not ours."†

The following further suggestions are added as possible clews to the more precise interpretation of organic evolution. The first suggestion is: That wherever the environment or complex of natural conditions is the same it could hardly be but that the same organic type should be developed. And this not merely on one planet, but on any planet, whatever its location in space. So also, on the other hand, wherever the conditions vary, the organic type developed must vary in corresponding degree. And since the World-Energy can be conceived only as infinitely rich in its Method, it is evident that Creation must be inexhaustible in the variety of forms through which that Method is forever unfolded into its infinitely rich actuality. But, again, for any particular sphere, as our own world, the conditions—that is, the special aspects of the World-Energy constituting the environment—cannot but present a limited range in so far as they are productive of special physical forms which are organic to Life. In other words, the types of organisms cannot but be limited in number and in variability. At the same time, with the increasing specialization of the

---

* "Die Erkenntniss ist beendigt, wenn es als die nothwendige Folge bestimmter Ursachen sich nachweisen lässt. Dieses *ursächliche* Erkennen nennen wir im Gebiete des Stofflichen auch ein *mechanistisches*, etc." Naegeli: "*Mechanisch-physiologische Theorie der Abstammungslehre*." S. 8.

† Agassiz. "*Methods of Study in Natural History*." 11th ed. p. 14.

earth itself, through its own condensation and consequent increasing tension of energy throughout its mass, the differences in the conditions of life on its surface must have continuously become, and cannot for an indefinitely extended future cease to become, more and more pronounced. And, as already suggested, and as elaborately shown in Darwin's writings, the continuance of life for any type of organisms is possible only through the continuous adaptation of the organisms constituting the type to their environment. Or, as Mr. Spencer puts it: " Life is the continuous adjustment of internal relations to external relations."* And this adaptation must keep pace with whatever changes the environment itself undergoes. Similarly, those that fail of such adaptation can not but become extinct. Fitness to survive consists in fullest correspondence on the part of the living unit to the aspects of Reason constituting the environment of such unit. Since such environment is itself a process, and since it is a constantly varying complex of conditions, it is evident that the types of organisms existing in the midst of and dependent upon that constantly varying complex of conditions, must undergo equally constant and corresponding variations as a condition precedent to their survival. The variation of the type that survives can be measured by no less a standard than that of the variation in the environment itself. The longer the period the greater must be the variation in the environment, and hence the greater the variation in the organic types involved. The environment is, indeed, not merely something *else* than the given unit determined by the environment. It is also, and far more,

* "*Principles of Biology*," (N. Y. Ed.) I., 80.

a complex of conditions *focusing itself into, and unfolding as,* that given unit; just as an image on a screen is not something else than the light, but just the light itself developed in one particular mode.

The conception, then, of the variation of organic species in nature — even to˙ the development of more from less complex species—so far from being in conflict with the highest conception of a divine order of the world, would seem to be itself a necessary aspect of any really consistent view we can form of a divine or rational World-Order. It is demanded by the very principle of Continuity itself, and cannot be got rid of, as it seems to me, in any other way than by renouncing all claim that the world is a world of established order, rather than a world of chance; that is, by admitting that the world whose order is one we are persistently endeavoring to think out is really a world in which thought is not only superfluous, but impossible.

At the same time, it is to be carefully noted that the "variation" is something which takes place on the part of individuals within a given type, while the type in its largest significance is itself invariable. Nor can the variation of any individual or series of individuals within a type ever carry such individual or individuals beyond the type. The truth discovered by von Baer, that all animals originate from eggs which at first are identical in substance and structure, is of utmost importance; for it points distinctly to a genuine simplest grade of organic matter, a *proto*-plasm, out of which all types of animals primarily arose. So also, as Agassiz insists, it is of the utmost significance that "each egg has such tenacity of its individual principle of life that no egg was ever known to swerve from the pattern of the parent animal that gave it birth"*—only, the "pattern" is nothing more nor less than that general, unchangeable type within which the individual—nay, countless generations of individuals—may and must vary in their ceaseless struggle for that degree of existence in which the type is most fully realized. Doubtless no egg that owes its parentage to a vertebrate can ever develop into any other than a vertebrate animal. But this does not in the least invalidate the conception that while in one locality of the primitive world the eggs of the primal vertebrate were developing in the direction of the fish, in another locality where the conditions were different the eggs of the primal vertebrate were developing in the direction of the mammal. Thus proceeded, as it would seem, the differentiation of the primal "generalized" (that is, as yet for the earth unspecialized) type of vertebrate animals; and always it proceeded in accordance with, as the progressive realization of, the perfect plan, the unalterable method, by which the divine World-Energy is forever unfolding itself in Creation as a whole.

It may very well be that there are "sundry traits in common," as between certain molluscoid animals and the lowest vertebrate animal.† *But this is only to say that the nearer we approach the beginning point in the development of animal forms on the earth, the more manifest is the homogeneity characterizing those forms. In other words, it simply indicates their common origin in an undifferentiated animal unit already developing in myriad duplications in the primal sea.

---

* "*Methods of Study in Natural History*," p. 29.
† Herbert Spencer: "*Principles of Biology*," II., 567.

On the other hand, none could protest more vigorously than would the evolutionist himself against the supposition that the vertebrate type as such is an offshoot of the molluscan type as such. That would be substantially to deny the existence of that "established order" of the world upon which Mr. Spencer insists, and which I should prefer to call the rational Method of Creation, without which science itself must be wholly impossible.

And now, not to extend this statement beyond what is necessary to indicate clearly the contrast between the real significance of organic evolution and the mythical significance popularly attached to it, I will only add a word in reference to the tender point of man's own origin. So far as I am aware, no evolutionist really supposes that the initial primate was any more an ape than it was a man.* In fact, it was not sufficiently advanced (differentiated) to be either ape or man. What the theory of evolution really claims is: that apes and men have alike descended from an animal with general characteristics at once manlike and apelike; but not so far developed as to be specifically and in fact either the one or the other. It was potentially both; actually, neither. Developed in the one direction, it gave rise to apes; developed in the other direction, it gave rise to men. And it is not to be forgotten that the primitive apes were far from being the same as the apes of to-day, and that primitive men were still farther from being the same as the men of to-day. Let us note further that these two "directions" of development are radii from

---

* Some color is given to the popular illusion that "Darwinism" means mainly "the descent of man from apes" by an occasional unguarded statement in works by pronounced evolutionists—as, for example, in Romanes' important contribution to the subject under the title: "*Mental Evolution in Man.*"

the same (logical) point. Whence it is evident that from the very outset the ape type and the human type were necessarily divergent, and that, therefore, neither could by any possibility have descended from the other. However complex the "pattern," the threads in the great loom of Creation never become tangled. Or, to change the figure, Nature is the perfect "logical machine." But it is so only because it is nothing else than the outer form, the infinitely extended self-manifestation of the *Logos*, or divine Reason.

Many professed evolutionists, indeed, would stop short of this latter statement, though they would concur heartily in the affirmation of a fixed order as the very core of any rational theory of evolution. It is the more amazing, therefore, that Agassiz should have antagonized the doctrine of organic evolution on the ground that it implies the descent of vertebrate animals from the specialized types of invertebrate animals — in other words, that it assumes the arbitrary intermingling of types. And this missing of the central thread of the doctrine of evolution by such a man is no less unfortunate than amazing, since his "*Methods of Study in Natural History*," embodying as it does his (mis-)interpretation of the only doctrine of organic evolution that Darwin or any other real scientist ever advanced, has been, in America at least, the one authoritative text-book seemingly justifying those who hate Darwinism because they have never understood it, and who refuse to make any effort to understand it because they hate it.

We come now to a further suggestion. It is: That primarily the conditions of life on any sphere that comes to be inhabited at all must be practically uniform over a large extent of the surface of that sphere. From which we cannot but conclude that the transition of inorganic into organic matter on the earth must have taken place simultaneously over wide areas. In other words, the center of the creation of organisms is not a geometrical center, but a rational or logical center. It is not one exclusive locality in space, but only a center in kind. Physical identity is necessarily local and particular. Logical or rational identity is universal, and, as such, is without relation to space. That is, centrality in kind is wholly indifferent to space as such, and consists only of the grouping of such conditions as tend to the development of units bearing certain generic or typical marks. The unit is a particular case of the more or less adequate realization of the universal or typical "plan;" whether the "plan" be that of a star, or a crystal, or a plant, or an animal, or a soul. Thus in this higher, concrete sense, centrality is seen to be co-extensive with space from the very fact that it is indifferent to space. No doubt each particular instance must be localized in space. But it is equally evident that wherever in space the conditions are favorable to the development of units of any given type, there is the center of creation for that type. And no matter at how many or at what remote points in space this grouping of conditions may occur, each point is equally the center of creation for the given type.

Again, one must be on his guard with reference to another point also. It is this: The arising of a given type is no more a matter of time, than it is a matter of space. Time, as was seen at the outset, is nothing else than the abstract form of change. Hence it is by no means necessary to suppose that the "origin" or process of coming into existence of any given type should be something which has occurred but once in an infinitely extended duration. On the contrary, such origination must occur *when*ever as well as *wher*ever the conditions favorable to such process become focused into reality. In fact, as already intimated, just this focusing of "favorable conditions" is itself the process of the origination of the units constituting the type. And, as the argument of the present volume goes to show, the order here, though necessarily chronological locally, is and can be only logical for the Universe as a whole, seeing that in the Universe as a whole every phase of existence possible to a rational world must be perpetual. That is, in the Universe as a whole the "moment" of creation for each type must be eternal, just as the "center" of creation for each type must be co-extensive with space.

Such is the second suggestion in its universal and more abstract form. The special application it is intended to lead up (or down) to is: That the same phase of organic differentiation must have occurred simultaneously over more or less widely *extended* areas, as also (and especially in case of land animals) over more or less widely *separated* areas of the earth — the type in any given case remaining essentially the same throughout the given area or areas so long as the environment remained substantially the same over such area or areas.

Whether in the history of the earth such coincidence of environment actually existed over areas widely separated from each other, is of course a question to be decided upon geological evidence. And such evidence is not absolutely wanting. Besides the *a priori* consideration that all beginnings are in the very nature of the case characterized by homogeneity, there are the familiar facts of the abundant remains of subtropical flora and fauna, even those of high orders and therefore of a relatively late period, in regions where now their development would be impossible. It would seem, then, that we have here a clue to the simplest possible explanation of the coincident existence of the same species of organisms in regions so widely separated as to make the hypothesis of migration from either area to the other very difficult to accept, especially in those cases where oceanic barriers intervene — ingenious and plausible as is Darwin's argument in support of such possibility.*

In this connection, too, it would seem that we have here a possible clue to the primary cause of the extreme differences as between one and another of the races of man. On the hypothesis here suggested these differences would be due, not merely to differences of climatic conditions working through indefinite periods upon descendants from the same ancestors. On the contrary, they would be due primarily to inherited peculiarities running back through lines of ancestry that were distinct possibly from the very beginnings of life on the earth. And this, it may be remarked by the way, seems to present a possible ground of reconciliation as between the views of Darwin and those of Agassiz respecting the mode of origination of the human race, since it would show that instead of their hypotheses respecting the

---

* Darwin was certainly mistaken when he assumed that the hypothesis of the simultaneous arising of the same species at many points of the earth's surface is equivalent to calling in the " agency of a miracle." See " *Origin of Species*," (N. Y. Ed.) p. 320.

"descent of man" being mutually exclusive, those hypotheses are in reality but different threads of the same fabric of truth.

Evidently, too, in case the several races of men originated separately in the manner above indicated, it would seem extremely probable that the human type was realized within some one more or less extended area long ages before the actual development of that type in any other area; the earlier development in the one region being due, primarily, to gradual changes through which the environment there became relatively more stimulating in the direction of mental activity. And it is not wholly without significance in this connection that the region in which the Aryan race has been found as far back in time as it can be traced, is a region in which such change in the environment actually took place. If, indeed, we were to follow up the clew here presented, and to suppose that the Aryan race arose through a Darwinian autochthon over the greater part of the area which they have inhabited from the earliest known period, we would also have in this hypothesis the simple natural settlement of the controversy as to whether this race was of Asiatic or of European origin. And thus, as in so many other cases, the "either—or" would here prove to be but a restless, if not profitless, oscillation between the two complementary aspects of the one real truth. In such case, too, the "race" thus originating would really develop as a race from the gradual fusion of a multitude of tribes originally in isolation, and of more or less contrasted characteristics, the language of the most intellectual tribe gradually becoming (with dialectic differences) the language of the entire race. And this would be quite in keeping with the remark of Prof. Sayce* that "For anything we know, the parent-Aryan may have been the language of a race essentially different from that to which we belong; indeed, it is highly probable that it was spoken by more than one race."

And now, allowing that the hypothesis presented in this second suggestion should be found to be justified by the facts, when once (if ever) the facts come to be adequately known, it would seem to contain an intimation of the primary reason why at the present day the various races of man present such striking contrasts in the degrees of civilization which they have severally attained. I do not forget, or lightly esteem, the fact that the existing differences are far greater than those separating race from race three or four thousand years ago; nor do I forget, or lightly esteem, the fact that the increased superiority of the more advanced races is due, mainly, to their own superior self-activity. But the real question would seem to be this: How came the superior races to be superior primarily? To what could this be due, if not to an earlier start in the human degree of life? And what could be the cause of this earlier start unless it be the greater stimulus of a more favorable environment?

"Modern" man has reduced nature to the grade of mere instrumentality. "Ancient" man bowed in fear before the various aspects of nature, worshiping them as gods. But by "ancient" man we who use the term commonly mean the "primitive" men who were our own forefathers. On the other hand, the "ancient" men of

* "*Science of Language,*" II., 122.

other races seem to have scarcely emerged even yet from their "primitive" condition. From which it would seem to be easy to account for the otherwise startling simian marks which some of the races still exhibit. It may also be remarked, finally, that upon the hypothesis here indicated it would seem that Malthus failed to seize the true perspective of history. The multiplicity of ancestry, the fact that the higher the type of organism the less prolific its members, the further fact that Nature's productivity in vegetation is largely in direct ratio of the degree of man's intelligence in cultivating the soil — all this seems to indicate that the "Malthusian law" is a vanishing aspect of history and not a permanent phase.*

* Compare Mr. Spencer's "*Principles of Biology*," concluding chapter.

CHAPTER XXVI.

CULMINATION OF THE LIFE-PROCESS IN A LIVING UNIT WHICH IS CHARACTERIZED BY REFLECTIVE CONSCIOUSNESS.

IN the last chapter we considered some of the leading aspects of the doctrine of Evolution with reference to continuity of development in life-forms, and found that this doctrine in its larger outlines presents nothing to which reasonable objection can be urged, even when it includes the doctrine of the descent of man from lower orders of organisms. We have now finally to consider briefly what may reasonably be regarded as the culminating aspect of the life of Man, in whom the life-forms of the world culminate.

We have seen that in the physically constituted living unit externality predominates, and that thus its dissolution sooner or later is inevitable. While, therefore, the life-process exhibits or is characterized by universality, yet that universality is by no means ultimate. In itself it has no genuine vitality. It is only when considered as a phase of the absolute universality of the World-Energy itself, that the universality involved in any special process presents its truth as an actual, concrete, working principle.

And to thus consider each specialized phase of universality is but to follow the obvious demand of reason.

For any special fact or phase of the world can be truly comprehended only when viewed in its relations. And the wider the range of relations included in the view, the more adequate the judgment formed of the fact or phase of existence upon which the view is directed. And thus again do we reach a conclusion already indicated in the progress of this inquiry: That each special fact or phase of existence is itself, thus far, the manifestation of the universality involved in the World-Energy. So that each and every fact or phase of existence thus presents the characteristic of universality in its very nature. It is, indeed, only through its possessing such degree of universality that it can so much as exist at all.

But the point of supreme significance here is that at the stage we have now reached the phase of universality everywhere appears as characterized by explicit *subjectivity*. The Universal is the Soul of things. But it is to be observed further that, as already proven, the ultimate truth of subjectivity is shown in its unfolding itself as an absolute process of self-objectification; that is, once more, in a process of self-particularization. Whence its infinitely varied discrete forms are characterized by measureless elasticity and that aspect of concrete continuity by which such forms undergo transmutation, the one into the other. There is no absolute line of separation between individual fact and individual fact, between species and species, nor even between the physical and the spiritual aspects of existence. The physical would have no meaning, or rather it could have no existence, apart from the spiritual; just as, on the other hand, the spiritual, in its character of spontaneity as concrete process of self-realization, necessarily develops, along with its other phases, the less adequate ones constituting the external, physical world.

All possible forms and modes of existence, then, are but so many phases of the self-objectification of the one absolutely self-complete Subject.

But the *complete* self-objectification of the World-Energy as subject necessarily involves precisely this: That the highest or most adequate phase of self-objectification, shall itself *as object* still bear the character of a subject. The objective itself must develop to subjectivity and become reflective consciousness and contemplative knowing. The created must itself take on the character of the creative. The external must become once more explicitly internal.

Now it is toward this very end that the successive phases of the unfolding of the objective world thus far considered have been seen to tend. Even centrality implies some slight degree of vague subjectivity. In affinity the phase of internality is more definitely developed; while in the life-process there are presented all the phases of spontaneity from the automatic process of selection and assimilation in the protozoan to the complex preferences and voluntary movements of the most highly developed organisms. Here as elsewhere the principle of continuity remains unbroken. The widely extended variations in degree constitute no exception to the law.

The striking fact is that throughout the series there is more and more complete blending of the inner and the outer in the given object—the object itself being "given" as we have seen, through the *outering* of the inner.

And now, more precisely, the "inner" is the universal, the pervasive, the spontaneous. As universal and pervasive, it possesses absolute, indestructible self-continuity. As spontaneous, it is *self-realizing process*.

But, as already so often repeated, its self-realization is nothing more nor less than its self-specialization, its self-differentiation. It is thus precisely that the universal assumes particularity and exhibits this as the necessary mode of its own self-realization.

At the same time, this blending of the universal with the particular, or rather, this unfolding of the universal in the particular, gives rise to definite realized existences which, *as such*, present the characteristic of *individuality*. Such individuality, however, is a self-contradictory one so long as the universal and the particular are imperfectly fused therein. For just so long is the individual pervaded by externality; or more precisely, it thus far fails to attain to genuine, self-sufficing, dominating subjectivity or spontaneity. It is, therefore destined to undergo dissolution and thus proves to be a *divisible individual*.

The individuality thus far examined, then, proves to be an illusory one.

Nevertheless, it is evident that the elements of genuine individuality have already presented themselves, even though they have not yet been shown in such relation as to remove all doubt of the actual realization of such genuine individuality as a phase of the created world.

It is this which constitutes the one remaining point of our inquiry.

What conditions, if any, are there tending toward and rendering certain and necessary the actual realization of genuine individuals — indivisible, spontaneous units — in that aspect of the world known as creation? The simplest (and complementary) factors in the process of creation, as we have seen, are universality and particularity.

We have now to note and emphasize the fact that it is the complete fusion of these factors in a self-renewing process that must constitute genuine, concrete individuality. This, too, we have already seen to be the vital characteristic of the World-Energy itself, considered as Spirit. That is, genuine individuality is an essentially spiritual characteristic. The genuine, adequate conception of an individual is that of a spiritual, self-conscious, self-active unit. An individual is a subject which unfolds itself as object. It is, then, legitimate, as well as of utmost interest to ourselves to inquire whether there is, as many have actually believed, but one genuine, abiding individual? whether all "other" individualities, including the human, are in fact only relative, vanishing, illusory forms or modes of the One?

We have seen that the World-Energy, as Spirit, is its own end—its own final purpose. Consistently with this, too, we have seen that its total activity is a process in which the subjective forever unfolds into the objective. Nor is this the whole truth. Rather it so develops the objective aspect of its own existence that through and in this objective aspect the subjective comes ever into greater and greater prominence—so that the particularized object, as such, proves to be dominated by, and with increasing degree to express, a specialized phase of subjectivity. The specialized object, let us repeat, is, in its specific character of specialized object, itself but an outerance or manifestation of the absolute Subject.

But the more complex and adequate this particular manifestation of the absolute Subject, only so much the more must such manifestation itself bear the character of subjectivity and ultimately suffice as a distinct, independent *subject*.

It would seem, then, that the World-Energy as Spirit not only objectifies itself in the forms of existence pertaining to the space-world, but that it also differentiates itself as spiritual essence. In the first place, indeed, the latter underlies the former. But also, in its more adequate phase of self-objectification, it must approximate ever toward the development of actual, independent spiritual units, or true *individuals*.

Nor can the subjectivity or spirituality of the World-Energy itself completely realize itself save through perfectly fusing the inner and the outer in the units arising through the highest phases of its activity. Not merely must it blend these phases in general in its own single Individuality. It must also develop itself in its own differentiated phases up to the point of the fusion of universality and particularity in the highest type of these differentiated phases. Not otherwise, indeed, could creation be really conceived as complete. Thus the highest type of existence in the created world is seen to be at once the culmination of the whole process through which particular forms of existence arise, and also the development through that process of actually realized genuine individuals, as the fused unities of universality and particularity necessarily arising through the eternal self-differentiation of the World-Energy as Spirit.

Thus the universal, absolute Subjectivity or spontaneous creative Power, self-specialized in the forms of individual *subjects*, proves to be also in that very fact a definitely constituted *object* of the most complex type; while at the same time the special object thus developed to subjectivity is able as subject to regard the World-Process itself as object. In other words, the self-objectifying of the World-Energy, or absolute, self-realizing Subject, attains actual completeness only in the development in the objective world of a specialized unit, in which universality and particularity are completely blended, in which the objective and the subjective are completely interfused.

Thus constituted the unit not only exhibits subjectivity as its dominant characteristic, but also exhibits it developed to genuine spontaneity. Whence the unit shows itself to be already an actually unfolded individual, possessing in more or less highly developed form all the fundamental characteristics of the absolute divine Individual.

In its fundamental nature this finite individual is, then, a genuine subject or concrete thinking agency; and as such it proves to be in its type the absolute culmination of the created world. For it is true *subject;* and yet in that very fact it is already the highest possible form of *object* which the absolute, divine Subject can put forth from itself. For it is, in its true or ideal nature, one with the divine Subject.

And this it further proves itself to be in the fact that it makes itself its own object; while, at the same time, as subject or thinking agency, it also opposes itself to (that is, contrasts itself with) the absolute divine Subject which, as such, now bears the character of absolute Object to the created subject.

Thus the absolute spontaneity of the divine Spirit is seen to return to itself in the culmination of its own creative process of self-objectification. And this return again is but one aspect of the total process. For the created subject must again, as spontaneous energy, unfold itself into realized objectivity—which it does in all its creations, economic, social, civil, religious, artistic, scientific.

It cannot be too strongly insisted upon that man, as an individual and also as a type in creation, is a manifestation of Thought, which is primarily not his own individual thought. Nor is he alone or unique in this respect. Every other animal—nay, every crystal and every atom—is also in its own degree a manifestation of the same Thought—that is, of the creative Thought constituting the very Substance of the Universe. Every man, animal, crystal, atom, is a particular form of existence. And yet each is universal in the fact that it is an embodiment or realization of a type, and as such presents the essential or universal characteristics of that type. But these essential or universal characteristics can exist as such only in and as thought. Each is, in short, just one specialized phase of the perfect Thought constituting the Method of the World-Energy. On the other hand, the well-nigh immeasurable superiority of man to these other manifestations of the perfect Thought consists in the fact that man is something more than a mere "manifestation" or outer form of Thought. He is, besides this, nothing less than the progressive reproduction of the very *Thought-Process* whose one perfect expression is the whole, eternal Creation. That is, man is able progressively to make that universal, perfect

Thought his own individual thought. Or, in other words, the "environment" of Man the thinker is precisely the Process of Creation seen as the actualized world of Reason or Thought. So that the real or true life of Man is the continuous adjustment of the internal relations consisting of his own individual thought-process to that total round of "external" relations consisting of the perfect Thought-Process unfolded in the divine World-Energy. And this is "external" *to* man only in so far as it remains unrealized *in* man.

Thus the descent of man must be considered from two points of view which at first sight seem to exclude each other. He is an animal and he is also a thinker, by which latter fact he is not only contrasted with, but, it would seem, separated by an impassable gulf from, all other animals, and even from himself as an animal. And yet, as we have seen, all animals, along with all other realities in the Universe, are also manifestations of Thought and owe their very existence to this fact. Nor is this all. On the contrary, the classification of animals, which, not so long since, was based largely upon the external characteristics of form and color, has gradually come to be based upon the internal characteristics of structure and function. It is not a little significant, too, that in this new method of classification the nervous system, as the more immediate external measure of the inmost function of *consciousness*, has come to be regarded as the final test of superiority in the comparison of animal types. Measured by this test, Man simply stands at the head of the whole series of forms of the animal kingdom. For this series of forms presents a scale of consciousness grading upward by scarcely perceptible differences, from the amœba to that unit of the organic world which is marked off from all the rest by his power of comparing, of judging, of thinking, of measuring all things by himself as the standard — by his power of *self*-consciousness, which may be described as consciousness raised, if not to the actual power whose exponent is infinity, at least to infinite potentiality. In short, Mind in its infinite nature, is the ultimate function of whatever can be called Matter. Or, more precisely, Mind unfolds itself into Matter as its own spontaneously produced organic expression. The continuity of Matter has its truth in the continuity of Mind as the original, creative Fact, Deed, Activity, or Actuality.

Evidently, then, the descent of man from successively lower and lower orders of animals, which themselves constitute a minutely graded series of thought-forms, and even of thought-functions, is, after all, nothing else than his ascent or evolution in the scale of godhood. And always it is to be remembered that the descent of man cannot possibly have been from animals, merely as animals, merely as physical, or material, or brute natures (allowing that such "natures" were thinkable). On the contrary, every step, every factor in this ascending scale of his evolution is possible for man only because each step and each factor is expressive simply of the method by which Man, the Son, is born of God, the Father. Just as Life can come only from the living, though it may be through units which are in themselves not-living; so Man the thinker can come only from God the Thinker, though it may be through a marvelous series of complex, more or less conscious forms, which in and of themselves cannot be said to think.

Doubtless Man was made of the dust of the earth, and, still more remotely, of cosmic dust. But the process of his development is nothing less than the process of Reason by which the concurrence of elements has tended unfalteringly toward ever greater complexity of relation, until at length there arose a unit which, though it could not be said to think, yet was itself a marvelous embodiment of Thought, and which, by further advance, grew into that degree of complexity of relations which may be termed self-relation—a characteristic better known under the name of self-consciousness, which is, in fact, the highest term of centrality, and without which the word centrality itself would be altogether meaningless; nay, without which all words and all things were impossible.

It would seem, then, that Darwin and his associates have only indicated to us in rough outline the more conspicuous physical aspects of the mode or method by which Man, the progressively unfolding thinker, has descended from the eternally perfect, creative Thinker. The intermediate links may very likely be: savage, primate, worm, protoplasmic pulp, nebula; but these are in reality only roots that still have their origin in and draw their sole nutriment from the primal World-Energy. This is the real secret of their incessantly struggling upward through darkness and time into more and more complex forms of Reason, to emerge at length into the light of Eternity, which for every man is but the ever increasingly clear consciousness of his own identity in nature with the primal Thinker, of whose Thought the whole Universe is but the outer, organic form.

And yet this ideal identity in nature of the created thinker with the divine Thinker can be realized only through progressive stages in time. Only thus can the created thinker or subject unfold into realized, objective existence, through a spontaneous process which, as essentially the self-objectification of ideally true subjectivity, is in its nature one with the eternal Process which constitutes the concrete truth and vitality of the divine Subject.

Following any other way the finite subject must fail of self-realization. Following this and no other way, the finite subject learns that in so doing it is but obeying the law of its own nature; for this law is the law of absolute Reason—the absolute, unchangeable law inherent in the true nature of every thinking agency.

But thus it realizes its own freedom. For freedom consists in conscious obedience to the law of Reason, whereby alone self-realization is attainable.* It is evident at the same time that freedom can belong only to a thinking unit, to a genuine individual, to whom, and to none other, is conscious obedience possible.

But not only does the finite subject prove to be in its nature capable of attaining to genuine, concrete freedom; but another infinitely significant inference is warranted from the fact of its identity in nature with the divine Subject. In that fact lies the assurance that the *finite subject* possesses an *infinite destiny*.

It bears within itself, indeed, the most extraordinary contradiction. It is created, and therefore finite. At the same time it is a subject of identical nature with the absolute, divine Subject, and is therefore infinite. Its

---

* Here, indeed, in this conscious, glad obedience to the law of Reason, we have the clue to the highest significance of that ultimate equilibration of which Mr. Spencer ("*First Principles*," ch. xxii,) writes so suggestively, and yet, in the outcome, as it seems to me, so unsatisfactorily.

finitude, however, is on the side of its present realization, while its infinitude is on the side of its ideal—that is, its typical nature.

It has, therefore, an infinite ideal to fulfil; and yet must fulfil that ideal through a process the steps of which are involved in succession. Whence it appears that it can never absolutely, exhaustively fulfil its destiny; though at every stage in its approximation toward the fulfilment of that destiny, its vigor as a self-identical, vital unit must be by so much enhanced.

We may fairly conclude, therefore, that there can be no period in the self-consistent existence of the subject or spiritual unit in which the tendency toward dissolution can so much as balance, much less predominate over, the tendency toward increase of vigor involving its assured permanence as precisely the self-same, self-identical spiritual unit whose free, self-consistent activity necessarily tends ever toward its own perfection.

Thus the created subject proves to be in its very nature a genuine *individual*, an indivisible, immortal, self-completing ideal totality. It is characterized by substantial universality, and hence possesses genuine continuity. Its perpetuated existence, then, is one in which its self-identity could not be lost.

On the other hand, as a vital, concrete universal, it must persistently prove itself an active unit, a unit which, through its own spontaneous activity, unfolds itself into continuously multiplied complexity of specialization.

As universal it particularizes itself. As possessing genuine continuity it spontaneously develops itself into ever more manifold discrete modes. As self-specializing universal it is, once more, a divinely constituted individual possessing an infinite destiny. It is lord of time and heir of Eternity.

The World-Energy is God. Its self-conservation is the eternal process of Creation. "Evolution" is the temporal aspect of this process. The self-unfolding of God culminates in man. For man is the Son of God.

INDEX.

A.

Action, at a distance, explanation of, 152; chemical, 184; and re-action, 108, 196.
Actual, the, the total round of possibilities is, 118.
Affinity, chemical and its development, 250; higher aspects of, 251, 257.
Affirmation involves negation, *i. e.*, differentiation, 237.
Agassiz, 276; misinterpretation of Darwinism, 279.
Agnosticism, 266.
Aristotle, 210; on law of contradiction, 25, 116; categories of, 105; doctrine of substance, 117.
Aryan race, 283.
Atom, 58, 151; definition of, given by science, 59; as force-center, 66, 144; as a phase of the physical universe, 67.
Atomic theory, 58, 92.
Attraction, 49.
Attraction and repulsion, as complementary modes of energy, 52; the initial qualitative differences constituting the reality of matter, 89; unity of, under the form of electricity, 191.
Attributes, of substance, 107; Spinoza's definition of, 105.

B.

Baer, von, 276.
Becoming, 116.
Being and non-being, 115.
Biogenesis, 259.
"Bodies," discrete phases of force, 140.
Brahm, 223.

C.

Categories of Aristotle, 105.
Cause, doctrine of, 207; final, as method, 254; four phases of, 210.
Cause and effect, reciprocal aspects in every event, 209.
Centrality, 246, 249, 256; in kind, contrasted with c. in space, 280; highest term of, 296.
Certitude, absolute test of, 29; Descartes on, 20.
Change, possible only through impressed force, 146; meaning of, 28, 213.
Chemistry, a form of applied mathematics, 91; an aspect of physics, 186.
Conception, how inducive of thought, 19, *note;* implies perception, 18; a seizure of relations, 16.
Consciousness, function of, 3; individual, 5, 19; power of, not creative, but transforming, 3, 5; ultimate range of, 5-7; degree of, measured in nervous system, 294.
Conservation of Energy, 199, 202.
Continuity, principle of, 276, 288; and discreteness of quantity in matter, 83.
Contradiction, law of, an advanced phase of law of consistency, 25; as stated by Aristotle, 25; true significance of, 27.
Creation, the one eternal fact, 253.
Creator and creation, 215.
Crystallization, 181.

D.

Dalton, 92.
Darwin, Charles, 268, 270.
Definite proportions, Dalton's law of, 92.
Death, 262.

Democritus, theory of, 58, 60.
Descartes, on the ultimate ground of certitude, 20; on creation and preservation, 253.
Descent, doctrine of, what it really is, 278.
Discoverers, typical, 228.
Discoveries, definition of, 227.
Discrete, the, implies the continuous, 83, 261.
Divine, early form of conception of the, as Unity, 222.

E.

Elasticity, defined as interfusion of attraction and repulsion, 193.
Electricity, 95, 191; and magnetism, 187.
Elements, chemical, 75; specialized conditions of homogeneous "matter," 77, 185.
Ellipse, 176.
Emanation and absorption, 152, 236.
Energy, absolute unity of, 202; Aristotle's definition of as absolute Divine Spirit, 148; as adequate cause of motion, 143; as an all-inclusive process, 108; conservation of, 196; conservation of, doctrine of, 199; Herbert Spencer on conservation of, 202; first law of thought implies the conservation of, 24; differentiation of, 205; dissipation of, a phase in a wider process, 198-9; self-conserved, 214; kinetic, 168; the substance of all reality, 204; totality of, always in equilibrium, 200; significant change in use of term, 148.
"Environment," 271, 275, 294.
Equilibrium, of the total, 143; of energy, an eternally accomplished fact, 241; various aspects of, 104, 143, 199, 222, 238, 297, *note*.
Ether, 73, 91.
Evolution, doctrine of, first presented in metaphysical form, 120; and involution, 252; Herbert Spencer on, 265; method of, 272; of life forms, 255; philosophy, 232.
Excluded middle, law of, 28.
Experience, limit of, 5; is realization of knowledge, 23.
Experiment, must begin in thought, 119.

F.

Fact, the one changeless, is the infinitely complex fact of change, 247; true significance of, 228; creation, the one eternal, 253.
"Fact," in part the creation of consciousness, 4.
Facts, dependent upon theory for their value, 2; intelligible only on interpretation, 2.
Falling bodies, laws of, 163.
Finite, the, phase of the infinite, 100.
Force, centrifugal, 174; exerted only in opposing force, 62; manifestation of dual, 180; is force only through action, 143; persistence of, Herbert Spencer on, 149; motion as a realized form of, 167; the "active" phase of the world, 62; sole reality of matter, 64.
Forces, chemical, identity of with other natural forces, 186; correlation of, 196.
Force-centre (atom), focus of an indefinitely extended force-sphere, 144.
Freedom and necessity, 238.

G.

Generation, spontaneous, 260.
God, the only reality, 241; Christian conception of, 224.
Gravitation, dependent upon quantity, not quality, of matter, 155; law of, 145, 150.
Gravity, center of, 50; a necessary aspect or mode of things, 158, 172.

H.

Haeckel, Ernest, 268.
Heat, 181; a mode of matter, 183.
Hegel, as an organizer of science, 29, 118, 231; "*Naturphilosophie*," 233.
Heraclitus, doctrine of, 109, 115, 118.
Hindu conception of creation, 223.
Human race, origin of, theories of Agassiz and Darwin, reconciliation of, 282.
Hypotheses, what are acceptable, 227.

I.

Idealism, various aspects of, 31.
Identity, absolute, includes all differences, 28; law of, 24; excludes change from existence as a whole, 27.
Individual, the World-Energy as an all-inclusive, 236; the created, 298.
Individuality, 248, 289.
Inertia, law of, 133.
Infinite, the, in relation to finite, 100; as an object of thought, 224; true, 237.
Intelligence, individual, limit of possible development of, 7; universal type of, 6, 252.
Internal and external, 108, 239, 245, 251, 256, 259, 288.

K.

Kant, on space, empirical and absolute, 11, 111; on conceptions and perceptions, 18; on value of universal logic, 120.
Knowledge, coincident with experience, 23; objective and subjective in its nature, 30; of relations and "relative" k., 98, 126.
Known and unknown, fundamentally related through the transforming power of mind, 6.

L.

Law of multiple proportions, 93.
Laws of thought, 24; as laws of things, 241; necessary, 29.

Life, attempts to artificially produce, 266; origin of, in and through the World-Energy, 259, 271; H. Spencer's definition of, 275.
Life-forms, evolution of, 255.
Life-process, the fusion of the internal and the external, 258; culmination of, in man, 286.
Light, 191; as a subjective creation, 193.
Living unit and its environment, 271, 275, 294.
Lockyer, J. Norman, 77.
Logic, formal, 231; universal, Kant on, 120; of Hegel, 232; of events, 231.
Logos, the, 272.

M.

Magnet, action of, 153.
Magnetism, 187.
Malthus, 285.
Man, descent of, 278, 295; development of, as a process of reason, 296; modern and ancient, 284; the Son of God, 299.
Many, the, as aspect of the "total," complementary to the "one," 17, 82, 220, 235.
Matter, 40; continuous, but also discrete, 83; extensive and intensive phases of quantity in, 86; G. H. Lewes' definition of, 63; infinite divisibility of, 84; actual infinite division of, 152; organic and inorganic, 268; penetrability of, 68; properties of, 55; quantitative relations in, 80; total volume of unlimited, 47; consists primarily of attraction and repulsion, 73.
Maxims, abridged statement of theories, 1.
Maxwell, Clerk, on matter and motion, 125.
Measure, a comparison with a fixed standard, 97.
Measurable, a phase of the measureless, 100.
Mind, active, as well as passive,

3; a function of matter, 295; identity of with the world, 7.
Molecular and mechanical energy, identity in kind of, 189.
Momentum, 157, 161.
Motion, curvilinear, 170; energy as adequate cause of, 143; laws of, 131; molecular, 178; nature of, 122; possibility of, 109; relativity of, 123.

N.

Nature, the organic aspect of thought, 267; the "outer," as distinguished from thought the "inner," 37.
Necessity and freedom, 238.
Negative, equivalent to affirmative, 235, 237.
Noumenon and phenomenon, 53.
Number, infinite, has no meaning, 114.
Numbers, powers of, 101.

O.

Object and subject, as phases of the universe, 38, 239, 288.
Object (matter), presented to consciousness as resistance, 40.
"One," the, an aspect of the "total," complementary to "the many," 17, 82, 220, 235.
Order, logical and chronological, 221, 243, 281.
Origin, 265; of species, 273; continuous aspect of, 280.

P.

Pantheism, 253.
Parallelogram of forces, 138.
Parmenides, 109.
Perception, 8; implies conception, 17; the simplest, a complex fact, 15.
Phenomenon and noumenon, 53.
Philosophy and science, no antagonism between, 233.
Physical, the, the initial phase of the spiritual, 23.
Plato, 53, 215.
Potentiality, in relation to potency, 221, 242, 250.

Process, the, of the world, 253.

Q.

Qualitative difference, 88; determined by variations of intensive quantity, 88, 94.
Quality and quantity, different aspects of the same sum of facts in the universe, 89; real only as attributes of substance, 105, 106; the intensive phase of matter, 185.
Quantity, extensive and intensive in matter, 86, 97; varying relations between, determine qualitative differences in matter, 94; continuity and discreteness of, in matter, 83, 120.

R.

Reality, ultimate, 54.
Reason, absolute, 240.
Receptivity, another name for reaction, 107.
Relations, logical and chronological order of, 221, 243, 281.
Relativity of knowledge, 21, 98, 126.
Repulsion, 40; attraction and, 52; a relation of reciprocal action, 43; a form of attraction, 48.
Revelation, an eternally accomplished fact, 229; in what sense progressive, 230.

S.

Sensation as primary phase of consciousness, 7.
Science, exact, must keep within the limits of measure, 99; and philosophy, no antagonism between, 233; mathematical, purpose of, 99.
Self-consistency, law of, 22.
Self-consciousness, primary unity of, 19; unity of, the condition of all knowledge, 20; of World-Energy, 226, 234, 240.
Sound, 191; as subjective creation, 193.
Space, 8; a condition of sensation, 9; fourth dimension of,

102; movable, 111; infinite, 125; its unreality, 122, 127; negation of, 13, *note*.

Species, origin of, 273; variable, 275.

Spectrum analysis, 75.

Spencer, Herbert, 268; on absolute being, 54; definition of life, 275.

Sphericity, 249.

Spinoza, 105, 120.

Spirit, as self-realizing method equal to the World-Energy, 234; as self-externalizing internality, 239; modes of activity of, independent of space relations, 244.

Spontaneity of World-Energy, 143, 149, 226, 229, 251, 292.

Stewart, Balfour, 198.

Subject and object, as phases of the universe, 38, 245, 288.

Subject, finite, identity of, in its true nature, with divine subject, 292, 297.

Substance, as defined by Spinoza, 105; by Aristotle, 106.

T.

Tension, electric, analogy of, to that of Prince Rupert's drop, 188; varying degrees of, resulting in qualities, 102.

Theory, 2, 228.

Thinking, distinguished from imagining, 260, *note*.

"Things" in relation to thought, 29, 271.

Thought, as the substance of the universe, 293; central truth and essence of the world, 226; human, struggle for self-development of, 228; "inner," as distinguished from nature, which is the "outer," 37; laws of, 24; formulated as the laws of things, 29; and justly so, 241; as such necessarily abstract, but also necessarily self-affirming, 234; system of, is the system of the world, 230.

Time, a condition of sensation, 13; essential element of motion, 159; real only as form of change, 265.

Totality of world a self-related totality, 147.

Truth, how attained, 39; the correct interpretation of fact, 2.

Types, organic, invariable, 276.

U.

Unity, abstract and concrete, phases of, 101.

Universality, particularity and individuality, 221, 236, 248, 287.

Unknowable, 6, 100, 230.

W.

Weight, an accident of matter, 72.

World, the, as a self-related totality, 147; identity of, with mind, 7; sum total of Energy, 194; the only possible, to be known, 6, 7; no "material" apart from the spiritual, 241.

World-Energy, and the process of its unfolding, 205; as absolute spirit, 237, 260; as absolute vitality, 259; as absolute process of Reason, 238; as knowing subject and known object, 226; as method, 272; as self-objectifying subject, 239, 288; as self-realizing Reason or as will, 238, 240; as spirit, 218; as system, 226; as the expression of necessity, 238; bears the aspect of absolute potentiality, 220; characterized by universality, particularity and individuality, 221; manifestations of, as spirit, 242; unity of, 219; self-differentiation of, 104, 205, 220, 235, 244, 289.

Z.

Zeno, 109; paradox of, 112.

Zero, absolute, 183; absolute of temperature, 103; a point of transition or of equilibrium, 104; in number, purely subjective, 103.

www.ingramcontent.com/pod-product-compliance
Lightning Source LLC
Chambersburg PA
CBHW030016240426
43672CB00007B/973